Canadian Literature Today

Canadian Literature Today

Edited by

R.K. Dhawan

PRESTIGE

Published by
Prestige Books
New Delhi 110 008

1995

ISBN: 81-85218-95-1

Photo Typesetting by
Pivot Computers
Delhi 110 006
Ph. 2934490

Printed at
Mehra Offset Press
New Delhi 110 002

Contents

Literary Criticism

Contributors

P.A. Abraham, M.S. University, Baroda

Madhumalati Adhikari, Jabalpur

Urbashi Barat, Jabalpur

Indira Bhatt, C.U. Shah Sc. College, Ahmedabad

N. Rama Devi, S.K. University, Anantapur

Vandana Garg, Shimla

Christine Gomez, Holy Cross College, Trichy

A. Hariprasanna, S.V. University, Tirupati

Ranjana Harish, Gujarat University, Ahmedabad

N. Kalaamani, Bharathidasan University, Trichy

Usha Pathania, H.P. University, Shimla

N.E. Pavithra, Pondicherry Engineering College

M. Prabhakar, Kakatiya University, Warangal

Vimala Rama Rao, Bangalore University

V. Sam Sahayam, M.S. University, Tirunelveli

Nandita Sinha, M.S. College, University of Delhi

G.R. Taneja, R.L.A. College, University of Delhi

Gerry Turcotte, University of Wollongong, Australia

Coomi S. Vevaina, S.N.D.T. University, Bombay

Canadian Literature Today

R.K. DHAWAN

The nineteen eighties and nineties have witnessed a remarkable flowering of Canadian literature in all forms—poetry, drama and fiction. It has been realized now that Canadian literature is worthy of a serious study. Margaret Atwood, the best-known Canadian woman novelist, has aptly pointed out that, notwithstanding criticism from its detractors, Canadian literature has demonstrated its 'own existence.' To regard this literature as a minor one, as some critics tend to do, will only be taking a myopic view of the immense body of writing that has come from Canada since the end of the Second World War. In the first half of the twentieth century, Canadian literary writing did make a mark but it was 'invisible' to the outside world and thus failed to draw the international attention it deserved. That it was not noticed beyond its own borders had its own advantages: it took a definite shape in form and content.

The earliest growth of Canadian literature can be traced to the oral voices of the original people, the Indian tribes spread out in the temperate regions. Theirs was an oral tradition; their songs and stories were formed from one generation to another. The aboriginal people, in their songs and stories, talk about the world around them, for Canada has had no heroic issues, no gigantic war or adventurous event. Myths and legends of the first peoples existed long before the Europeans arrived. These were followed by the literature of the first explorations and entrepreneurial ventures, marking the first impact of the European mind. Subsequently Canada has witnessed the evolution of two national cultures, developing autonomously and simultaneously. We all know about these two 'home cultures' French and British and also the fact that Canada is quite vulnerable to the domineering American culture to the immediate south.

Like India's own complex literary heritage, Canadian literature is written in more than one language; it reflects a regionally diverse and multicultural society. Canadian culture, like Indian, is a mosaic rather than a melting pot. The wide variety of literatures in both the countries—Canada and India—foster the growth of a unique, composite identity in each case. Canada, today, is a complete world in microcosm, because it has various distinctive ethnocultural groups and political, social and religious differences. Its citizens come from every corner of the globe who retain their own distinctive heritage. It publishes every year some three hundred newspapers and periodicals in various ethnic languages.

There has of course been some controversy as to what constitutes the actual Canadian literary tradition, and who its best writers are, and also, which of the foreigners who have settled in Canada and which of the Canadians settled abroad are part of their national literature. This leads us to a debate over larger issues like the genuineness and the true identity of Canadian literature. The dual nature of Canadian literature—French and English—is partially responsible for this situation. Critics, belonging to this school, fail to acknowledge the advantages of bilingual cultures. It must be realized that literary works coming from bilingual cultures demonstrate how the tension or interaction between different language systems can be utilized for narrative, dramatic and analytic ends. The appearance of fiction as a literary form following Western models is in itself a cross-cultural phenomenon. It is the emergence of a new genre of writing resulting from the meeting of two cultures. A literary genre that belongs to a particular culture is often the form in which the values of that culture find expression. Hence we witness, in the culture contact, two sets of values coming into conflict with each other, each struggling for supremacy over the other. The genre introduced from outside has to adapt itself to a new milieu, and in doing so, it undergoes transformation both in form as well as in content. Chinua Achebe, Wole Soyinka, George Lamming and V.S. Naipaul, for instance, reinforce their stylistic resources by drawing upon the native speech.

Diversity of cultures has given rise to the emergence of varied literatures, the most noteworthy being South Asian Canadian literature. It constitutes the works of writers which show South Asian sensibility or their writers maintaining a distinct South Asian identity. New immigration legislation in the 1970s opened Canada's borders to a larger number of Asian immigrants, whose impact on Canadian writing started surfacing in the mid-eighties, in the journals such as *The Toronto South Asian Review* and in the works of individual writers like Saros Cowasjee, Rohinton Mistry, Bharati Mukherjee, Surjeet Kalsey and M.G. Vassanji.

There are more than 3,00,000 Canadians of Asian origin, including those who have settled there from Europe, Africa and South America. Emigrants from South Asia normally speak English in addition to the South Asian language of their origin. They have their own distinct values and heritages, which have enriched and are enriching the mosaic of tapestry of the Canadian culture. In many cases, immigration experience is central to their work. Whileas these are the voices of change, they speak for their love for Canada, and even issues like race discrimination and the process of acculturation. Their literature seeks to serve as a bridge between them and white Canadians, as also among ethnic groups themselves, to serve understanding and multiculturalism.

The substantial body of South Asian Canadian literature is written in English, but there is an appreciable output in Punjabi and Urdu. Writing of this kind has its own value, but its readership is limited. Those writing in English, on the other hand, have attained national recognition. Like Sadhu Binning, Surjeet Kalsey, Stephen Gill, Akbar Khan and a host of writers.

Many of the South Asian writers are univ.-bred, and were writing before coming to Canada. Like Bharati Mukherjee, Saros Cowasjee, Uma Parameswaran and Rohinton Mistry. There are others who started writing in Canada and achieved fame. Bharati Mukherjee, who belongs to the first category, was born in Calcutta, had her education there, before she migrated to Canada. She, along with her husband Clark Blaise, came to live in Montreal in 1966. She taught fiction-writing at McGill and, for a longish time, directed McGill's creative writing programme. Though she had been writing earlier too, her first novel was published in 1972. She achieved sufficient recognition as a literary artist, before she migrated to America. There she has been working as Professor of creative writing at Columbia.

Past and present merge in the writings of another writer of South Asian origin—Rohinton Mistry. He emigrated to Canada but in *Tales from Firozsha Baag*, he nostalgically produces the effect of an insider to Ferozsha Baag, Bombay. He achieves this target by reenacting, re-creating the place and people, with the skill of a miniature painter. In *Such a Long Journey,* published in 1991, Mistry unfolds a long vista of varied interests all along the development of a dexterous plot. The title of the book has a symbolic significance and refers to the life of Dr Gustad Noble, the central character, covering at the same time a vast canvas of Indian life. It discusses the facets of life of an average Indian and reflects on certain explosive chapters of the Indian politics and the three wars that took place between 1962 and 1971.

Another South Asian Canadian, M.G. Vassanji, author of *The Gunny Sack* and *No New Land* has made a mark on the literary scene. Recently he has won the first Giller Prize, Canada's newest and largest award for fiction. He won the $ 25,000 award for his novel *The Book of Secrets.* Moyez Vassanji's novel beat four other finalists—Bonnie Burnad's *Casino,* Eliza Clark's *What You Need,* Shyam Selvadurai's *Funny Boy* and Steve Weiner's *The Museum of Love.* Literature written by South Asian Canadian writers has a special appeal for Indians here. This has significantly helped the growth of Canadian literature in this country.

Let us now assess the position of Canadian literature in India. English literature, regarded as the cannon, has reigned supreme in Indian curriculum. Majority of English programmes at Indian universities remain steadfastly Anglocentric elevating British literature over all others. Introduction of non-British studies has undoubtedly been a slower and more difficult process. Commonwealth literature, has earned a small niche for itself as recently as the eighties and nineties. There has been a lively curiosity about new literary phenomenon in various Commonwealth countries, especially Canada, Australia, and Nigeria. Amongst the new literatures, Canadian literature has drawn an enormous attention.

In the recent years, more and more universities have included Canadian writers and areas of study as a part of academic programmes. In some universities, Canadian literature is offered as a separate course. But most of the departments teach representative Canadian texts in courses on 'Post-Colonial Literature,' 'The New Literatures in English,' 'Women's Writing' but the large majority subsume Canadian literature under the umbrella of 'Commonwealth Literature.' Under the circumstances, a Canadianist is confronted with the problem of selecting one or two texts to represent the literary output of the entire country. An enquiry regarding this aspect reveals that the two extremely popular writers in Indian curriculum are—Margaret Laurence and Margaret Atwood.

Nature in Early Canadian Poetry

NANDITA SINHA

In a country of vast landscapes and distinctive natural configurations, it is hardly surprising that nature forms a dominant theme in early Canadian poetry, especially in the lyric verse of the Confederation poets—Charles G.D. Roberts (1860-1943), Archibald Lampman (1862-1947). Though all of them were inheritors of the romantic tradition, echoing Wordsworth, Keats and Tennyson, their poetry nevertheless expressed the typical Canadian dilemma of a dichotomy between literary landscape conventions and the real landscape that they inhabited. The sentimental, pastoral tradition is thus crossed by a more immediate one that imaged the terrifying coldness, emptiness and vastness of the Canadian environment in terms that emphasize terror rather than beauty. The verse of these poets shows, in varying degrees of effort, their struggle to relate imported poetic imagery to a direct experience of Canadian scenery. They achieve distinctiveness of utterance and a sureness of tone only when they manage to abandon stereotypes for a poetry of personal awareness.

Roberts's best poetry is contained in the reminiscences of his boyhood surroundings—the vista across the marshes of Tantramar on the border of New Brunswick and Nova Scotia and the waters of the Bay of Fundy to the Minudie Hills. His ability to record impressions with exactitude is memorable, especially when he is able to resist vague moralizing. He observes "the low wind wash the softening snow" ("The Flight of the Geese," 103),[1] "Tons upon tons of brown green hay" ("In an Old Barn," 102); he remembers "those wide red flats, above tide mark\Pale with scurf of the salt seamed and baked in the sun" ("Tantramar Revisited," 101). This poem is probably Roberts's most Wordsworthian, concerned as it is, like "Tintern Abbey" with loss and the return to a remembered landscape. But the return is in the imagination; the poet prefers memory to actuality, wishing to protect the "darling illusion" from "the hands of chance and change." This unsentimental, bleak clarity of vision is characteristic of the Canadian ethos, the poem imbued with the feeling which Northrop Frye defines as typically Canadian "a feeling of the melancholy of a thinly settled country under a bleak northern sky."[2]

The precarious balance between established traditions and a distinctive voice and approach is evident in Archibald Lampman, whose boyhood was spent in Gore's Landing on Rice Lake near Peterborough, Ontario, a locale of woods and lakes and fields which nourished his poetic temperament. Lampman's greatest pleasure was walking in the countryside and on several occasions he went on canoeing and hiking trips into the northern Ontario wilderness. His love of the outdoor embodies itself in the precise and concrete images of his best nature poetry. Lampman's personal life was full of unhappiness and frustration and so he retreated into nature, which was to him both an escape and a source of inspiration. The echoes of Wordsworth are very strong, especially the Wordsworthian experience of being "laid asleep in body" to "become a living soul." All of Lampman's poems lead up to this central moment of dream or trancelike state of consciousness. In his experience of nature, Lampman's observation of the outer world is at the same time an affirmation of the autonomy and creativity of the human mind. It is a sensation of being both rooted in the surroundings and being lifted above it into another sphere of cosmic consciousness. In "Late November" (126) the poet watches the "thick-driving snow" relentlessly covering all landmarks. It is a scene of bleakness and melancholy, observed with careful fidelity to the colours and contours of particular objects. "Wrapped round with thought, content to watch and dream," the poet feels strangely sheltered and uplifted. Melancholy is the dominant mood of "In November" (127) with its images of bleakness, emptiness, decay and death. It describes a wintry day when the poet comes upon a clearing in the woods "peopled" by dead mullein stalks. It is an eerie, almost sinister scene. Then in an epiphanic moment, a ray of sunlight suddenly shines out and conveys upon the scene "A sort of spectral happiness" "A pleasure secret and austere." The sense of affirmation and renewal delicately offsets the haunting quality of the poem.

In the much-acclaimed poem "Heat" (121) Lampman exquisitely renders the sun-scorched panorama of the Ontario landscape:

The burning sky-line blinds my sight
The woods far off are blue with haze
The hills are drenched in light.

It vividly recreates the shimmering effect of the heat waves. The poem is structured round oppositions—movement and stillness, coolness and heat, fields and sky, earth and water, sound and silence, darkness and light. The understated conclusion, "In the full furnace of this hour\My thoughts grow keen and clear" grows out of the poet's awareness of the paradox of nature, both "sharp and sweet."

Lampman's handling of the sonnet form was masterly. It allowed him both personal expression and the reticence imposed by the stylized structure. Lampman's temperamental affinity to Keats finds expression in his sonnets of the same paradox that is central to Keats's poetry—that beauty is fleeting, only in art can it survive.

Nature, in Lampman's poems has its terrors as well as its beauties. In "Winter Evening" (132):

Soon from height to height
With silence and the sharp, unpitying stars
Stern creeping frosts, and winds that touch like steel,
Out of the depth beyond the eastern bars
Glittering and still shall come the awful night.

We have here the idea of the essential neutrality of the non-human world, its indifference to man's problems, which will emerge again in later poets like E.J. Pratt and early Birney. Northrop Frye comments: "the winter, with its long shadows and its abstract black and white patterns does reinforce themes of desolation and more particularly, of the indifference of nature to human values, which I should say was the central Canadian tragic theme.[3]

Carman's response to nature was instinctive, impressionistic and traditional. His drawbacks lay in vagueness and imprecision, his strengths in his ability to evoke a mood or atmosphere. His "Low Tide on Grand Pre" (111) has been called the most nearly perfect poem to come out of Canada in the nineteenth century. It is a nostalgic, emotional recreation of a past love. The landscape expresses both his remembered ecstasy and the sorrow, that followed

Was it a year or lives ago
We took the grasses in our hands
And caught the summer flying low
Over the waving meadow lands
And held it there between our hands?

Ralph Gustafson in his preface to *The Penguin Book of Canadian Verse* says: "In Carman's best is a clear beautiful music, and honesty that is the daring of innocence, and over all, a joyousness of spirit and a gentleness of soul that are heedlessly winning—an imagination which Lampman found 'that of our northern land.'" (29)

The difficulties of matching the idiom of European Romanticism with the experience of the Canadian landscape is keenly felt in the poetry of Duncan Campbell Scott, especially since Scott was intimately concerned with the northern wilderness, as head of the Department of Indian affairs. Scott was more open to experimenting with poetic modes than his contemporaries and sometimes is able to achieve a terse rhythm wholly appropriate to the presentation of the Canadian reality. He succeeded in creating a kind of free verse, irregular in rhythm, plain in diction and restrained in tone—that was eminently suitable to stark narratives about Indian trappers and other inhabitants of the north. Nature, primitive and untamed, reveals herself to him in two opposed aspects of serenity and violence, the conflict in nature imaging man's own inner conflicts. In "Night Hymns of Lake Nipigon" (513) the natural background of darkness and storm mirrors the human conflict of the doomed Indian way of life. The storm becomes an image of the inexorable violence of human history which "whelms them in splendid hollows of booming thunder/wraps them in rain, that sweeping breaks and onrushes/Ringing like cymbals."

Until the late 1920s, Canadian poets were content to continue in the Romantic tradition. But the publication in 1936 of an anthology called *New Provinces* revealed that the modernist sensibility was slowly but surely establishing itself. The poetry of Finch, Kennedy, Klein, Pratt, F.R. Scott and A.J.M. Smith brought in metaphysical wit, a spare lyricism, science, satire and terseness. For these poets, it has been wryly remarked, "trips to the Canadian fields and streams in a wondrous frame of mind would no longer do." A.J.M. Smith, in an essay which formed the original preface to the anthology, first published in *Canadian Literature* (Spring 1965), was more biting:

"The bulk of Canadian verse is romantic in conception and conventional in form. Its two great themes are Nature and Love—Nature humanized endowed with feeling and made sentimental, Love idealized, sanctified and inflated. . . . The most popular experience is to be pained, hurt, stabbed or seared by Beauty—preferably by the yellow flame of a crocus in the spring or the red flame of a maple leaf in autumn."[4]

A bridge between these two traditions was provided by the poetry of E.J. Pratt (1882-1964). Pratt's roots in the older poetic tradition enabled him to write descriptively and lyrically about the Canadian landscape particularly its starkness, severity and grandeur. Pratt is preeminently a poet of the sea, in particular of the rock-bound, storm-lashed Newfoundland coast that provided him with his earliest, most deeply felt images. His poetry showed what was rugged and violent in the beauty of Canada. His youth spent beside the North Atlantic made him aware of life as a struggle with the harsh environment, where men and women wage an endless battle to make a living from the sea. The natural forces of wind, water and rock can have a terrifying malignant aspect, and Pratt particularly has an eye for the forms of nature that threaten to destroy civilization—the shark, the iceberg, the granite cliffs on a rocky coast line. Pratt's fascination is for all forms of strength and power:

> Here the crags
> Meet with winds and tides
> Not with that blind interchange
> of blow for blow
> That spills the thunder of insentient seas,
> But with the mind that reads assault
> In crouch and leap and the quick stealth
> Stiffening the muscles of the waves ("Newfoundland")[5]

Pratt's perception of the tragic has been conditioned by what he called "the ironic enigma of Nature and its relation to the Christian view of the world." By this he meant the difference between the Christian, romantic view of nature as a manifestation of a beneficent God and the brutal reality of the experience of Newfoundland life. Deterministic philosophy and Hardy's pessimism influenced his own tendency to see man's struggle against nature from an ironic fatalistic perspective. His central concern is evolution and its implications for man and nature, and he works out this theme in long narratives of epic proportions.

Margaret Atwood in *Survival* defines four basic Victim Positions into which she fits in Canadian literature, putting the nature poetry of the nineteenth century in Position one—To deny the fact that you are a victim. As she says wittily: "Pretending that nature is the all-good Divine Mother when you're being eaten by mosquitoes or falling into bogs is position one. It can't really stand up very long against the Canadian climate and the Canadian terrain, measured against which Wordsworth's Lake District—Divine Mother Country—is merely a smallish lukewarm pimple."[6] Other positions move from Nature as dead or indifferent through Nature as hostile, to Position four, which she defines as, To be a creative non-vicitim. In terms of poetry it connotes an attitude of acceptance, of seeing oneself as part of the process. Such moments are rare in Canadian poetry, but as we have seen, the early poets did make tentative forays into this ambivalence. If, in general, these poets remained close to the established traditions, they charted fresh territory often enough to belie the assumption that early Canadian nature poetry was a mere pale imitation of the British inheritance.

NOTES

1. Carl F. Klinck and Reginald E. Walters, ed., *Canadian Anthology* (Toronto: Gage Educational Publishing, 1974).
2. Northrop Frye, "The Narrative Tradition in English-Canadian Poetry," in *Canadian Anthology*, p. 604.
3. Northrop Frye, "Preface to an Uncollected Anthology," *Ibid.*, p. 599.
4. A.J.M. Smith, "A Rejected Preface," *Ibid.*, p. 586.
5. Peter Buitenhuis, ed., *Selected Poems of E.J. Pratt* (Macmillan of Canada, 1968), p. 3.
6. Margaret Atwood, *Survival. A Thematic Guide to Canadian Literature* (Toronto: Anansi, 1972).

Voice of Violence—A Reading of Irving Layton's Poems

V. SAM SAHAYAM

> Ghetto of the elect. A wall, a ditch.
> Expect no mercy. In this most Christian
> of worlds, the poet is a Jew. Mariana Tsvetayeva

The wounds of the war are still green in Irving Layton, a contemporary Canadian Jewish poet. He speaks for the Jew; and for the Jew alone. He is unforgiving, for he feels the Jew has been callously let down by the Christian nations. Some lyric poets invent their own world, he says,

> With sunsets and petunias
> skylarks
> a heart a great love
> has cracked.

But Layton confesses:

> Mine's made
> from charred bones
> the smiles of fair-haired
> humans
> looking at them. ("The Lyric")

According to Layton, all the Europeans were involved in the persecution of the Jews, either actively, like the Germans or passively, like those who allowed the holocaust to happen. In "Whom I Write For," the poet frankly confesses that he has no patience to plead or preach:

I do not write to improve your soul
or to make you feel better, or more humane

His is a poetry of 'emotion,' but there is hardly anything 'tranquil' about it. It is, in brief, nothing but the nursing of the grief, and the poet exhorts his readers to become totally involved in the feeling of his own sense of outrage:

I want you to feel as if I had slammed
   your child's head against a spike,
And cut off your member and stuck it in your
   wife's mouth to smoke like a cigar.

He has utter contempt for the "lying poets"—"toadies and trained seals"—who allow "their envy and impotence flower into poems/And their anality into love of man." As for himself, the poet would rather spit fire and brimstone for he has already made his judgement, once and for all:

Give me words fierce and jagged enough,
   to tear your skin like sharpnel, . . .
Words with the sound of crunching bones
   or bursting eyeballs;
or a nose being smashed with a gun butt.

Layton employs surrealistic imagery to drive home the Fall of Man from the grace of Eden. The entire tone of his poem "Wagschal Exhibition" that deals with man's post-lapsarian state is reeking with a sense of disgust and nausea. Eden's birds, according to the poet,

                                        drape
the gangrenous vegetation
like monstrous black snowflakes.

There is no 'milk of human kindness' flowing in the verses of Layton and his poems are the very antithesis of those pleading for humanity, empathy and synthesis, themselves being assertions bordering on the anarchistic. Layton's fury remains to this day unmitigated, as can be discerned from his apathy for his contemporary Canadians, even the Canadian Jews:

> Living, they are as dead.
> The failed violinist
> The self-despising lawyer.
> The art teacher, his soft belly
> pink and sleek. And
> several middle-aged women, a smirk
> betraying the dirty secret in their skulls. . . .

Layton's affinity for his forebears springs out of a gut feeling and not from any source of sentimental piety or ardent veneration for their exemplary lives, as can be discerned from the blatantly irreverential tone in which he refers to them in "The Benediction":

> I gaze entranced
> at those of long departed
> rabbinical ancestors
> lecherous great-uncles
> murdered skin
> famed disputants in seminaries.

There is no doubt that Layton seems to be reliving all the agonies of his ancestors in his veins, and in his verses. However, his capacity for vicarious feeling as a poet, begins and ends with the Jew. Such a myopic obsession with the 'clan' lends a peculiar—and unmistakable—edge to his verse in "The Search":

> Alien and bitter the road my forebears knew:
> fugitives forever eating unleavened bread
> and hated pariahs. . . .
> Times there were the living envied the dead.

Layton puts the entire blame for the persecution suffered by the Jews on Christ:

> that one Jew
> who taught the tenderest Christian how to hate
> and harry them to whatever holes they sped.

Layton's poems like "The Crucifixion," "The Galilean," "Shlemihl," "The Luminous Bagel," "Jeshua" and others present the poet's utterly irreverential attitude towards Christ and also a certain helpless obsession with Christ as we find in D.H. Lawrence:

> Brother, if it's the last thing I do
> in this rotten beautiful world
> I'm going to paint you
> with your white robe parted
> and your circumscribed cock showing
> caught in the fringes
> of your *talith*. ("The True Picture")

The words with which Layton addresses Boris Pasternak, the author of *Dr. Zhivago*, as can be expected, are far from being complimentary, as according to the poet, Pasternak betrayed the Jews by becoming a 'Christian':

> Boris, you were soft as a boiled potato
> No Hemingway women had you by your balls . . .
> Was it weakness made you write the gospel poems,
> blubbering at the foot of the Cross
> where you flung yourself—a baptized unheroic Jew?
> ("Boris Pasternak")

Layton can admire only those Jews who participated in violent struggles for the Semitic cause. For this reason he praises Osip Mandelstam (1891-1940), calling him "a surreal Son of David": "We yet speak to each other, brother to brother." And he has positive contempt for his fellow Canadians who preferred to live a life of comfort, having failed to sustain and nourish their racial need for rancour and revenge:

> So they chew branflakes and crabmeat, gossip, make love
> take out insurance against fires and death
> while our poetesses explore their depressions
> in delicate complaints regular as menstruation. . . .
> they are mankind's gold and ivory toilet bowls
> where brute or dictator relieves himself
> when reading their grave messages to posterity.
> ("Osip Mandelstam")

Langston's lack of self-control and his irrepressible fury, no doubt, borders on the maniacal, for he makes no bones about his uncompromising desire for revenge in "For Nadezhda Mandelstam":

> When freedom flings his fiery horseshoes they explode,
> Sending scorching hails with a loud noise
> At the heads, eyes and groins of my enemies. . . .
> The Stalins hatch everywhere. The poet must break
> Their backs with a hammer's blow.

Layton's impatience and vehemence, at times, drive the poet in him to seek a parallel for his own image in Satan or Lucifer, standing on "the burning marle":

> I dreamt that I was Satan
> Being warmed by molten stones. ("Heinrich Heine")

Layton makes frequent mention of his defiance and rejection of Christ as he tends to associate Christ with all what the so-called 'Christian' nations have done to the Jews in Europe:

> what imbecilities have been said and done
> in your name, what madness. . . . ("Incident at the Cathedral")

He calls Jesus "whoreson, bastard, *meshumad*" for neither the Church nor the Christians spoke for the Jews in the days of their persecution:

> Priests and nuns
> were blots on the snow
> —forbidding birds, crows

To Layton, Christ is a simple demagogue "haranguing and haloing." However, ironically enough, in the sign of the Cross, he finds

> not a symbol
> of impotence and failure
> nor of humiliation and defeat
> But of spiritual power, forever
> beyond the reach of nails or bullets. . . .
> Of the eternal Jew crucified
> for freedom and creativity ("The Sign of the Cross")

Layton sees Christ only as a sinful human being, who called upon himself a summary punishment, because of his own pride. In one of his poems entitled "The Sinner," Christ himself figures as the protagonist:

> Arrogantly I cursed the fig tree
> the scribes and pharisees

and "only with my last groan did I give up my pride.

Thus one finds in Layton's verse a remarkable poetic energy stemming out his Semitic rancour, as he refashions history, surveying with his jaundiced eyes. To him, the other victims of poverty and war in the post-war period like the displaced Palestinian Arabs or the Vietnamese 'Boat People' do not merit the kind of sympathy the Jews need.

Beyond any shade of doubt, Layton's extremism has seriously jeopardized the quality of his verse. His poems may not only lack the universal appeal, but may well turn out to be works triggering off serious conflicts in a world which is already fraught with political strife over other issues. Nevertheless, the extraordinary energy of his poems deserves critical attention and invites comparisons from other contemporary poets. In particular, Layton's poems can be studied for the thematic contrast they provide, when contrasted against the humane, synthetic vision of the poems of Eli Mandel, a fellow Canadian Jewish poet, whose poems stress on the 'pity of war' (Wilfred Owen).

Thematically, Layton's poems invite comparison with the poems of Stephen Spender, the British poet, who too has inherited some Jewish blood, and whose poems make an emotional and moving document on war, embracing all humanity. Even more interestingly, Layton's poems have much in common with those of Nissim Ezekiel in their skepticism with regard to religion and in their mockery of the scriptures, though they present a striking contrast to the vision of the contemporay Indian Jewish poet in the final analysis.

National Interpretation in Terms of Individual Expression through Drama: A Study of Two Plays of Robertson Davies

N. KALAAMANI

"Our drama is not characterised by a garrison mentality, or its offspring survival, nor even . . . by leaving home, but rather by arriving, exploring, questioning and above all, by celebrating the discovery of place," observes Ann Saddlemyer in her essay "Thoughts on National Drama and the Founding of Theatres."[1] This celebration and discovery could have been the chief concerns of dramatists, until 1920, but after this period playwrighting found a new focus and a new phase of exploration as if in answer to Harcourt Farmer, who was raising the pertinent question: "Where are the Canadian playwrights—I mean persons of Canadian descent or adoption, who have written plays, the subject matter of which deals with some intrinsic part of Canadian life—past or present, and whose plays are directly artistic representations of Canadian life, or interpretation of Canadian temperament?"[2] What sort of identity could be presented in a bilingual, multi-cultural, pluralistic society?

It is true that Canadian literature was prolific in its various forms of literature, like poetry, and fiction. But as far as drama was concerned, there were very few names, until and during the second world war, when a handful of dramatists came to the forefront. Most memorable among them were the three dramatists—Given Pharis Ringwood, John Coulter and Robertson Davies. It would not be superfluous to add, that of the three, it was Robertson Davies, who was able to feel the pulse of an immigrant culture.

As against literary works whose primal focus was on landscape, Robertson Davies essayed to present the immigrant world of thoughts, dreams and emotional responses. The struggle to come to terms with a landscape, a people, and more than that to aspire for a psychological identification and imaginative oneness with their physical environment—these were Robertson's primal concerns in his dramatic works. The immigrant race's intellectual pioneers, their struggle to find an artistic atmosphere, was a theme that attracted the writer. Playwriting became his chief medium. He had a good theatre experience. For ten years he had thrown his considerable energies into theatre writing and directing plays for the 'Little Theatre' and for several professional companies. He sat on the board of the Stratford Drama Festival from 1953 to 1971.

His dramatic carrer was eventful. Before marrying the stage manager of the old Vic Company, Brenda Mathews, for whom he acted bit parts, he had acted briefly with a provincial acting company. Besides this, he had taught theatre history at school and done a major part of the literary work for the director. His Oxford thesis, published on Shakespeare's boy actors (1939) was an indepth study of the capacities of the boy actors and what they may be trained to do. Till his retirement (1981), he had been contributing much, to the then newly established Drama Centre at Toronto, where he was Master of Massey College.

Beginning as a playwright fighting the issues and impacts of colonialism, Robertson Davies was determined to break away from the British influences and recreate a literary dramatic landscape for Canada. He had established his claims as a novelist. Nevertheless, as a playwright, he ventured on new Canadian subjects, spangling on his canvas a wide variety of themes on Canadian life, art and ideas, that one could see him at once pioneering and as a powerful voice on the emerging dramatic front.

Like many of his journalistic writings, his plays emphasize the need of intelligent liberate people, who could stimulate and inspire writers. Such a reading public or audience, Robertson Davies was convinced, could be the basis of a civilized life. The Canadian writer had been persistently preoccupied with encounters with the landscape that he had lost all concerns with the intellectual life. Robertson Davies sought to emphasize this aspect of Canadian culture in his plays. As a result, his early works harbour on themes of Canada's failure to see art as essential to its development as a civilized nation. And good art needs a good environment. In him was a fervent desire to establish an ideal intellectual climate for writers to flourish, that in many of his works, as in *A Voice* Davies appears in the role of an educator arguing that Canada needs intelligent masses. The same urge towards education, stimulation and liberation appears in his fiction from *A Mixture of Frailties* (1958) onwards.

His two plays, *At My Heart's Core* and *Overlaid*, are investigations into the intellectual struggles of pioneers. *At My Heart's Core* is an idyllic picture of an immigrant culture, presenting a variety of moods, ranging from curiosity and adventure to exploration, discovery, fear, anger, confrontation, protest and reconciliation. In his Epilogue to the two plays, Davies observes: "*At My Heart's Core* came directly from my sense of intellectual loneliness of the pioneers who had left the world of the mind behind them, and tried to keep up their contact with it from the depth of wilderness."[3]

At My Heart's Core pivots round a group of intellectuals emigrated from Ireland. Presenting the multifarious conflicts in the lives of these immigrants, Robertson Davies throws a kaleidoscopic insight into the physical, social, economic, cultural and religious milieus of Canada. And amidst the orchestration of these various notes, is the struggle of the intellectual pioneers searching for an environment.

The Bushes and the Backwoods of Canada offer no environment for creative ventures; aspiring for a suitable climate and unable to find one, the handful of intellectuals, and women of refinement, Mrs. Catherine Parr Traill, Mrs. Susanna Moodie and Frances Stewart nostalgically look back to a past. The past brings back memories of not only a congenial landscape, but temptations of different kinds. The temptations are objectified in the figure of Cantwell.

Cantwell, an immigrant coming from the unknown, is by far the most interesting character in the play. He comes uninvited, he leaves boldly and stays in the house of Frances Stewart, quite defiantly. He obviously has quite a store of knowledge about each of these women and angles them with their own weakness. In fact, the temptation of Cantwell, far from being sexual, is one that attunes to their innate intellectual cravings.

Frances Stewart is a woman of rank and refinement. She is well-bred, pleasant and hospitable, a typical Irish landlady. Mr. Stewart, her magistrate-husband, has power, but in a newfoundland lacking social consciousness and an atmosphere agitated with the politico-religious upheaval, her rank and refinement are vainglorious.

She is denied a social environment which could give her life a meaning. It is this innate desire in her that Cantwell picks up subtly and works on: "You are beautiful, highly born, witty and possessed of that wonderful generosity of spirit—that quality of giving—which raises beauty and charm to the level of great and holy virtues. What need has the backwoods of these things? You should not be here. You choose wrongly." He compares her to Lady Rossmore, who, so to say, has usurped her place—in the midst of that brilliant and fashionable society, with the light of a hundred candles falling upon her jewels—and, she, Frances, sitting on a rush chair by the light of a backwood's fire. Frances, momentarily is carried away by the temptation, but intelligent as she is, checks him.

Next, he tempts Mrs. Traill, a scientist. Having stood in such high regard of Mr. Sheppard the renowned naturalist, it was criminal to waste her life here in a climate intellectually barren and devoid of stimulation. His provocation is subtle: "If you have it in you to do notable scientific work is of not my concern, as a man of some education myself, to ask why you make it a bad second to the drudgery of a settler's wife." He goes to the extent of driving her against her husband: "I'm suggesting that for your sake, and your children's sake and for the sake of the advancement of knowledge, your husband should play second fiddle to you." In fact, he grudgingly remarks: "We are not animals, and the female does not live at the sufferance of male."

Everytime he succeeds in tempting, though momentarily, a horn is heard in the background. This again happens when he tempts Mrs. Moodie. He talks to her about her artistic ability:

> We are not man and woman, Mrs. Moodie, but artist and connoisseur—a vastly more delicate relationship and I tell you that you may strangle all your children in their beds, murder Moodie with the cleaver, trample the British flag under your feet and Almighty God will find some mercy for you; but if you for an idiotic scruple refuse to write your best, he will put you into hellfire and I, as a critic will applaud His Judgement. Do you understand me?

Mrs. Moodie stops him: "You make my scribbling seem very important." But Cantwell rebukes her with the words,

> Do you suppose that the importance of literature is

> diminished because nobody hereabout understands it. Would music cease to exist because your neighbours were deaf? I have said that Mrs. Traill's work is important. But that is science—a chilly business at best. Your work is art, and art is what gives form and meaning to life. Dare you neglect the sacred obligation which has been laid upon you?

Mrs. Moodie begins to realize her importance and sees herself as the peer of Ms. Edgeworth.

But all the three ladies, intelligent as they are, instantly discard the desires that he stirs in them. However thoughts once been aroused, refuse to settle. The ladies become thoroughly agitated. Their anger finds the target in Cantwell. Thus when the magistrate appears on the scene, the three ladies jointly victimize him. In fact what interests us in the play is how the Magistrate tackles Cantwell and the ladies in a seemingly jocular fashion, but emerges as the most perceptive and enduring of all the others. With his catalytic appearance he makes each of the ladies see into their Heart's Core. Where Cantwell has made inroads into their hearts, he carefully brings them out of it. Finally he also gives them a path which they could traverse with the news for Catherine and Mrs. Moodie. His wife, as to his expectations, emerges all the more stronger for these temptations.

The play could be read as an exercise in intellectual pioneering. Most of the characters are real. These actual-life characters not only embody the struggle for an intellectual climate, but epitomize the angst, and the rootlessness of an immigrant culture. A particular reference should be made of Susanna Moodie. Interestingly Susanna Moodie has attracted the attention of many a writer, as for example Margaret Atwood, who in her *Journals of Susanna Moodie* has depicted the typical immigrant yearning in the person of Mrs. Moodie. Atwood even regarded Susanna Moodie as her cultural ancestor, the archetypal immigrant—typically reluctant, alienated, cut off from her new environment by consciousness of herself and of the cultural incongruities of her position—and at the same time, though less obviously, the fact that she is a woman, an artist, cultivated, critical, ill at ease in the wilderness, but strong and enduring. Atwood chose "Mrs. Moodie because she reflects many of the obsessions still with us," "she becomes a still current voice from the depths of the Canadian psyche." In Susanna Moodie and her sister, is the elucidation of the expatriate experience—the anxiety to possess some point of space to which they can relate emotionally and psychologically—searching for roots, where their intellectual ingenuities could bear fruition. For Robertson Davies, the Strickland sisters became the symbol of the intellectual loneliness of the pioneers who had left the world of the mind behind them.

Apart from the ventures of these handful of intellectuals, there is another character Phelim in this play. An Irish immigrant, Phelim is an ancient relic of the Irish bardic tradition. In every respect he reminds one of 'Pop,' his artistic counterpart in Robertson's other play *Overlaid.* He is revolutionary, audacious, unyielding: the unrecognized ministrel in an alien land. As a contrast to the intellectuals, he is a natural artist craving for identity. The craving for identity for the Arts and the Artistic has always been Davies' preoccupation. The idea finds better representation in Davies' *Overlaid.*

In *Overlaid* (1948) one of his five one-act plays which appeared in *Eros at Breakfast and Other Plays* (the other two are: *Hope Deferred* and *In the Gates of the Righteous*), the life enhancing force of art meets a temporary defeat at the hands of a death-centred religion of respectability as the father character Pop desires a cultural spree in New York to his daughter Ethel's yearning for a solid granite family tombstone.

The play draws a significant dialectic between the life-in-art and death-in-life paradigm in the central characters of Pop and Ethel—the father and his daughter. Pop in identifying himself with art and the artistic poses a violent contrast to his respectable, religious-daughter. She is hard-working, "good," respectable, "all-sacrificing." Her father is rebellious, non-conformist, romantic and adventurous. Ethel appears as a hard-faced woman of forty, with a basket of clothes for ironing; and Pop is presented as an epicurean wanting to relish the exotic pleasures of life. When the play opens, Pop is found all ears to the Saturday broadcast on the radio, to the performance given by the president of his Opera Guild. Ethel comes in, and unable to tolerate this noisy programme turns off the set.

A wordy argument ensues, only to be interrupted by the appearance of the Insurance Agent whose announcement of the maturity amount of twelve hundred dollars triggers off another kind of argument. Pop finds it an opening to the realization of his life-long dream for a cultural holiday at New York, only to be cut short by his well-meaning but most commonplace realist of a daughter. Pop is persistent. He wants to drink life to its very dregs; he has even charted out a programme as to how he would spend the money:

> I'd tell you what I'd do, since you're so nosey: I'd get some stylish clothes, and I'd go into one o' these restrunts, and I'd order vittles you never heard of better than the burnt truck Ethel calls food—and I'd get a bottle of wine—cost a dollar—may be two—and drink it all, and then I'd nosey along to the Opera House and I'd buy me a seat right down beside the trap drummer, and there I'd sit an' listen, and holler and hoot and raise hell whenever I liked the music an' throw bookies to the gals, an' wish at the chorus, and when it was over I'd go to one of these here night-clubs an' eat some more, an' drink whiskey, and watch the gals' take off their clothes—every last dud, kinda slow an' Devilish till they're bare naked—an' may be I'd one of them fifty bucks for her brazeer—

Ethel could only stare at him in disbelief. She is stunned, scandalized. When she collects herself, she raves at him: "Is that what your soul feeds on, Restrunts with shameless women in 'em?" But Pop is nonchalant. He is determined. His goal is set. He is regardless of ethics or ecclesiastics, effects or ettiquettes, God is life-giving and not life-denying. Starving and tormenting the soul in the name of religion is blaspheming god. Anything joy-yielding, life-yielding is divine. One cannot catch the Niagara in a tea-cup. So is god. Anything that maims or restricts life, or the life-forces is restricting god, and therefore a profanity. In the Lawrentian sense, Pop propogates. The man-alive concept. And like Whitman, he avers that man contains multitudes. The body, he affirms is as sacred as the soul. In fact, Pop staunchly proclaims: "God likes music an' naked women an' I'm happy to follow his example—" Pop's vision is essentially epicurean.

But, what interests us in the play is not Pop's dreams, but how he enkindles, tempts, intimidates, corners his daughter to stir up the dormant dream in her, the dream that she has buried so deeply within her that no amount of levering on the part of Pop is successful until eventually he pretends that he has sharked on his holidaying tour. But when Ethel comes out with her innate desire, it is sadly unfortunate that she requires only a tombstone, perhaps an expensive granite family tombstone.

From beginning to the end, Ethel is a striking contrast to Pop. Whenever Pop is involved in a life-giving venture, Ethel quiets him. His last act of endorsing the cheque to Ethel, giving her an opportunity to accomplish that her life-dream is an unexpected twist in the play. In this instant, one reckons in the stead of the whimsical, inadvertent, aged epicurean a soft-natured, benevolent, all-sacrificing father figure in Pop. His apparent indifference is only an apparel that unfolds the most-ennobling and endearing sentiments for a daughter who left him for the sake of religion: "and I guess it was as if you'd died to me, and everything I liked. So far as I'm concerned, 'his here tombstone's mostly for the little one I lost." Pop had been cherishing the love for his daughter, but she was lost to him. In giving her what she requires, he finds his fulfilment. Throughout the play, Pop finds himself a symbol of everything that is artistic, ennobling and life-giving. The mind, body and life are his soul, his god. Art is the life-force. If religion, or any institution should restrain man, curb him of his spontaneity, they should be abhorred. Life should be emotionally enriching, soul-stimulating, mind-ennobling. Life in co-ordination with the Art is therefore what Man should aspire.

Pop emerges as the Daviesian voice imploring a recognition for all that is life-giving, that is artistic. For all that is beautiful and ennobling in life. The radio-set is only an externalization of his inner self, his quest for art and beauty: "If our lives lack beauty, we are poor indeed"—he aspires for the fulfilment which the noblest art can give. He experiences this fulfilment in listenin' to the radio every Saturday afternoon, in being a member of the Op'ry Radio guild, wearing its hat and gloves etc. . . .

To Robertson Davies, Pop becomes the embodiment of the Intellect—the aims, dreams, imagination and art. As in *At My Heart's Core,* in this play he rediscovers life, the life of the mind which does not negate the life of the senses (emotional understimulation). At best, his plays are an affirmation of life, the best, the happiest and the most ennobling.

NOTES

1. Ann Saddlemyer, "Thoughts on National Drama and the

Founding of Theatres" in L.W. Conolly, ed., *Theatrical Touring and Founding in North America* (Westport, Connecticut: Greenwood Press, 1982).

2. Harcourt Farmer, "Play-Writing in Canada," *Canadian Bookman* (April 1919).
3. Robertson Davies, from the Epilogue of the Author to *At My Heart's Core* and *Overlaid*, *An Anthology of Canadian Literature in English*, ed. Russell Brown (Toronto: OUP, 1982).

The Female Attempt to Exorcise the Cruel Patriarchy: A Comparative Study of Claire Martin and Sharan-Jeet Shan

RANJANA HARISH

The contemporary feminist critic Patricia Meyer Spacks defines autobiography as a means to exorcise one's past. In her famous book *Imagining a Self* (1976) she writes, "Autobiography assures the author of his [her] existence beyond all possibilities of philosophical denial. Through it he [she] comes to terms with his past or exorcises it."[1]

Women's autobiography writing is very often an attempt to mark a point of departure from their old selves, the selves which were handed down to them by the patriarchal culture of their society, into a new world of self-sufficiency with an ample space for the self. The attempt to exorcise the past, which in Spacks' view is the goal of both male as well as female autobiographies. In case of women autobiography doesn't spring from a common intention to assess the past and define it as do men. Instead, it springs from women autobiographer's deep sex/gender awareness of their marginalized existence in the world dominated by the male culture.

The early critics of the genre like Gusdorf Misch and Olney have looked on an isolated individualistic autobiographical self as a precondition for any autobiography. But in the hands of women autobiographers it becomes a genre of the collective identity. Modern feminist critics of the genre like Nancy Chodorow, Susan Stanford and Shari Benstock have established that for women the definition of self lies in a collective awareness. Woman's identity is rooted in, if not limited to, a collective awareness. This principle of female individuation process is amply supported by Indian psychoanalysts like Sudhir Kakar and Ashis Nandy. Women's autobiography doesn't construct an isolate self, on the contrary it projects a self which is a representative and an extension of others. And thus, with women, autobiography becomes a means to fight back oppression in the patriarchal culture, in which they are constantly pushed to the fringes. Virginia Woolf had rightly called it "the genre of the oppressed."[2]

Sheila Rowbotham the known feminist theorist in her interesting article "The Trouble with 'Patriarchy'" defines patriarchy as "an ideology which arouses out of men's power to exchange women between kinship groups; as a symbolic male principle, and as the power of the father. It has been used to express men's control over women's sexuality and fertility; to describe the institutional structure of male domination."[3] When the members of the oppressed group lift their pen to write autobiography very often they do so with a pronounced determination to reject the suppressing patriarchy. It is, as if, their declaration of defiance.

Claire Martin's Governor General's prize-winning autobiography *In An Iron Glove* (1976) and Sharan-Jeet Shan's autobiography *In My Own Name* (1991) are two striking attempts of members of the "muted group" to turn eloquent against their oppression by the dominant group. The creation of past in both the autobiographies is done with an intention to recreate the memories of the atrocities inflicted on them by men and to exorcise them from their world for ever. In order to carve out a well-defined female space for themselves, they must get rid of the dark, frightening, overpowering shadow of the cruel patriarchs lurking over their lives.

Introducing Claire Martin's autobiography Philip Stratford says, "It was a book that had to be written. From the author's point of view, undoubtedly as a kind of exorcism." Writing about the book Claire Martin herself tells her readers that it was written to fight back the oppression. She writes, "To be a child or a woman will always be like being destitute or coloured—a hazardous situation. And it seems that mankind is always very eager to point out that whenever anyone is strong enough, male enough rich enough or white enough to persecute the weak, he will gladly do so." (1)

Both these women authored autobiographies open with the death-bed scenes of the monstrous patriarchs. Despite their avowed determination not to forgive such cruel men ever, both the autobiographers are surprised to find that their contempt for the men who made their lives a hell melt in the face of death. They forgive the tyrants. But forgiving them is not enough. To exorcise the very memory of the oppressed life under such men, they recreate these cruel patriarchs in the pages of their autobiographies with a well deserved lack of sympathy. Rejecting the slightest pity for the monstrous father, Claire begins her story with the words, "I must put aside the pity that came to me like a late visitor who rings at the door in the middle of the night, someone for whom you must set up a bed and make room." (2)

Claire Martin was a child "born of a marriage between a tiger and a dove." (3) Her father was a terrorizing patriarch who would frighten his children and wife to death, would eat away all the "chosen morsels" and would enjoy iron-handed control over them. He firmly believed that it was his fundamental right to rule over the family with an iron hand as it was a hand which earned for them. Claire writes, "He automatically defined himself as the hand that fed as that didn't impress us unduly. His was the hand that beat us too." (111) Little Claire could feel reassured sitting next to her mother at the dining table only when she put her hand on Claire's legs under the table-cloth. She hated her monstrous father. She loved her timid mother dearly but often she resented the fact that she had married that man: "She had given him to me as a father." (98) Often she prayed for the death of such a cruel father after his "beating sessions" were over. "You Know, mother, I don't like him. I wish he would die," (73) the child would say. Recalling his cruelties, she says, "He enjoyed our cringing silence. He wanted us chronologically terrified. We were. He could take full credit for that." (99)

For first twenty years of her life Claire had to live under such a terrifying father. Her autobiography recreates her deprivation, discrimination, and depression in the rigid patriarchal set-up most vividly. The final chapter, however, shows her growing out of her father's overpowering shadow. Defying the authority of the code of conduct prescribed by the patriarch, she takes to smoking. With a thrill of an unbelievable adventure she records her first experience of defiance against the father thus: "My whole destiny seems altered. I had the feeling I had won a victory over my father that would be followed by many others." (166) The death of her suppressed mother in the final chapter stands as a point of departure from her old self. On her mother's death she makes a vow to herself. She would never forgive and forget the atrocities that the cruel patriarch inflicted on the women of the house, i.e. she, her sister and their mother. She says that until she wrote her autobiography, "Not a single day went by that I didn't take it [hatred for the father] out and give it a good shake. Not to get rid of it. To make sure that it was still as fresh as ever. To hear the lanking of those old chains again." (1) But by putting a handful of earth on the cruel man's coffin she finally forgives him and by giving vent to her memories of his cruelties in her autobiography she exorcises her past and seals it with a hope to create an independent future with ample space for the self.

Sharan-Jeet Shan's experience of patriarchy is no different from that of French Canadian Claire Martin. She too writes to seal her past. In the preface to her autobiography she writes, "In writing my story, in reliving the past, the healing process has begun. It has helped me to throw away the valium and clean out the acrimonious wrath from my soul."

As a girl-child she too had experienced lack of space very acutely. She was born to be "Parai" and hence it was most natural that her status in the family was of a transient, an unwanted guest. One full chapter "Born to be Parai," out of total eighteen chapters of her autobiography, depicts most vividly the deprivation that a girl-child has to suffer and the discrimination that she has to take. She tells us that she was repeatedly told that this was not her home. The little girl observed that all the privileges were meant for males only. They could do whatever they liked while a woman was always to take humiliations at everybody's hands. Her brother, for instance, was served special food as it was he who would carry on the family name. When the kind boy wished to share his special food with his sister he was told by the mother not to do so: "you mustn't spoil your sister. She is 'parai'. She must bear to suppress such temptation." (12)[6] Claire Martin also notes that privileges like possessing fur coats and good food were meant for males in her home.

When Sharan-Jeet objected against such a discrimination the explanation that the senior women of the house, her mother and grandmother, offered her was that she was born a woman. In their view, "It was simply 'bure karam' bad deeds in past lives, which caused one to be born a woman or to be a scheduled caste. If God had meant for me to enjoy the privileges of a man, he would have made me so," (12) recalls Sharan-Jeet.[7]

However, the girl was sent to school and later to medical college as that would make the task of finding a match for her easier. During the first year of her medical studies this love-starved girl came to know a senior medical student Aziz Mohammed and fell in love with him. She knew it was a crime to fall in love in their community and the crime became manifold when the man hailed from another caste, that too a Muslim. When the conservative father came to know about the daughter's love affair, he burst with anger. He discontinued her education and ordered her not to step out of the house. The daughter questioned his authority over her life and received a good deal of thrashing in return. Enraged by such a cruel treatment her determination to marry Aziz became stronger. Finally one night she eloped with Aziz and married him secretly. But the couple was soon found out by Sharan-Jeet's father who dragged the girl home. He was mad with anger as the girl had spoilt "Khandaan ki izzat."

Sharan-Jeet was taken to a far-off village of Punjab where she was kept in captivity in the back room of an old house. The only person who saw her was her enraged father. He visited her twice a day to give her beating. The beating sessions lasted long and stopped only when the cruel patriarch had no more energy to continue. This used to leave the girl with blue patches all over the body. He was pressing her to agree to marry a man of his choice. But the girl was stubborn. She recalls, "I decided to defy all traditions and customs to go on saying no. . . . After all, God could not belong to my father and his relatives alone." She had her own justification based on the concept of the equality of the sexes. Sitting in her dark isolated room she used to wonder whether there existed any justice for the members of female sex. "Nobody had decided his [father's] future for him. No dogma had cut short his career so drastically. Why did he want to destroy mine?" she questioned. (43) But nobody cared to answer her questions. She was a woman born to be treated the way men liked. Her economic dependence made her helpless.

Finally, two months's constant beating and isolation broke Sharan-Jeet's spirits and she gave in. The marriage was fixed. She was to marry a well-to-do London-based Sikh man. After the marriage ceremony when the bride was leaving her father's home, her father blessed her and gave her a hundred rupee note as a token of his love. Under the pretext of giving a parting hug, the bride returned the money and whispered in the man's ear, "Keep it Babuji, as my contribution towards the sale of my body." (49) She would never forgive him, she promised herself and entered one more world of cruel patriarchy filled with inequality and dependence. The bride knew she could carve out her own space only if she could earn. The traditional role-model of "pativrata istree [sic]" handed down to her from her timid mother was of no avail to her. She must shed off her fear, exorcise her past, to grow out of the old, suppressed feminine self to attain her identity.

The last pages of the autobiography show Sharan-Jeet attaining a well-defined identity with the help of economic independence. Her autobiography concludes on the note of fellow-feeling for women and anger for the male culture which feels empowered to decide a woman's fate. She concludes, "As women, we give birth, suffer miscarriages, share the agony of abortion, understand the torment of rape and bring up children. White or black, it is often the man who decides what is to be done with our bodies and minds." (176) She objects to such prevailing reality and calls for the members of the oppressed group to unite to fight back the oppressing patriarchy.

Whether French Canadian or Indian the reality of female life in the patriarchal world remains the same. They must remain satisfied with their marginal existence or discover their way to exorcise the cruel experience of patriarchy to create their well-defined space as do Claire and Sharan-Jeet.

NOTES

1. Patricia Meyer Spacks, *Imagining a Self* (Cambridge: Harvard Univ. Press, 1976), p. 15.
2. Virginia Woolf, "The Lives of the Obscure," *Dial*, May 1925, p. 381.
3. Sheila Rowbotham, "The Trouble with 'Patriarchy'" in *The Women Question*, ed. Mary Evans (Oxford: Fontana Paperbacks), p. 74.
4. Claire Martin, *In an Iron Glove: An Autobiography*, trans. Philip Stratford (Montreal: Harvest House, 1976).
5. Sharan-Jeet Shan, *In My Own Name: An Autobiography* (Delhi: Rupa, 1991).

6. Malvika Karlekar's *Voices from Within: Early Personal Narratives of Bengali Women* (Delhi: OUP, 1991), records many such incidents of girls' starvation and discrimination.
7. Renuka Singh's *Oppression of Women by Women* (New Delhi: Vishwa Yuvak Kendra, 1980) is an excellent study of this theme. She holds that most of the times it is a woman who is responsible for the miseries of the other woman.

Finding an "Immigrant" Voice: Michael Ondaatje's *In the Skin of a Lion*

GERRY TURCOTTE

> The event that will light the way for immigration in North America is the talking picture. The silent film brings nothing but entertainment—a pie in the face, a fop being dragged by a bear out of a department store—all events governed by fate and timing, not language and argument. The tramp never changes the opinion of the policeman. The truncheon swings, the tramp scuttles through a corner window and disturbs the fat lady's ablutions. These comedies are nightmares. The audience emits horrified laughter as Chaplin, blind-folded, rollerskates near the edge of the unbalconied mezzanine. No one shouts to warn him. He cannot talk or listen. North America is still without language, gestures and work and bloodlines are the only currency.
>
> Michael Ondaatje, *In the Skin of a Lion*

In an article entitled "Michael Ondaatje and the Turn to Narrative," Ina Ferris suggests that *narrative* has increasingly "become the privileged form for serious literary inquiry and experimentation."[1] She makes this comment in reference to Michael Ondaatje's "turn to narrative" in a collection of related poems entitled *The Collected Works of Billy the Kid,* a series which won Ondaatje the coveted Governor General's Award for Poetry in Canada. Ferris goes further to suggest that the importance of narrative, versus, for example, lyric poetry, is a condition of contemporary society. Western culture, it would seem, has moved away from the Romantic lyric impulse, to that of the narrative tale.

Ferris is quick to point out, however, that Ondaatje's particular move is not clear-cut; rather, his is a blending of the lyric and the narrative modes, so that each is problematic and intertwined. It is not uncommon, for example, to find his novels called poetic both in style and in form.

This problematic narrative is ideal, Ferris goes on to say, for understanding and investigating the post-modern condition. At the heart of current literary theory is a preoccupation with words. Not, I should say, with *using* words, but with casting a critical eye on the very nature, function and form of language. Increasingly, contemporary criticism and philosophy is turning to words in an attempt to determine what words do, and how they do it. "And for a literary inquiry into such matters, narrative with its claim to referentiality presents itself as the mode that focuses most clearly the currently pressing questions about reality and language."[2]

Beginning with the 1970 volume, *The Collected Works of Billy the Kid,* Ondaatje has focused his own attention on historical figures, or on the act of recording history itself, in an attempt to question the very feasibility of historical verisimilitude. William Bonney, alias Billy the Kid, yields next to the pioneer of modern jazz, Buddy Bolden, the subject of a 1976 novel entitled *Coming through Slaughter*, and the latter, in turn, is succeeded by Ondaatje's own family in an autobiography-cum-novel entitled *Running in the Family*. Ondaatje's interest in the kernel of historical truth suggests his awareness of the mimetic role of fiction—fiction, that is, as a historical document, or, history as a recorder of the truth.

But Ondaatje's peculiar style, half poetry and half novel, half lyric and half narrative, and his very contemporary practice of invoking himself, or at least the fictional author, in the midst of his works, draws attention to the very unreliability of history itself. When he stands before us, as he does in *Running in the Family,* and says, "If those listed above disapprove of the fictional air I apologize and can only say that in Sri Lanka a well-told lie is worth a thousand facts," we are being told to be wary of the Authority of the author.

And Author/ity is what will be my keyword in the discussion that is to follow, because Authority is very much the ghost at the heart of *In the Skin of a Lion.* And I mean Authority here as in *Author*ity, with the Author underlined; and Authority as an entirely different though not unrelated sort of entity, one that represents the mainstream, one that signals established History, the Central Voice that records History and so forth.

Because this novel, *In the Skin of a Lion*, is very much a book about what versions of the truth we ultimately believe in; it is a book about those in power, and their ability to make their word the Law, both metaphorically and actually. And in the end, this book becomes the voice of all those relegated to the margins of society, the so-called migrants of a community, the working-class, the undervalued.

It is also a book about story-tellers, and about the *artist's* potential for exposing any measure of truth through "art." Can the artist's imagination, in other words, resuscitate meaning from "fact"—from "history?" Can fiction truly discover "a moment in the past?" (75) In order for Ondaatje to question these ideas, he must create a text which is, to some measure, meta-fictional. What do I mean by meta-fiction?

Meta-fiction is the term we now use to discuss fiction which is self-conscious of the very devices at its disposal; a fiction, usually, which comments on itself *as* fiction and so, which troubles the boundaries of its very fictionality.

So far, all of this is very theoretical, and it may be useful at this point to start working our way through specific examples in the text. From the very first, we are told that this book will be about *versions* of stories. The epigraph by John Berger states, "Never again will a single story be told as though it were the only one," a comment which echoes an earlier statement in *Running in the Family*: "No story is ever told just once. Whether a memory or funny hideous scandal, we will return to it an hour later and retell the story with additions and this time a few judgements thrown in. In this way history is organized." We are told, point blank, that history is subjective, and ever changing. If history is the record of the winners, to quote the cliché, we are about to engage in a history of the margins.

From this beginning, that is, from the comment "Never again will a single story be told as though it were the only one," we are then given what could also be termed another epigraph, though slightly lengthier in nature, and written by the author himself. It is an opening which tells us, although few readers seem to remember this, that the entire novel which follows, is told during a car ride. The speaker is Patrick, the listener Hana:

> This is a story a young girl gathers in a car during the early hours of the morning. She listens and asks questions as the

> vehicle travels through darkness. . . . She listens to the man as he picks up and brings together various corners of the story, attempting to carry it all in his arms. . . . She stays awake to keep him company.

As one critic has put it, "The first page of the frame-story makes sense only with regard to the last two pages of the novel."[3] What we realize in retrospect, is that this is a story, told in difficult circumstances, so that it is a narrative of dubious reliability. After all, our narrator is sleepy and preoccupied. But we also know, if we dig a little deeper, that the narrator is himself suspect. Hana, one could argue, is the one recording the tale; it is she who "listens" to the man, and who "gathers" the story. This cryptic and elusive note, then is our introduction to the novel.

In the Skin of a Lion signals, from its opening pages, that this will be a novel about story-telling, about naming, about whose version of the world will triumph and be remembered. And it is about those people who are part of all stories, although they are rarely written about, and it is about their place in the narrative.

Because this book will take such an antagonistic approach to official history, it seems pointless to focus needlessly on the "facts" of this story. Yes, the character of Ambrose Small really existed; yes the bridge was built in much the same way that it is described herein; the Union Strikes occurred, and the shootings; and the opening of the bridge itself was "marred" according to official documents, by a figure who "escaped by bicycle through the police barriers—the first member of the public. Not the expected show car containing officials, but this one anonymous and cycling like hell to the east end of the city." (27)

It would be difficult for Australians to read this passage and not think of a similar moment in Australian history, when the Sydney Harbour Bridge was itself seized by a Captain De Groot, who galloped ahead of the officials, sliced the ribbon of Authority and in so doing cut himself a piece of history. Who remembers the officials who were meant to cut the ribbon? Who, indeed, would remember such moments, were it not for these "illegal" figures who emerge from the sidelines to seize the day? Ondaatje's novel, and this particular moment, stand as testaments to the artificiality of official historical records, and to the strength and effectiveness of political protest.

In a way, it is possible to see this thin ribbon stretched across either the Sydney Harbour Bridge or the Prince Edward Bridge, as the strand of official history. Such is its thinness, its delicacy. History and authority is as fragile as that strip of cloth so easily torn. These figures—our blurred cyclist or our mounted Captain—establish the presence of other stories, other lives, other versions of history which want their say, and which are always present, sometimes in focus other times not.

In Ondaatje's novel we are told that there are photographs which record the cyclist's act: "he is a blur of intent. He wants the virginity of it, the luxury of such space." (27) He goes on to say that "the cyclist . . . claimed the bridge in that blurred moment, alone and illegal. Thunderous applause greeted him at the far end." (27) But we are also told that even this cyclist "was not the first. The previous midnight the workers had arrived and brushed away officials who guarded the bridge in preparation for the ceremonies the next day," (27) and had their own ceremony. In one brief, eliptical moment, Ondaatje makes clear the difference between sanctioned ideas of History—of what happened "officially"—and counter-history.

This episode, occurring as it does early in the novel, together with the scene which features Nicholas and the vanishing Nun highlights Ondaatje's preoccupation with borders, with what is left out of the official story. And if we are to make any sense of this eliptical novel, we will have to look to these outskirts for meaning.

The outskirts are, of course, where we normally relegate the migrants. This spurious term—who, after all, isn't a migrant?—is used to describe a number of people in the novel, people who will stand in opposition to authority figures. Patrick, for one, is called an "immigrant" to the city when he leaves his rural home to find work; and of course the workers on the bridge, and later on the tunnel, are more "obviously" migrants. They speak a language other than the controlling tongue; they have their own quarters and cook their own food. And, as one critic puts it, "Their desire to belong to and be accepted by the mainstream is in essence a desire for language, a language appropriate for the metropolitan Canadian experience." (93)

Of course, these figures *are* part of the mainstream. They are the people who built the city of Toronto between 1914 and 1938. It is their labour, their deaths, their sacrifice which has shaped the city. But this contribution is easy to ignore if we read official documents. What is valued is the imagination of Commissioner Harris—his vision of the bridge and later of the Waterworks is considered more real than the work of the builders, so that Harris buys his way into the history books.

But Ondaatje shows us that this imagination is limited; or at least that it is only one variety. Nicholas Temelcoff, for his part, comes to represent one of the many artist figures throughout the novel, an artist figure who rivals Harris, and who comes, at last, to recognize his own role in the fabric of history. And to establish this I have to digress for a moment.

In his early writing, in a poem called "Spider Blues" to be precise, Ondaatje created a metaphor of the writer as spider, a spider poet "making lines out of the juice of his own abdomen." For Ondaatje, the poet's role was one who "thinks a path and travels/the emptiness that was there/leaves his bridge behind."[4] The image of the poet spinning in space, leaving his or her arc behind, and though self-centred, still creating *something*, can easily be super-imposed on the figure of Temelcoff.

Temelcoff is a "daredevil" who swings through space, who "falls off the bridge like a diver over the edge of a boat," (34) and whose timing is described punningly as "immaculate" (32) when he catches the nun. But Temelcoff, despite his ability, has no place in the official picture. His role is to be invisible in his usefulness and skill: "even in archive photographs," we're told, "it is difficult to find him." (34) Temelcoff, I would argue, is just one of Ondaatje's artist figures. His function, for example, is described in literary terms: he is "the speck of burned paper across the valley" in one shot, or an "exclamation mark," a figure who knits "the bridge together. The moment of cubism." (34)

These artistic references, to writing and to painting, together with the image of the spider, suggest that Temelcoff is part of a continuum of artist figures in Ondaatje's pantheon. But he is a symbol of the artist on the outskirts, which is where the artist should or needs to be according to the text. Nicholas is not official history. If his art is cubism, it is the revision, even the rejection, of what seems apparent, in the same way that Picasso re-saw and represented reality as a cubist artist. His break from authority is not only signalled by the fact that he does not appear clearly in Official accounts, but also by the fact that he refuses to attach himself to the "travellers," the derricks which carry the heavy equipment and metal to the uncompleted bridge. "He is not attaching himself to a falling structure." (40) Rather, he is secured to what he has already built, and flings himself, like Ondaatje's spiders, through the air, creating as he goes.

Later in the story, Patrick will present a photograph to Temelcoff, which will show the latter that he was indeed part of the history of the city, and through this connection he will fulfill yet another artistic function: he will become a story-teller. Not surprisingly, Patrick discovers this photograph in a collection of archival material not readily presented to the public.

Caravaggio is another of the artist figures in this novel, a fact which Ondaatje signals to us in a mischievous way. Caravaggio may well be named after an Italian artist of the Renaissance period. Michaelangelo Merisis or Amerigi, as he may well have been known, was frequently in prison for a variety of offences, from libel to assault. As well as being an unstable or volatile figure, a possible pederast and an exile (he was banished by His Holiness for capital crime), he is also largely credited with having introduced the "low-life" of Rome to paintings—the denizens of taverns, thieves and prostitutes were an obsessive fixation of his. As John Gash has put it, "The lives of few artists have contributed as much to the formation of the notion of the artist as an outsider," a preoccupation which would make him ideal for Ondaatje's own particular emphasis in this novel.

To some extent, however, this may be one of the many instances where Ondaatje throws in references to deceive the reader; to make it appear, in other words, that there is more at stake here than there really is. Part of the post-modern novel's game is, as has already been suggested, meta-fictional, and one of the major aspects of this meta-fictionality is intertextuality. This simply means that there is in all texts the presence, the suggestion, even the evocation of a plethora of other texts, and, moreover, that the novel is not only aware of this, but deliberately draws attention to these texts.

In the case of Ondaatje's Caravaggio, we know he is an artist figure in the very literal way he escapes from jail. In the section which bears this character's name, we are presented with yet another metaphor of the migrant situation. Imprisoned by the Authority, the major figures in the novel—including Patrick—realize as they sit painting the roof of the penitentiary that each time they smear themselves with paint, "they became partly invisible." Patrick goes on to think that "If they painted long enough they would be eradicated," (179) and indeed, Caravaggio uses this realization to escape. At one stage we are told that Patrick and Buck "painted him, covering his hands and boots and hair with blue. They daubed his clothes and then, laying a strip of handkerchief over his eyes, painted his face blue, so he was gone—to the guards who looked up and saw nothing." (180)

We have already seen the metaphor of the colour emerging to identify migrants. In an earlier section of the novel, the Dyers are said to be all different colours. They step into the various dyes "as if into separate countries," (130) and gather together, "the representatives from separate nations," standing like the different colours of the map. (130) This coloration is, of course, imposed upon them by capitalism; they are made to sacrifice their very essence, their health, their scent, their colour, for the sake of Business. Like the cattle on the "killing-floors" who are stunned with sledge hammers and whose eyes will flicker as they're skinned, these men become the sacrificial offerings to New World enterprise, men who are "left . . . invisibly with tuberculosis and arthritis and rhematism." (131) These men are even said to be re-named by the Establishment, by the English-speaking bosses who cannot pronounce the migrant names.

So when Ondaatje refers to Caravaggio *becoming* his surroundings in order to escape them, it is not difficult to think of one of the traditional migrant scenarios where one does indeed blur all differences in order to escape labels and limitations. For some, this escape is made through story-telling; for others, such as Caravaggio, the escape is made through a direct attack on the bourgeois values of the New World. Caravaggio is a thief—even a shape changer—becoming invisible, or becoming a pirate, as he does when he becomes Randolf Frog in order to deceive the owners of an exclusive yacht. The fact that this duplicity takes place at a costume ball, where identity in general is unreliable, is proof enough that Ondaatje is himself suspicious of the stability of identity. Caravaggio, to be effective, must be anonymous. Unlike the "Bosses" he does not seek to be part of the official History—to be so, he would lose his effectiveness to exploit and undermine the makers of such Authority.

It was suggested earlier that *In the Skin of a Lion* was about the discovery of language, and also about the oppression of speech by those in power. It may be useful, at this stage, to look at this more closely, remembering all the while the image of the artist as he or she has been drawn thus far. I have offered a reading of the less "obvious" migrant and artist figures—I've focused on metaphoric equivalents, which, as Alice points out, is one of the most effective ways of communicating an idea. At one stage she says, "You reach people through metaphor." (123) But the novel is also filled with direct comments on the situation of migrants in a new country.

The talking picture, for example, is said to "light the way for immigration in North America," suggesting that the power of the New World is one of language. "The silent film brings nothing but entertainment" but the talkies bring "language and argument." And what is the power of these? It is one which promises the possibility of the reversal of Authority, or the reversal of fortune. As the text suggests about the silent movies, "The *tramp* never changes the opinion of the *policeman.*" (43, emphasis added) Why? Because he cannot *speak*—he cannot debate. "He cannot talk or listen." (43)

North America, moreover, is a land of opportunity because, in principle, it is free of the hierarchies which restrict the "migrants" in their own countries. "North America is still without language, gestures and work and bloodlines are the only currency." (43) It is "a spell of language that brought Nicholas here, arriving in Canada without a passport in 1914, a great journey made in silence." (43) The passport, and speech, are both considered to be signifiers of identity. Without either, Nicholas can be said not to exist. His will be a journey, therefore, toward achieving identity through language. As he himself puts it, "If he did not learn the language he would be lost." (46) To avoid this, then, he takes ESL classes, and becomes "obsessive" about the language.

Unfortunately, unlike his fellow migrants who learn English from plays, movies or records, Nicholas chooses Fats Waller as his model and "so his emphasis on usually unnoticed syllables and the throwaway lines made him seem high-strung or dangerously anti-social or too loving." (47) Part of the problem, of course, is that until he begins to talk about his own history, his language is mis-placed. When he regains his confidence, through Patrick's discovery of the photograph which establishes Nicholas's role in the building of history, he moves from denial to communication of the story. On page 149 we're told that "Nicholas Temelcoff never looks back. He will drive the bakery van over the bridge with his wife and children and only casually mention his work there." *After* viewing the photograph, Nicholas makes a new realization:

> Nicholas is aware of himself standing there within the pleasure of recall. It is something new to him. This is what history means. He came to his country like a torch on fire and he swallowed air as he walked forward and he gave out light. Energy poured through him. That was all he had time for in those years. Language, customs, family, salaries. Patrick's gift, that arrow into the past, shows him the wealth in himself, how he has been sewn into history. Now he will begin to tell stories. He is a tentative man, even with his family. That night in bed shyly he tells his wife the story of the nun. (149)

The most dramatic metaphor of the migrant situation is probably the puppet show. Held illegally at the half-finished waterworks, only a hundred yards from Queen street, the puppet show is a synechdoche of the migrant impulse to conform and simultaneously to excel in the new world. It is also patently clear that language, particularly the English language, "can by no means be openheartedly adopted. This non-acceptance is due to the immigrants' illiteracy and the long working hours, which leave them neither time nor energy to deal with a new idiom. In addition, English is perceived as the language of the oppressor and the enemy of the working class, who attempts to enforce his discourse on the immigrants."[5] You'll remember that it has become illegal for them to assemble in protest in public, "in any language other than English." (133)

The tiny puppets, who represent the masses of migrants, take exaggerated steps "on this dangerous new country of the stage. Their costumes were a blend of several nations." (116) The large "human" puppet is common to all the other puppets: "The hero linked them all." (116) The hero, however, wants to break out of the mass. But ultimately, the mass is conservative and cautious. They warn the "hero of his ambition, gesturing him down with laws." (117)

The play becomes the story of conformity and Authority, with the hero being "brought before the authorities, unable to speak their language." (117) Ondaatje's language in describing this scene is telling: it is a "caricature of a culture;" the audience is "silent;"

the only "sounds on stage were grunts of authority" while they wait for the "puppet to speak, but it could say nothing." Ultimately, the puppet kneels and begins to pound the floor, "pleading for help—a terrible loudness entering the silent performance." This ritual continues, becoming louder and louder, more and more frantic, until Patrick finally stumbles onto the stage and stops her. She is, of course, Alice Gull.

The moment is yet another instance of transformation, both symbolically, with the migrant reaching through ignorance and puppetry to connect with another human being; and concretely, with the puppet becoming human, changing from male to female, and also from nun to performer. It is also a shift back from the early part of the book to the latter. This moment of Alice's return brings us to another feature of the narrative, therefore, and that is its inter-connectedness. It is shortly after this scene, in fact, that the novel reaches its "heart"—where it declares its central theme.

Patrick Lewis, a central character who has very easily been left out of my analysis so far, ventures from the Riverdale Library where he has been reading the documentation on Commissioner Harris' Bloor Street Viaduct. It is here, as I said before, that he discovers Nicholas Temelcoff, and where he reads about the nun whose body was never found. It is here that he realizes that "His own life was no longer a single story but part of a mural, which was a falling together of accomplices. Patrick saw a wondrous night web—all of these fragments of a human order." (145) Again, the idea of the spider poet is suggested here.

The articles he discovers deal with "everything but information on those who built the bridge. . . . Official histories and news stories were always soft as rhetoric, like that of a politician making a speech after a bridge is built, a man who does not even cut the grass on his own lawn." (145) The point of "art," Ondaatje seems to be saying, is to do what the photographer Lewis Hines' pictures did, which is to "betray official history." (145) Art, however, is always "too late" whilst "Official histories, news stories surround us daily." (146) The section here ends with the comment, "The first sentence of every novel should be: 'Trust me, this will take time but there is order here, very faint, very human.' Meander if you want to get to town." (146)

If "Only the best art can order the chaotic tumble of events," then Ondaatje deliberately produces a fragmented novel, apparently disjointed and meandering, only to bring all the pieces together at the end. The game is an artifice, however, and Ondaatje is aware of his "fictional" ordering. Part of the exercise here is to demonstrate how "history itself," like art, is a construct; that at best, the record which we have of human activity is an artificially constructed document which is subject to continued and varied re-interpretation. And this re-interpretative act is the only hope for those whose stories have been brutally suppressed.

Patrick, the quiet "searcher," is an observer throughout the novel. He never really does anything; he *looks* for things, and he is acted upon. And although he does torch the hotel, he is imprisoned quite easily for his crime, an imprisonment which sees him retreat to silence. Even his goal to blow up the Waterworks comes to nothing. Or does it? In the end, Patrick finally "tells." He, like Temelcoff and all the others, becomes a story-teller. This is his act. In the *Epic of Gilgamesh*, a tale which precedes Homer's *The Iliad* by some 1000 years, Gilgamesh goes out into the wilderness to fight the lions, and wears their skins while grieving for the loss of his friend. Gilgamesh, too, is a hybrid, a migrant of sorts, two thirds god and one third human; he is a figure searching for a place to belong.

The idea of wearing the skins of lions suggests very much the idea of assuming the mantle of the powerful. But the connection with this idea of power, and role-playing, is made clearest in reference to one scene where we are told of a play

> in which several actresses shared the role of the heroine. After half an hour the powerful matriarch removed her large coat from which animal pelts dangled and she passed it, along with her strength, to one of the minor characters. In this way even a silent daughter could put on the cloak and be able to break through her chrysalis into language. Each person had their moment when they assumed the skins of wild animals, when they took responsibility for the story. (157)

In the Skin of a Lion is a novel about the responsibility of seizing the lion skin—of grabbing hold of the mantle of the story-teller and of speaking one's way into a version of history.

NOTES

1. Ina Ferris, "Michael Ondaatje and the Turn to Narrative," *The Canadian Novel: Present Tense,* ed. John Moss (Toronto: NC Press, 1985), p. 74.
2. *Ibid.*
3. Armando E. Jannetta, "Onomastic Devices in Michael Ondaatje's *In the Skin of a Lion," Commonwealth: Essays and Studies*, vol. 13, no. 2 (Spring 1991): 92-103, p. 93.
4. Ina Ferris, p. 76.
5. Armando E. Jannetta, p. 96.

Hanging on a Question Mark: A Critical Analysis of Michael Ondaatje's *Coming through Slaughter*

COOMI S. VEVAINA

Michael Ondaatje was among the more important writers to emerge in Toronto in the 1960s. Born in Ceylon (now Sri Lanka) in 1943, he joined his mother in England in 1954 and moved to Canada in 1962. Since then he has published four books of poetry, a critical study of the writer Leonard Cohen, a collage of poetry, prose, photographs and found material entitled, *The Collected Works of Billy the Kid*, an experimental novel *Coming through Slaughter* in which he mixes medias and genres, an autobiographical work, *Running in the Family* in which he has erased the boundary between autobiography and fiction and a "rare and exotic novel" *In the Skin of a Lion* which as Leon Edel says, deals with "human situations through verbal cinema."[1] Ondaatje's writings show the influence of the visual arts, of contemporary cinema artists like Louis Malle, Alfred Hitchcock and Sergio Leone and of the "connoisseur of chaos," Wallace Stevens. Fascinated by borders and the exotic, he tends towards the surrealistic dislocation of actuality and expresses the tensions in art and in life in the form of fantastic narratives which border on the gothic.

Ondaatje who regards himself as an "arch-romantic"[2] has often been regarded as "the least obviously Canadian writer in his subject-matter and vision and in the verbal texture of his work."[3] However, a closer look at his works reveals a distinctly Canadian sensibility. Canada's "situation on the North American continent . . . deeply involves it in the Machine Age."[4] Ondaatje strongly rejects the mechanistic, materialistic existence, literal-mindedness and brash optimism of Americans. He sees the insistence on rationality and the unerring faith in the ability to control the irrational forces within oneself and the wilderness around one, as both superficial and false. Like Buddy Bolden in *Coming through Slaughter*, we are often unable to reconcile the warring forces within us. The "existential complexity" and the fundamentally chaotic nature of lived experience, is devoid of "facts." In an interview with Sam Solecki he openly confesses having put in geographical names into *Billy the Kid* only because he "liked the sound of them."[5] His distrust of reason is as complete as that of his poet-friend bp. nichol who in *martyrology book II*, says,

ah reason
there is only feeling
knowing the words are
is am
This moment is
every-thing present and tense
I write despite my own misgivings
say things as they do occur
the mind moves truly
is it free[6]

"The concept of movement is central to Ondaatje's work."[7] Sheila Watson in an article entitled, "Michael Ondaatje: The Mechanization of Death," says that Ondaatje was born two years before Siegfried Giedon published *Space, Time and Architecture, The Growth of a New Tradition*. Giedon's work "concentrated on the renewed interest in organic form 'the ten-fingered grasp of reality' which had been destroyed when Descartes had unlocked the door to mechanization."[8] Einstein's concern with simultaneity, and concepts like "space-time," "acoustic space" and the "optical revolution" emphasize the need to revision the notion of reality which is essentially "surreal, absurd, inchoate, dynamic and most importantly, ambiguous."[9] Furthermore, American public myths like the American Dream and the Frontier Myth reject the value of private or individual myths. In novel after novel Ondaatje staunchly asserts the "raw power"[10] of private myths and exploits their dramatic possibilities as fully as possible. The only "true" story is the one which does not pretend to be historically accurate. In his own words, "Man becomes a pulse of light in a dark landscape. He disappears into historical time and re-emerges in an echo."[11] In the manner of other major Canadian writers like Margaret Laurence, Adele Wiseman, Eli Mandel and Robert Kroetsch, Ondaatje too believes that fiction is more true than fact.

Coming through Slaughter (1976), which won the Books in Canada First Novel Award, fictionalizes and creates a myth out of the tormented life and tragic death of the turn-of-this-century black American cornetist, Charles (Buddy) Bolden, who is believed to have been one of the first and most powerful musicians to play what was subsequently called hard jazz and blues for dancing. The novel offers "a brisk series of cameos and vignettes which show Bolden and his various allies in vivid detail, yet more spectral than real."[12] Bolden's popularity during his life-time is clearly indicated in the following lines by the jazz critic, Jelly Roll Morton: "Anytime it was a quiet night at Lincoln Park because maybe the affair hadn't been so well publicized, Buddy Bolden would publicize it! He'd turn his big trumpet around toward the city and blow his blues, calling children home, as he used to say. The whole town would know that Buddy Bolden was at the Park, ten or twelve miles from the center of town. He was the blowingest man ever lived since Gabriel."[13] However, since Bolden's career predated the making of commercial records of his kind of music, there is nothing left of him but legend. "The thin sheaf of information"[14] by way of historical facts enables Ondaatje to play fast and loose with history and manipulate characters and events "to suit the truth of fiction." (159) Historical facts and fiction fuse to form mists and shadows. The echoes and silences in the novel are crucial to the myth in it. Commenting on this aspect of Ondaatje's art, Audrey Thomas says, "I sometimes think there are two Michael Ondaatjes, identical twins and famous acrobats—high-wire artists. One gathers information—dates, times, places, etc.—the other gathers the secrets of the human heart. At a pre-arranged moment, they swing out towards one another and clasp hands. At that moment of clasped hands his amazing books are born." The elaborate display of factuality in *Coming through Slaughter* in the form of dates, interviews and tape transcripts is often cheerfully deceptive. The darkly romantic vision of the writer is expressed through the maze-like form of the work. Cluttered with names of persons, places, events, numerous flashbacks and comments on Bolden by members of his band, friends and family, interviews, hospital entries, thoughts and feelings of the author himself, bits of conversations and songs, the structure of the novel brilliantly mirrors the formless and chaotic life of the protagonist and provides us with Ondaatje's vision of Bolden. Beneath the jagged surface form lies a unity of effect created by themes and images which may legitimately be termed as "poetic." The form of the novel, according to John Moss, "is not skeletal but fluid and alive, like blood flowing in the reader's veins."[15] Ondaatje's sheer love of language and mastery over it is evident in the scene which describes Bolden's fight with the Fly King, Tom Pickett: "Language does not report reality: it creates reality."[16] Depending on the speaker, the tone of his prose ranges from the starkly journalistic to the poetic and visionary.

Bolden's spontaneous, anarchic and transient music was an expression of his life. Essentially post-modern in his preference for fragments, his music sharply contrasted with the perfect arches and "mechanistic pleasure" (93) of that of his contemporary John Robichaux. Despite the surface anarchy "there was a discipline" (37) which his contemporaries did not understand. Frank Lewis who was part of Bolden's band describes his music as that which had "so little wisdom you wanted to clean nearly every note he passed, passed it seemed along the way as if travelling in a car, passed before he even approached it and saw it properly. There was no control except the mood of his power. He tore apart the plot—see his music was immediately on top of his own life. Echoing, as if, when he was playing he was lost and hunting for the right accidental notes. Listening to him was like talking to Coleman. You were both changing directions with every sentence, sometimes in the middle, using each other as a springboard through the dark. You were moving so fast it was unimportant to finish and clear everything. He would be describing something in 27 ways. There was pain and gentleness everything jammed into each number." (37) Bolden's music was regarded as formless but the fact was that he was "tormented by order." (37) A similar split between the rival desires for order and disorder, compelled him to madly oscillate between the two till the moment of his mental breakdown at the public prade in New Orleans in 1907. Bolden's friends Bellocq and Webb symbolize the contrasting attractions between order and disorder in the novel. "Never professional in the brain" (14) like Bolden, the radical outsider Bellocq, symbolizes the force of disorder. Indifferent to Bolden's music and teetering on the edge of society, this crippled, neurotic photographer tries to lure Bolden out of the world of audiences into an area of silence. His steady job as a photographer for a ship-building firm provides him with the money he needs for photographing whores naked or clothed, with pets or alone and preferably with scars on their bodies. Like the artist Henri Rosseau, "he even talked to his photographs he was that lonely." (127) Bellocq reluctantly makes a print of Bolden's band for Webb before bleaching out the negative he possesses. Making and destroying came from the same source within him. Later in the novel we learn that Bellocq set fire to the wallpaper in his room and burnt himself to death. His unexplained suicide indicates a path Bolden could follow in case of necessity.

The police detective, Webb, is the antithesis of Bellocq. He represents order and public life which Bolden desperately needs but rejects as unbearably claustrophobic. True to his name, he attempts to weave a web for the wayward fly, Buddy Bolden. Clapping for encores and forcing Bolden to return from his voluntary exile with the Brewitts, he symbolizes Bolden's most pitilessly demanding audience. Unlike Bolden and Bellocq he holds himself back from emotional involvement, aware that sexual passion disrupts ordered systems. In his attempt to understand Bolden, Webb interviews his friends and family members only to conclude: "Their stories were like spokes on a rimless wheel ending in air. Buddy had lived a different life with every one of them." (63) Bolden's multiple selves resemble the fan in his shop called N. Joseph's Shaving Parlour. Living in a low-life district amidst prostitutes, hustlers, gamblers, alcoholics and drug addicts, Bolden "dreams" of the death of his children and is obsessed with death. The newspaper he published from 1899 to 1905 called 'The Cricket' contained excessive reference to death. The possibilities were terrifying to Bolden and he hunted out examples obsessively as if building a wall. A boy with a fear of heignts clilmbing slowly up a tree. There were descriptions of referees slashed to death by fighting cocks, pigs taking off the hand of a farmer, the unfortunate heart attack of the ninety-year-old Miss Bandeen who opened her door one night to let in her cats and let in someone's pet iguana instead. There was the freak electrocution of Kenneth Store who stood up in his bathtub to straighten a crooked light bulb and was found the next morning by his brother Gordon, the first reaction of Gordon being to turn the switch off so that Kenneth fell stiff to the floor and broke his nose."

(24) Bolden attempts suicide twice by cutting or biting his wrist. The image of the "suicide of his hands" is the last of the numerous images of wrists being cut on windows or hands going through glass as his hand is the source of both his creativity and his tensions. Unable to control the conflicting forces within him, he is at peace with himself only after his breakdown at the age of thirty-one. Ondaatje, like bp nichol, is, in his own words, "very interested in silence."[17] In a section of his poem *White Dwarfs* he says,

> There are those burned out stars
> who implode into silence
> after parading in the sky
> after such choreography what would they wish to speak of anyway[18]

In death Bolden moves into his parade of silence having come through the experience of slaughter—and undoubtedly through the town of slaughter; the country which John James Audubon depicted in his paintings along with its damned birds who, like Bolden, "felt their skin was on fire and screamed/ and were led away."[19]

The making-destroying duality in Bellocq, Webb and Bolden is also present among the women in Bolden's life. Nora Bass, as her name suggests, is a basic reality to which Bolden must return, "the home of his wife's mouth." (122) Robin Brewitt likewise, true to her name, offers Bolden flight from the world of the stage and helps him find peace in her white room "with no history and no parading." (86) However, for Bolden, there can never be any final escape from his art as even while making love to her he tries to improve upon Cakewalking Babies, pressing the flesh on her back "as though he were plunging into a cornet." (59) While both the women consciously desire to lead Bolden away from the self-destruction of the stage, they unconsciously lead him back to it. Bolden's sexual jealousy for Nora prompts his assault on the handsome hustler, Pickett and his passion for Robin disrupts the order in the lives of the Brewitts. Several scenes in the novel reveal "the tremendous force of the connection between violence and sexuality."[20] The girl fan at the parade who encourages him to play more brilliantly than ever before, drives him to a state of frenzy and causes his breakdown and consequent plunge into silence and death. It is possible to see her as a psychic externalization of the insanely demanding audience both Bolden and Ondaatje desire and fear.

"Private and fictional magnets" (158) drew Ondaatje and Bolden together. In a section in *White Dwarfs,* Ondaatje asks himself:

> Why do I love most
> among my heroes those
> who sail to that perfect edge
> when there is no social fuel.[21]

The author seems to identify completely with Bolden when he says, "When he went mad he was the same age as I am now." (133) The differences between them are further erased in the following brilliant paragraph charged with elements of magic realism: "When I read he stood in front of mirrors and attacked himself, there was the shock of memory. For I had done that. Stood, and with a razor-blade cut into cheeks and forehead, shaved hair. Defiling people we did not wish to be." (133) Like Bolden, Ondaatje too understands the restrictive power of audiences and reputation and wants his audience to be volatile and respond to new forms in his art. However, despite his empathy with Bolden, Ondaatje's art unlike that of the musician is highly controlled and ingeniously patterned. Though it teeters on the edge of chaos, it does not lapse into it even momentarily as at no stage does Ondaatje let his emotionally charged material slip into hysteria. His fascination with Bolden is with a certain kind of creativity in certain artists in whom making and destroying are of necessity co-extensive. The tensions within such artists can be resolved only by being transmitted into art, madness and\or suicide. Such art calls to mind names like Hart Crone, Randall Jarrell, John Berryman, Sylvia Plath and Anne Sexton. "The 20th century game of fame" (134) creates immense unheavals in the lives of artists who, "hanging on a question mark" (Robert Lowell), cannot decide whether it is a death rope or a lifeline.

NOTES

1. Michael Ondaatje, *In The Skin of a Lion* (Toronto: McClelland and Stewart, 1987).

2. Stephen Scobie and Douglas Barbour, "A Conversation with Michael Ondaatje," *White Helican* (Spring 1971), p. 10.
3. Sam Solecki, "Michael Ondaatje," *The Oxford Companion to Canadian Literature,* ed. William Toye (Toronto: Oxford University Press, 1903), p. 620.
4. Sheila Watson, "Michael Ondaatje: The Mechanization of Death," *Open Letter—Third Series* (Winter 1974), p. 165.
5. Sam Solecki, An Interview, *Rune* (Spring 175), p. 47.
6. bp. nichol, *martyrology book II* (Toronto: Coach House Press, 1972), n.p.
7. Sheila Watson, p. 168.
8. *Ibid.*
9. Sam Solecki, "Nets and Chaos: The Poetry of Michael Ondaatje," *Brave New Wave,* ed. Jack David Windsor: Black Moss Press, 1978), p. 2.
10. Michael Ondaatje, "O'Hagan's Rough-Edged Chronicle," *Canadian Literature,* 61 (Summer 1974), p. 24.
11. *Ibid.,* p. 27.
12. John Moss, "Michael Ondaatje," in *A Reader's Guide to the Canadian Novel* (Toronto: McClelland and Stewart, 1987), p. 224.
13. *Biographical Dictionary of Jazz,* ed. Charles E. Claghorn (New Jersey: Prentice-Hall, 1902), p. 44.
14. Michael Ondaatje, *Coming through Slaughter* (Toronto: House of Anansi Press, 1976), p. 184.
15. Moss, p. 223.
16. Stephen Scobie, "Two Authors in Search of a Character: bp. nichol and Michael Ondaatje," in *Poets and Critics—Essays from Canadian Literature* 1966-1974, ed. George Woodcock (Toronto: Oxford University Press, 1974), p. 229.
17. Scobie and Barbour, p. 13.
18. Michael Ondaatje, *White Dwarfs,* p. 71.
19. Michael Ondaatje, "Herson Rex" in *Rat Jelly,* p. 52.
20. Scobie, p. 235.
21. Michael Ondaatje, *White Dwarfs*, p. 71.

The Other Solitude: The Jew and the Gentile in Mordecai Richler's *The Acrobats*

P.A. ABRAHAM

Region, nation, race and religion have quite dramatically come to occupy today the consciousness of the world. While 'unity in diversity' is an ideal principle, it should be admitted that uniformity is not the law of life. Life exists by diversity. In spite of the differences what man has to learn is the value of reconciliation, tolerance and love for mankind. In his novel *The Acrobats*[1] Richler is pre-occupied with the problem of relationship between the Jew and the Gentile, the question of freedom and survival in an indifferent world, the discrepancy between love and the power struggle and the loss of values in the modern age.

Richler belongs to a generation of Canadian Jews born to immigrants who came to Canada in the beginning of the century to escape organized prosecution in Eastern Europe. He grew up in Montreal where his childhood was filled with anti-semitic events. Although Richler observed the Holocaust from the safety of Canada, his novels reveal the extent to which the knowledge of Nazi atrocities affected the Canadian Jewish consciousness. Anti-semitism was also openly propagated by the fascist movement in Quebec. This, in turn, created a sense of insecurity and alienation on the part of the Canadian Jew. It can be marked that the Jewish individual moves between an obsessive aspiration to be assimilated into the Gentile world and a powerful need to confront the Gentile world pointing an accusing finger to the terrible injustice committed against Jews. Paradoxically, he wishes to obliterate his Jewish identity by embracing the ideals of liberal humanism and at the same time, experiences a powerful urge to assert his Jewishness and expose the hypocrisy of liberal ideals.

The defeat of fascism in Hitler's Germany did not kill anti-semitism. Nor in self-proclaimed tolerant France. In both countries Jewish synagogues and cemeteries were desecrated in recent times.

In Canada and US they still have their exclusive country clubs and resorts which refuse admittance to Jews. This, despite the fact that many of the best brains, best musicians, artists, writers, industrialists and philanthropists are Jewish. Albert Einstein put it succinctly in his address to Sorbonne University in Paris: "If my theory of relativity is proved successful Germany will claim me as a German, and France will declare that I am a citizen of the world. Should my theory prove untrue, France will say I am a German and Germany will declare I am a Jew."

All this proves that traditionally the Jews have represented the exiled people. In the post-war period, however, the liberal Gentile man also becomes an exile in both the literal and moral sense of the term. In Richler's novels, the interaction that evolves between the Gentile exiles and their Jewish counterparts reveals an unusual situational shift.

In this paper I shall try to examine Richler's treatment of racial hatred and discrimination and the impact of racism on the consciousness of the Canadian Jew. It can be seen that the tension between assertion of the Jewish heritage and rejection of Jewish roots constitutes the spectrum of Richler's exploration of Jewish survival in the post-war world. Thematically, *The Acrobats* demonstrates constant vacillation between the poles of identity and assimilation.

A number of critical readings of *The Acrobats* have identified the obvious influence of Hemingway and the philosophy of existentialism on the structure and ideology of the novel. The title of George Bowering's essay "And the Sun Goes Down: Richler's First Novel" clearly implies Richler's resemblance to Hemingway. Bowering finds that in many instances Richler imitates Hemingway quite openly. Thematically according to Bowering, Richler describes the post-Hemingway world, the character's inner struggle and existential choices are made in a world in which the heroic romantic stance presented by Hemingway exists more.[2] Arnold Davidson shares Bowering's views when he says that Richler portrays the loss of direction and alienation of his Hemingway-like protagonist.[3] It is George Woodcock who establishes a properly balanced view of Mordecai Richler's novels. While not denying his imitation and appropriating of themes emerging from fashionable literary trends, he draws the reader's attention to Richler's preoccupation with the problems of the relationships between people, the discrepancy between love and the power struggle, and the loss of values in the modern age. Woodcock also observes that *The Acrobats* initiated the motif of "the tensions between the Jews and the Goyim [which] recur in every Richler novel."

The episode which introduces the conflict between the Jews and the Gentiles in the novel occurs long before the actual plot of the novel, which takes place during the three-day-long festival in Valencia, begins to unfold. The Montreal incident describes the love affair between Andre Bennett, the Gentile protagonist in the novel, and his Jewish lover Ida Blumberg.

Andre, the only son of the rich Bennetts, and Ida, the only daughter of poor Jewish immigrants from Poland, meet at the University and they fall in love with each other. When Ida gets pregnant, she refuses Andre's offer of marriage because he is a Gentile. She dies as a result of the abortion which was financed by Andre. Ida's father, old Mr. Blumberg, accuses Andre of murdering Ida out of his hatred for the Jewish people. Andre cannot tolerate this allegation and he hits the old man. Feeling guilty Andre gives up his wealth and status and leaves for Europe where he tries to come to terms with his traumatic experience. However, he cannot develop his talent for painting due to the terrible depression he has undergone.

Since Andre is the only witness to the true nature of his relationship with Ida, it is structurally plausible that the story is narrated only from Andre's point of view. But as R.F. Brenner has pointed out in *The Acrobats*, "the device of recollection juxtaposed with the unfolding present and the use of the subjective point of view are also thematically operative."[4]

The subjective aspect of the narrative presents the theme of the tension between the Jew and the Gentile from the point of view of the Gentile. The voice registers the reaction of the Gentile to the Jewish world on the Gentile's psyche. The circumstances under which Andre tells his story reveal the extent to which the denouncement of his relationship with Ida has affected him. Shortly after making love to his new lover Toni, Andre tells her about his unfortunate love affair with Ida. The painful reminiscences of the past suggest the inner conflict of Andre which still persists.

Besides the death of Ida, the encounter between Andre and Ida's father also has shattered Andre's world, with the result that he has lost trust in himself and in humanity. It is the complete lack of personal contact between Andre and Blumberg which is the most unfortunate aspect of the encounter. Both of them look and act as stereotypes rather than individuals. Blumberg plays the role of the perennial Jewish victim and Andre finds himself responding accordingly as a brutal anti-semite.

Andre describes Blumberg like a typical East European ghetto Jew who lives under constant threat of pogroms and persecution. His appearance complements his conduct as an injured victimized Jew:

> Old Mr. Blumberg was seated at supper table reading from a prayer book by candle light. He was old and wizened. He rocked to and fro as he read. He had long side curls which made him look very sorrowful and he wore a square skullcap. He scrutinized me for an instant without saying anything. Suddenly he began to weep. It wasn't the sound of a man crying or even of an animal. He looked up at me as if he was afraid that I might whip him. (115-16)

Blumberg has been conditioned by his life experience to see every "goy" as a potential threat of suffering and persecution. Andre also instantly realizes that Blumberg sees him as yet another murderer of Jews. Blumberg clearly refers to the history of the pogroms and to the Holocaust when he addressed Andre impersonally as a representative of mob persecutors: "Why can't you leave me alone? Haven't you had enough amusement with us? Will you always murder us for your enjoyment?" (116)

Though, physically, Blumberg is the victim, the integrity of his perception makes him emerge as the morally stronger adversary in his confrontation with Andre. Acting on his conviction that all Gentiles are anti-semitic persecutors, he defiantly calls Andre "murderer." Blumberg's manner becomes ultimately hateful when he describes the baby that Ida tried to abort as "your filth inside her."

Ironically, Andre's behaviour fulfills Blumberg's belief that every "goy" is a persecutor of Jews. Andre is enraged by Blumberg's perception of him as a murderer and a rapist. He is also deeply insulted by Blumberg's disregard of his feelings for Ida and her aborted baby. Therefore, Andre hits Blumberg out of an impulse which as he later admits, he could not control: "I couldn't help it. I just couldn't help it! I hit him. You don't know how an old man can look at you, how." (116)

Andre's account of the encounter with Blumberg seems to imply that Jews' defiant manner has manipulated him into a violent response. To a certain extent, it is true that Blumberg has staged the classic situation of a "goy" hitting an old helpless Jew who just lost his only daughter. But Andre, as man of conscience, knows that there is some truth in Blumberg's accusations. He hits the Jew because he cannot bear the fact that the old man knows him well.

In his essay "Race the Dream and the Nightmare," Leslie Fiedler discusses the roots of the psychological trauma of the oppressor in relation to the oppressed: "The intelligent white man's burden of guilt consists not merely in knowing himself as oppressor but in knowing the oppressed know this too."[5] Andre's outburst of rage against Blumberg constitutes a projection of his shame and dismay at the exposure of his exploitative treatment of Ida.

Andre's own account of his affair with Ida reveals how he used Jewishness to gain social acceptance among his peers at the University and to rebel against his parents, and thus as an excuse for emotional withdrawal when she got pregnant. When Andre met Ida, her Jewishness had special appeal to him. He wanted to use this relationship to vindicate his unhappy childhood by disowning the world of his rich, uncaring parents. At the same time he understood that his relation with Ida, a Jewish working-class girl, who rebelled against all the middle-class conventions, would convince the socialist intellectuals to accept him as one of their own: "Secretly I was pleased that she was a Jewess and notorious. I would marry her and that would show everyone. My family, the intellectuals, the leftist clubs, the fraternities. It would be a sensation." (114) When Ida gets pregnant, Andre's feeling as a superior member of society offers to marry her: "After all even if I was such a fine socialist I was still Andre Bennet of the Canadian Bennets, and who was she? Just a frivolous little Jewess born of Polish immigrant parents." (115)

Andre acknowledges the extent of his hypocrisy, selfishness and racial bias only when it is too late. Ida dies leaving him with a terrible burden of guilt which, in turn, leads to his own death. Ironically, Andre's relationship with Ida prefigures another relationship between a Gentile and a Jewish woman in Mordecai Richler's later novel *The Incomparable Atuk*.[6] The marriage of Sejmour Bona and

Ruthy Rosental is a satiric comment on what the marriage of Sejmour Bona and Ruthy Rosental would have been like, had Ida agreed to marry Andre. The relationship of Sejmour and Ruthy, who have rebelled against their respective cultures and traditions, consists in mutual exploitation of each other as a member of a different faith. There is no long loyalty or friendship between them. What inspires the couple is the unrestrained wish to conform to the world which proclaims nonconformity to be the norm, and which disguises emotional exploitation and power under false ideas of liberalism and racial equality.

They became an inseparable campus couple and, the day after graduation, were married. A civil ceremony of course. Bona married Ruthy because 1. This, he hoped, would prove his ultimate liberation from a provincial anti-semitic family; 2. Let's face it, the girl, being a Jewess would be forever in his debt. She could never be unfaithful. On the contrary she would be respectful, grateful; 3. He had come to adore Jewish cooking even more than bananas. Ruthy married Bona because 1. She wished to give her family a fine slap in the face; 2. It would prove—especially to skeptical friends, who predicted she would end up married to a dentist with a house in the suburbs—that she wasn't ghetto-bound; 3. Being a goy he couldn't be as smart as she was. She could direct and control him. (125) Symbolically, the marriage contract exposes the hypocrisy and moral dishonesty which underlies the relationships between the Jews and the Gentiles.

In the final analysis, Andre is capable of appreciating the unworthiness of his feelings for Ida Seymour and Ruthy. They however, are totally incapable of seeing that their exploitative relationship has distorted their perception of each other's heritage.

In his discussion with the Spanish Communist Ouillermo, Andre idealistically equates humanity and beauty (68) realizing that from the moral point of view he has failed to live up to his ideal. It is in the person of colonel Kraus, a Nazi, that Andre identifies the ugly aspect of himself.

Structurally, the connection between Andre and Kraus is established through their rivalry for the Spanish girl, Toni. Andre sees Kraus as his evil alter ago whom he must find the courage to destroy. In his last encounter with Kraus, Andre has a vision of actually becoming the Nazi: "Andre looked hard at Kraus and he remembered him striking old Mr. Blumberg. He remembered him in bed with Toni (while he himself, Andre, sat stupid in a chair, listening to time passing) or Ida who was dead, his filth inside her. Yes, it was Kraus, it had been Kraus always." (162) Kraus admits to himself later that he killed Andre because the young man somehow conveyed to him that he was ugly and didn't matter. (179) Kraus' intuition is correct. Andre initiated the right by punching Kraus in the face because it was his face that was so ugly. (163) Thus at the cost of his life Andre liberates himself emotionally from the stigma of a murderous coward that has set him apart from the rest of humanity.

He tries to get a cathartic effect by having deadly fight with a Nazi. But Chaim, the Jewish character in the novel has been trying to show Andre that it is through love and acceptance that one has to become a better human being. Chaim in Hebrew means "life." So it is apt that he demonstrates an entirely different approach to the world from that of Blumberg. Unlike Blumberg, Chaim treats Andre as his own son, offering sympathy and hope. In one of his stories about Jewish sages and rabbis, Chaim tells Andre about the two great Jewish teachers, Hillel and Shamai: "One man was compounded of love and the other only of justice." (127) Richler seems to suggest that Chaim and Blumberg represent the polarity which characterizes the House of Hillel and the House of Shamai.

In the story about the two sages that Chaim tells Andre, Shamai refused to accept the Gentile tailor who wished to become a Jew, "on one foot" while Hillel converted the tailor to Judaism by teaching him the humanistic precept: "Do unto your neighbour as you would like your neighbour to do unto you; and you shall be a Jew." (128)

Similarly Blumberg's refusal to see Andre as his son-in-law is determined by the fact that Andre is not Jewish. Blumberg divides the world between Gentile murderer and victimized Jews. On the contrary Chaim believes life as a process where one makes it worth living through caring for and helping others.

Chaim also tries to help Andre by using the teachings of Maimonides, another great Jewish theologian. Maimonides submits that it is wrong to claim that there is more evil than good in the world. (50) God created a good world and a good man, but it is man who through mistakes contributes most of the evil.

Most of evils originate in ignorance; which is a lack of wis-

> dom.
> And, tell me, what is an ignorant man?
> An ignorant man is he who believes the whole universe exists only for him. As if nothing else required any consideration. (128)

Human beings tend to think of themselves as lords of the universe. They often judge the world from their self-centred perspective. Eventually, it becomes the source of evil and suffering in the world.

Maimonides' concept of the origin of evil helps Chaim to expose the source of Andre's social maladjustment. According to Chaim, human propensity toward self-aggrandizement also explains the reason why Andre as a Christian felt superior to the Jewish Ida. Richer wants to suggest that narcissism and self-inflation constitute the core of the historical antagonism between Christianity and Judaism.

> Jesus kept saying over and over again to Judas: I'am the son of God and very holy, God will never let me die. And Judas said: Everybody is the son of God and we all die and return to Him. No Jesus said, I'm special.
> Nobody is special before God, Judas said. . . . Jesus said you go tell the Romans where I am and they'll come to crucify me but in the last moment God won't let me die because I'm His son. . . . And the Romans came and got Jesus. When Pilate said to the people should I let him go? They said no! no! And in a way they were right because Jesus was always making them feel guilty and ashamed because they were human instead of godly. So poor Jesus was crucified and he died. (76)

Chaim argues that mankind has not benefitted from Christianity: "Without Christ who knows what might have been? Chaos? But that's what we've got now. Isn't it? For hundreds of years men have murdered in the name of Christ." (76) Chaim has seen the survivors of the concentration camps and the burnt down Warsaw ghetto. He may be associating the present chaotic condition of the world with the Holocaust which has just occurred.

The lesson about the purpose of life that Chaim teaches to Andre is deeply embedded in the Jewish tradition. In his last attempt to save Andre from self-destruction Chaim tells him: "There are times to fight and times to run. Knowing that is the difference between being a foolish hero or a useful man." (131)

Heroic death will not bring new hope to the world which has already experienced a number of deaths. The world does not need useless heroes. It needs people who can be useful to humanity. Chaim's reservation about heroism as a necessary element for the salvation of the world represents a long standing Jewish tradition which has avoided glorification of the heroic act. In his essay "The Heroic, the Beautiful, the Authentic," Lionel Trilling says, "in the Rabbinical literature there is no touch of the heroic ideas. The Rabbis, speaking of virtue never mention the virtue of courage. . . . The indifference of the Rabbis to the idea of courage is most remarkable in that they knew that many of their number would die for their faith. . . . The Rabbis never see themselves—as if the commandment which forbade the making of images extended their way of conceiving the personal moral existence as well."[7]

The lesson of the useful man that Chaim teaches to Andre gains relevance in the light of Chaim's own life-story. Chaim had gone through the pains of emigration from Europe to the United States and through the personal loss of his beloved Becky. In 1946 he went back to Europe. In the burnt-down Warsaw ghetto he saw "those who were not burnt now walked in the cold desert land tugging at their beards, mourning murdered sons and murdered daughters." (14-15) Then Chaim met a young survivor of the camps, "the thin frightened boy with a number and symbol on his arm." (30) He gave the boy, his American passport so that the young survivor could be reunited with his sister in Bronx. Since then Chaim has become the proverbial wandering Jew. He moved from place to place constantly chased by the police.

However, his qualities of infinite kindness, tolerance and compassion represent him as a Messianic figure. He disclaims any feeling of revenge against the Nazi colonel Kraus for murdering Andre. Moreover, he insists on Toni's having Kraus' baby and helps her to raise him. The baby whose name is Andre obviously represents a hope of reconciliation and salvation for the post-war world.

Andre's attitude towards Chaim is marked by ambivalence. He respects Chaim, but he also sees him as a persistently patronizing figure. Andre's ambivalence initiates the motif of tension between Gentiles and Jews emphasized in later novels.

However, the novel ends with a vision of a better world.

Through the character of Chaim, Richler declares faith in the inherently good nature of man in spite of the horror of the war. The novel concludes with Chaim's affirmation of his hope for the world.

> There is always hope. Always.
> There has to be. (189)

The optimistic conclusion of *The Acrobats* indicates the literary mode of social comedy. Northrop Frye in *Anatomy of Criticism* maintains that the comic vision is essentially of "social significance." Comedy progresses towards the establishment of "a desirable society" and it projects an image of an ideal "serene community."[8] This goal is usually achieved as defined by Northrop Frye, through "an integration of society which usually takes the form of incorporating a central character into it."[9]

Chaim's utopian vision of an integrated society is undermined to some extent by the irony of Andre's self-inflicted isolation and death. Nevertheless the comic assertion of life prevails in the novel. As mentioned earlier, the promise of social renewal, understanding and reconciliation is demonstrated in the birth of Toni's baby the son of the former Nazi, symbolically named after Andre. The novel leaves the reader with a hope and a vision of a world in which social order and harmony can be restored.

NOTES

1. Mordecai Richler, *The Acrobats* (London: Sphere, 1970).
2. *Mordecai Richler*, ed. G. David Shaps (Toronto: Ryerson Press, 1979), pp. 1-4.
3. *Mordecai Richler* (New York: Frederick Unger, 1971), p. 33.
4. *Assimilation and Assertion in the Response to the Holocaust in Mordecai Richler's Writing* (New York: Peter Long, 1989), p. 24.
5. "*Commentary* (October 1963), pp. 297-98.
6. (London: Granada, 1980).
7. Lionel Trilling, *Sincerity and Authenticity* (Cambridge and Massachusetts: Harvard University Press, 1973), p. 65.
8. (New York: Princeton University Press, 1973), p. 85.
9. *Ibid.*, p. 43.

M.G. Vassanji's *No New Land:* An Immigrant's Journey through Experience to Self-Awareness

INDIRA BHATT

M.G. Vassanji's novel *No New Land*[1] belongs to that school of novel-writing which commenced with E.M. Forster's *A Passage to India,* followed by Paul Scott's *The Day of the Scorpion*, exploring the social, cultural, racial and political issues that the white experienced when they ruled India, though Vassanji's main concern is not political but racial and cultural. Adella's hallucination of rape by an Indian Muslim Dr. Aziz causes an avalanche of reactions among the white Britishers and the patriotic Indians, so does Vassanji trigger off the action of the novel and the reaction of the people around Nurdin with the imagined rape of a white woman in Canada. In Forster and Scott, the white though rulers are aliens in India whereas in Vassanji, the protagonsit Nurdin is an alien in Canada, whereas the white are secure and powerful in India, Nurdin is not only insecure and frightened but has no footing in the country of the whites. With these differences in the set-up, Vassanji attempts to explore the immigrant's journey through experience to self-awareness. This paper attempts to examine how successfully Vassanji uses the oft-repeated motif of rape in apprehending reality of life and in fathoming the psyche of the major character in his novel *No New Land.*

The novel opens with two depressing events in the life of the Lalani family: the young daughter Fatima receiving news of her getting admission to Arts and Science instead of the coveted and prestigious pharmacy, and the father Nurdin being accused of assaulting a white woman. Though angry and dejected Fatima the young woman of seventeen could accept her plight and decide that "Arts and Science was not so bad after all" (207) and looks forward to joining the medical school later on. But Nurdin feels defeated and dejected and knows not where to look since the accusation of rape is a charge against not only his innocence but his inbred beliefs or morality. He had been brought up by the disciplines of Islamic religion and his father used to whip the children in German fashion. Sandwiched between the goddess Laxmi in the building of 'sixty nine Rosecliff Park Drive, a symbol of a burgeoning Toronto and the huge jabbing in the sky building of CN Tower,' between the dreams of riches, comforts and security and the constant futile battle against the harsh realities of the new land, between the values of his cultural origins and the problems of existence and survival in a new country, the Lalanis are at the crossroads of their life. The novelist comments: "We are but creatures of our origins and however stalwartly we march forward, paving new roads, seeking new worlds, the ghosts from our pasts stand not far behind and are not easily shaken off. An account of Nurdin Lalani's predicaments must therefore go back in time and begin at a different place." (9) Nurdin's father Haji Lalani who had settled in Dar-es-Salaam in East Africa was born in an Indian Muslim sect, the Shamsis and was a man of strict disposition, "to whom the harsh German justice-epitomized in the whip made of hippo hide and the name 'Hand of Blood' given its wielder by the natives—was not alien in spirit. He could have taken, bought a black woman . . . to while away the lonely nights. . . . Instead he prayed and fasted and became friendly with the fathers at the German Catholic Mission and spent his time in theological discussion and friendly debates with the fathers at the mission or with the sheikhs at the mosques." (13)

Vassanji creates a Forsterian situation when a German young girl comes into his shop to look at the gifts for her servants:

> As she stepped in from the glare of sunlight outside, it took a while for her presence to materialize in the relative darkness inside the shop, where Hazi Lalani sat with his servant. . . . As the fraulein raised her arm to point to a string of beads hanging from a nail, Haji found himself staring at her—she was flushed with the heat, her face lightly perspiring and her armpit a delicate wet patch—and he felt the faint stirrings of a desire inside him. (14)

He would have quashed these forbidden shadows of thought had not his face been brought alive by stinging slap from the girl's hand.

The novelist makes it quite clear that she was accompanied by her servant girl. There was no scope for Haji even to touch her yet he feels guilty as if he had really raped the girl and believes that he should have been whipped though neither the German father nor his friend the Missionary of the mosque considers him guilty of any crime. After this Haji Lalani decides to marry and settle down in the material world. Nurdin belongs to such family background where the father is a strict moralist of the old school where even the desires are considered immoral acts and must be punished. However in Nurdin's case there neither is any desire nor any deliberate action vis-a-vis the white woman.

One morning at eleven o'clock Nurdin was pushing a squeaking trolley heaped with bed linen at the Ontario Addiction Centre at the basement level which was quiet and windowless but bright and gleaming in artificial light. "As he approached the small lobby facing the two elevators, he saw in front of him a girl in blue jeans sitting on the floor, leaning against the side wall. Her legs were drawn up in front of her, her hands hung limp on the raised knees, and her head was lowered. Obviously she had been crying, the blonde hair was dishevelled. The face—what he could see of it—was puffy and red." (176)

Instinctive he hurries towards her, parking the trolley on the way, and asks: "Madam—Miss—is anything wrong? Can I be of any help?" (178) As there is no response he almost squats beside her with his hand on her shoulder waiting for her to respond to his offer of help. Though he has a pure intention of helping her, he realizes that he had never been so close to a white woman before and also becomes aware of her femaleness. But the response when it comes, was not quite what he expected. His hand is still on her shoulder when she suddenly gives the alarm: "'Rape!' she cried 'He's trying to rape me!'" He immediately backs away from her as the situation turns threateningly against him, gets into the elevator and goes to his friend Romesh in the same building: "There was an oppressive empty feeling in the pit of his stomach which was to stay with him for a long time to come." (179)

The accusations the father and the son face for the imagined rape remind us of the accusation Dr. Aziz in *A Passage to India* and Hari in *The Day of the Scorpion* face in India. Vassanji has created almost a cave-like situation, the darkness inside the shop and the windowless artificially lit part of the basement corridor near the elevator. The frustrated plain looking Adella suffers from hallucination in the mystic surrounding of the cave in India, whereas the young white woman cries "rape" to exploit and get money from the plain-looking Muslim immigrated from Africa. As Forster has exploited the situation to describe the political and racial responses of the colonizers and the colonialized, Vassanji exploits the situaton to highlight the problems that the immigrants face in a new country of the white. Be it India, Africa or Canada, the white consider themselves superior and easily accuse the black of crimes they have not even contemplated. The racial prejudices are the same everywhere. It is no Amarapur, not the country where the wells are of gold, pillars of silver, floors that smell of musk and the hearts that are sympathetic.

This episode is central to the novel and Vassanji explores the psyche of the rootless, frightened insecure immigrant Nurdin through this. Neither his father nor his wife ever considered him of any worth. In this alien country even his children despise him, since he could not find any good job and ultimately accepts a menial job quite undignified according to his wife Zera and his daughter Fatima. Zera never lets him near her and he finds himself a lonely unwanted man in the family. His relationship with Sushila, his playmate in Africa is now on the point of turning into a meaningful relationship when he is accused of rape. His existence has been so far very painful. In losing the sense of belonging to his country, even to his family, Nurdin has also lost the sense of his identity. In this new country he has only seen the unpleasant side of life both outside and inside his family. There is a sort of Kafkaesque painfulness, agony and isolation he suffers from. The novelist brings this out through the comments of Nanji the part-time professor at the university. It is through Nanji that we are made aware of the futility of the western philosophy in explaining the eastern way of life. "The only choice, real choice, man has in the world is whether to go on living . . . or to commit suicide, end this absurd existence," (76) comments Nanji who is always worried about the questions of morality and ethics. He is obsessed with the choice that he might have to make and believes that "to become Westernized, which is what we have opted for by coming here [Canada], we have to go back and battle by battle relive all their battles—spiritual struggles. How can you otherwise assimilate generations of experience?" (77) To which the novelist responds through the prosaic, pragmatic, realist lawyer Jamal: "Our God is not dead, we are better off." (77)

Nurdin survives his experience through this alternative—of God and the Missionary. His experience makes him realize his predicament, the harsh realities of survival and he becomes conscious of his plight:

> as if he had taken a tremendous fall, then getting up, not knowing how much of him was still intact. Most of the time there was this heaviness in the heart pulling him *inside, into himself* making him inattentive, vague, numb, as if what he suffered from was something terribly physical, the aftermath of a deafening explosion, whose echoes drove everything else from his mind, made discussion meaningless. (184)

He too begins his search, his purpose of his existence and feels depressed: "When does a man begin to rot?" (82) He thinks that he lacks that something that would take him far instead of bearing life's drudgeries. He had permitted first his father and then his wife to arrange his life. But "now he feels tremors of change inside him and new yearnings." (84) He cannot cut himself off from his past where 'a glass of water was brought by a servant,' here he has to become a menial and obey the orders of others. Besides his father's photograph is a constant threat to him especially the *fez* on the small head, the bushy eyebrows, the hard eyes, the small mouth, relentless in judgement here as the real person had been in Africa." (83)

It is through his relationship with the outer world, first with Romesh and then with Sushila that he breaks out of his rotten existence of his life, though the guilt of having a companionship of Sushila the other woman stays with him and he cannot look in the eyes of his father's photograph.

Next it is the false accusation of rape and his wife's and his children's suspicion that really awakens him to his despicable plight but he feels that if they really know about Sushila, they would not doubt his integrity. With the arrival of the Missionary the clouds of doubt and uncertainties disappear since the Missionary does not consider him guilty and cuts off the final fearful link to his father when putting on his own head the red fez of Hazi Lalani, the Missionary asks him "what punishment do you deserve? . . . with a hearty laugh he further asks Nurdin, 'does it still frighten you so?'"

(196) As the Missionary removes the hat from his head, it becomes lifeless. This action of the Missionary removes that last weakness in Nurdin and he feels released from his father's old ideas of morality, from his past and becomes a new man. "In one stroke the photograph on the wall had lost all potency, its once accusing eyes were now blank, its expression dumb. Suddenly they were here,.in the modern world, laughing at the past." (197)

The immigrant has now fully rejected the existential relationship with the culture of his past. He accepts the new cultural situation. It may be painful for the alien to accept it as a price of his awareness, it involves a recognition of his own situation in time and space to the total cultural complex of the new world. The absurd drama that his touching a white woman creates, is ironically comic and though he is tortured and tormented in a Kafkaesque manner it is neither on metaphysical level nor on tragic level.

At the end when the charge is withdrawn (as is done by Adella in *A Passage to India*) and his innocence is proved beyond doubt he feels that "the tryst he had almost agreed to—and the freedom it would have led him to—now seemed remote and *unreal*, had receded into the distance, into another and unknowable world." (205) But he also realizes that he does not need any such release. The past had been exorcised: "Before, the past tried to fix you from a distance, and you looked away, but Missionary had brought it across the chasm, vivid, devoid of mystery . . . you take on the future more evenly matched." (207) He must now think of his family and his job. He was not going to let a mere embarrassment rob him of the security the job brought to him. He becomes committed to himself. The experience of being accused of the rape brings about a thorough change in him and makes him aware of his own worth. The novelist has symbolically used the red fez of Haji Lalani to free him from his fear and sense of being unwanted and the CN Tower draws him out to the new path of his life—in the new country and new culture. On the other hand the motif of rape, what Lamming terms "Prospero-Caliban-Miranda syndrome is used by Vassanji to give new meaning to the existential—exiled life of the immigrant in the country of the white. In spite of Vassanji's reference to Lawrence Durrell's "There is no new land, no new sea, for the city will follow you, in the same streets you'll wander endlessly," the expatriate is unable to return to the old idea of home despite its certainties and he is unable to find a new one in his adopted land, he becomes aware of the new realities which have to be accepted and in them and through them, he must come to grips with himself.

Vassanji has not been able to fully exploit the rape-motif in exploring the international and inter-cultural sensibilities of the characters as Forster and Paul Scott have done. Nor does he give us the other point of view—what the Canadians feel about the immigrants except the stray episode of Ismail's being crippled by the young white boys. He simply portrays the Asian-African community, their own aloofness, and their isolation, from the mainstream of the country. There are also a few loose ends in the novel. *No New Land* moves onwards from the *The Gunny Sack* dilemma of the immigrants and tries to resolve successfully the conflicts of the protagonist attain self-awareness.

NOTES

1. M.G. Vassanji, *No New Land* (New Delhi: Penguin, 1992).

Images of Woman in Miles Franklin's *My Brilliant Career* and Alice Munro's *Who Do You Think You Are?*

N.E. PAVITHRA

Australian and Canadian literatures have had little more than a century of effective existence and women have been involved in the development of the two literatures since their inception. In the pattern of their development, three broad phases may be distinguished, from the beginning to the nineteenth century, from the 1900s to the 1940s, and from the 1940s to the present. In Australia, Catherine Spencer (1825-1910) has the distinction of being the first woman novelist to write about Australia and the first to deal with women's problems. In Canada, in the mid-1970s Francis Brooke began writing the work that has come to be called the first Canadian novel.

In the early years, the burdens and difficulties of the female immigrants were the major concern and women writers like Catherine Spencer, Rosa Praed and Jessie Convreur (Australian) and Susanna Moodie, Catherine Traill and Sara Duncan (Canadian) in their writing, combined the themes of unhappy marriage, the woman's lot in a predominantly male universe, the effect of a frightening wilderness and her longing to escape. Their involvement in the "woman question," that steadily fomenting and spreading movement of protest, involved much of the late nineteenth and early twentieth century energy and constituted an almost ubiquitous strand in fiction from the Canadian Lizars to the Australian Franklin and beyond. In 1901, Miles Franklin's *My Brilliant Career*,[1] like Sara Duncan's *A Daughter of Today*, sought a language for the unmarried woman living in a desert world where marriage is the idiom of life. Both novels explored the theme of the independent career woman who rebels against traditional social and sexual roles.

The social protest continued and there was a large body of

novels written by women, both Australian—Barbara Baynton, Katherine Prichard, Henry Handel Richardson and Christina Stead—and Canadian—Joanna Woods, Margaret Brown and Marian Keith—who concerned and identified themselves with a female consciousness and its relationship to a largely male world. But it is from the 1940s to the present, with the emergence of Australian writers like Judith Wright, Thea Astley, Kylie Tennant, Shirley Hazzard, Elizabeth Jolley, Elizabeth Harrower and Barbara Hanrahan, and Canadian writers like Margaret Laurence, Margaret Atwood, Marian Engel, Mavis Gallant, Alice Munro and Audrey Thomas—that women's literature really attained maturity. In their writing, a recurring theme is the woman's search for self-understanding and personal fulfilment, and in this paper I have examined how Miles Franklin and Alice Munro have dealt with the woman's search for self in their fiction. Set half a century and a hemisphere away from each other—Miles Franklin's *My Brilliant Career* published in 1901 is part of the Australian ethos of the 90s while Alice Munro's *Who Do You Think You Are*?[2] published in 1978, details the life of a woman, Rose, of a small town in Ontario—the two novels are bound by a common focus on the woman's experience and by a common tradition, the female tradition. As Elaine Showalter points out:

> When we look at women writers collectively we can see an imaginative continuum, the recurrence of certain patterns, themes, problems, and images from generation to generation. . . . [This is because] women themselves have constituted a subculture within the framework of a larger society, and have been unified by values, conventions, experiences, and behaviour impinging on each individual.[3]

The purpose of this paper is to place Miles Franklin and Alice Munro within a female rather than an Australian or Canadian tradition.

Franklin's novel, centers around a woman, Sybylla Melwyn, in rebellion against traditional, social and sexual roles because she wants to do something other than marry—she wants to be a writer more than a wife or mother. In Munro's novel, Rose, the central character struggles with her lack of self-esteem and the inability to regard herself as a sentient, autonomous person rather than an adjunct of a male. It is this chief thematic concern of the status and role of women within society which marks the novels as being part of the wider tradition of female literature. From the very early pages we are introduced to the notion that marriage is a financial and economic contract, that a woman has no future beyond that of being married off. In Franklin's world the only alternative seems the drudgery of schoolteaching and Sybylla cries in anguish at the matchmaking arrangements of her grandmother for her: "Grannie, dear old grannie, thought that I should marry any man who, from a financial point of view, was a good match for me." (72) She resolves to "never marry. I would procure some occupation in which I could tread my life out, independent of the degradation of marriage." (72) Though Sybylla thought that if marriage must occur, it should be between equals, she viewed the partner only as a "participant in my degradation," (70) and prefers a strictly platonic relationship with men. She muses: "Why did not social arrangements allow a man and a maid to be chums—chums such as two men or two maids may be to each other, enjoying each other without thought beyond pure platonic friendship? But no; it could not be. I understood the conceit of men." (69) Through Sybylla, Franklin moves in this novel into the Feminist phase of Showalter's categories, in that she rejects totally the male ideology of love and marriage and romance, and attempts to set up a feminist utopia where females are self-sufficient and no longer dependent on men. And, her decision to be a writer proves the possibility.

Interestingly, fifty years later, a hemisphere away, Rose, the protagonist of Munro's *Who,* is in a similar position as Sybylla. But their lives differ markedly in the way two women make their choices. Sybylla's rejection of the rich and very eligible squatter, Harold Beecham, is based on her clear sense of priorities, unlike Rose's choice to marry the affluent Patrick whose family owned a chain of stores in British Colombia, though she knows that she is making a mistake. Halfway through their courtship Rose feels she cannot go through it and apologizes to Patrick: "Oh, Patrick, listen, please, I can't marry you, please, I don't know why, I can't, please, I'm sorry, believe me, I can't." (122) But before a week had passed she was back in his arms. Later, when Rose reviewed and talked about this decision "she said that comradely compassion had overcome her. . . . Then she went further into it, and said greed, greed. . . When she was seeing life in economic terms . . . she said that only middle-class people had choices anyway, that if she had the price of a train ticket to Toronto her life would have been different." (127-28) She postulates the unfashionable thesis that marriage and the financial security it can bring is an indispensable precondition of a woman's life, and she and Patrick "could not separate until enough damage had been done, to keep them apart. And until Rose could get a job and make her own money, so perhaps there was a very ordinary reason after all." (128)

In neither Sybylla's nor Rose's world, is marriage a natural fulfilment of love between two people, the transformation of one life into a fuller and richer, if largely unseen, one. It is rather seen as simply inevitable for any woman who wishes to live free from physical want or the scorn with which unmarried women are viewed. Sybylla's first experience of the married state is as a child of Lucy and Dick Melvyn who are members of the Australian squattocracy but the narrator makes it explicit from the beginning that there is a great gulf between the parents in terms of class, sensibility and heritage: "His pedigree included nothing beyond a grandfather. My mother, however, was a full fledged aristocrat." (2) From here, the pattern is set for the female being degraded through marriage. Dick Melvyn subsequently takes to drink and plunges his children into poverty, his wife into the continual grind of childbearing. Against this, the wife is seen to be helpless, "afflicted with the curse of Eve," (14) so that her thralldom to maternity and her subsequent ill-treatment at the hands of the male is seen by the narrator as equivalent to the father's cruelty to the young cows on their dairy farm. Even her beloved Aunt Helen has been psychically destroyed by a male who cast her aside for a mistress. Set adrift in a society where a woman's place and status is determined solely through her relationship with a man she has, Sybylla feels "humiliated and outraged in the cruellest way by the man she loved and trusted. He had turned her adrift, neither a wife, widow nor maid." (49) Their lives affect Sybylla's relationship with men and she fights valiantly and instinctively against what she sees as the degradation of marriage. Spurning Harold Beecham's proposal she scornfully says:

> Marry you! Ha! Because the social laws are so arranged that a woman's only sphere is marriage, and because their endeavour is to secure a man who can give them a little more ease, you must not run away with the idea that it is yourself they are an-

> gling for, when you are only the bothersome appendage with which they would have to put up, for the sake of your property. (145)

Both Franklin and Munro concentrate relentlessly and exhaustively on the economic imperatives governing the structures of a society and finally even the individual lives of the citizens of that society.

As in *Brilliant Career,* money or the lack of it, is a central factor of *Who*. But it is not this which really influenced Rose's decision to marry Patrick:

> It was not the amount of money but the amount of love he offered that she could not ignore. . . . She had always thought that this would happen, that somebody would look at her and love her totally and helplessly. At the same time she had thought that nobody would want her at all, and up until now, nobody had. . . . She would look at herself in the glass and think: wife, sweetheart. . . . It was a miracle . . . (103-4)

This intense desire for romantic love of the kind that existed in story books makes her enter into a marriage which she realized "was a mistake. It was what she had dreamed of, it was not what she wanted." (104) And it is financial security that is obtained at a certain price. Rosie is virtually forced into playing a part, concealing from him many aspects of her real self: "All the time, moving and speaking, she was destroying herself for him." (110)

Patrick and Rose, like the married men and women of Franklin's world, are representatives of the "weak" man and the "strong" woman. But after their divorce, the roles are reversed. While Patrick appears self-sufficient and content, Rose seems dependent and unable to cope with loneliness. She flits from one relationship to another but still remains unfulfilled. Even her successful career does not fill the void. It is only when she returns to her childhood town and comes across Ralph Gillespie, a childhood friend with whom she identifies, "What could she say about her and Ralph Gillespie, except that she felt his life, close, closer than the lives of men she'd loved, one slot over from her own?" (276-77) that she finally finds and accepts herself.

Both *Career* and *Who* which deal in some detail with ruinous marriages and question the very rightness of marriage itself, are even more vitally concerned with the growing to adolescence of complex, young girls. Collectively they offer exhaustive and intense explorations of the progress of women towards selfhood. While Sybylla moves towards an awareness of and belief in her creative potential, Rose realizes and accepts her true self and the images in the two novels move from the disillusioned and imprisoned woman to the exultant and reborn woman. The emphasis on women which we find in Franklin's and Munro's novels appears to be symptomatic of an urge to describe the female side of the human condition, a synthesis of insight gained from their own feminity. Franklin, a sensitive young genius, part of the feminist movement in Australia protested against the restrictive patriarchal environment where a woman's role was either marriage or teaching, and produced, in *Career,* a document of both aspiration and frustration and the possibility for an alternative for women, while Munro, part of the female renaissance of the 1960s in Canada when the recurring concern in fiction was the search for self, in *Who* developed a level of perception which goes beyond the external, by creating an awareness of those contradictory or negative aspects of reality which the truly fulfilled woman confronts and accepts. We can thus see both Franklin and Munro believe as the latter puts it that "there's a change coming in the lives of girls and women."

NOTES

1. Miles Franklin, *My Brilliant Career* (1901; Sydney: Angus and Robertson, 1974).
2. Alice Munro, *Who Do You Think You Are?* (1978; Toronto: Penguin, 1991).
3. Elaine Showalter, *A Literature of Their Own: British Women Novelists from Bronte to Lessing* (London: Virago, 1978), pp. 11-13.

Umbilical Bondage: An Analysis of Marie-Clair Blais's *Mad Shadows*

USHA PATHANIA and VANDANA GARG

Family is the sheltered grove in which human beings are born, grow and develop before stepping out into a larger social context. The filial bonds, often have a lasting influence. Moreover, the child's mother and father are given and fixed for ever at the time of the procreative process. It is a part of the given order of nature, an "objective fact of nature, a natural phenomenon, a concrete or substantive part of nature. And this objective fact of nature cannot be terminated."[1] Sociologists, psychologists and educationists, therefore attach great significance to the parent-child relationship, because, according to them the patterning of emotion takes place particularly during childhood. Leland H. Stott, a pioneer in the field of developmental psychology, rates this relationship very high. He argues: "Psychological research suggests that the prevailing quality of the experience the child has with his parents, particularly the mother, during early childhood is of paramount importance."[2]

Keeping in view these observations, an attempt is made here to analyze the complexities of the mother-child dyad as portrayed by Marie-Claire Blais, a prominent Canadian novelist, in her first novel *Mad Shadows*.[3] The paper proposes to establish how, at times, the primary and intimate bonds like the one between a child and his mother can prove dangerous and stifling and impede the development of an integrated wholesome personality on the one hand and on the other hand, rob one of the capacity to interact warmly at the personal and social levels.

That the mother plays the most important part in the child's life and exercises the happiest influence upon him, is a truism on which there is no need to enlarge. But there exist less obvious aspects of the mother-child relation that are not so frequently mentioned, even though they have a profound effect upon the child's subsequent relationships in the adult life. No other member of the human family has been more exalted and more sentimentalized over than the mother. The idealized picture of her that emerges from conventional religious teaching, from novels, the theatre and the cinema, and from memoirs usually written long after the death of the author's mother, has, as a rule, little in common with the mothers of flesh and blood we meet in the novels of Marie-Claire Blais. She presents these intimate ties essentially in terms of conflict. Though the entire gamut of kin relationships has been presented in her novel *Mad Shadows*, yet her prime concern is to portray some disturbing aspects of the mother-child dyad. The relations between mother and child in the novel are strange and superficial. Selfless love, genuine concern and trust does not characterize the bond between Louise and her son Partice. Isabelle, the daughter is a pathetic victim of emotional deprivation.

It is a universally acknowledged fact that it is through constant exchanges with the mothering person, that the infant takes his first step on the road to selfhood. But Louise's relationship with her son is peculiar. She is a dominating mother whose desire to possess her son denies him the opportunity to grow and develop into an independent personality. Louise does not encourage him to become physically independent even: "His mother caressed the nape of his neck with the palm of her hand. With a gentle slip of her all too supple wrist she could lower Patrice's head to her bosom and hear his breathing more clearly." (15) She is happy to keep his attention to herself only: "Patrice did not seem to worry about himself. He presses even closer to his mother, his large eyes empty at the night." (16) He gives the impression of being mentally retarded, unable to understand or remember anything that goes on in his life.

Minimal demands are placed on Patrice by his mother to master the world around him and to function independently. Socialization process which leads to the development of a healthy personality is being severely hampered. Louise is so protective that she encourages him neither to play with the children of his own age group nor participate in community activities. Her unduly protective attitude is the greatest obstacle in the development of her son as a complete being because it is believed that the mother should provide a facilitating environment for the process of development, without which, "the infant's first experience takes place in a psychosocial void, and his development is likely to be severely disturbed."[4] It can be argued here that Louise's undesirable possessiveness about her son is an offshoot of her unsatisfying relationship with her ex-husband. Both were opposite personalities and such mothers, argues Samuel Lowy, "pour all their emotional interest over their children, and so unduly intensify the bonds of natural infantile fixation in them thus obstructing the free path of their children to mental independence and fitness for their after life."[5] Patrice's predicament is all the more disturbing because of the absence of a father figure in his emotional world. There have been several investigations which reveal that the "father absent child often suffers from intellectual deficits. . . . Father absent boys have more difficulty in forming peer relationships than do father present boys."[6]

A healthy parent-child relationship provides the children an opportunity to grow mentally and emotionally and prepares them to establish healthy interpersonal relations with others. But in this case the mother-child bond totally incapacitates Patrice. In spite of the emotional riches that an all powerful and over-shadowing mother stores in Patrice's inner world, the same power tends to hinder the growth of the son's autonomy, thereby leaving the psychic structure relatively undifferentiated, the boundaries of self vague, and the inner convictions more or less uncompromised. Mother has such a strong hold on her son that he is unable to interact with anyone else. Such peculiar relationships are explained by Lindgren when he observes, "Parents have a need to have their children depend on them, and they often prolong and intensify the dependency relationship for this reason. It is hard for them to accept the fact that when children grow up parents are no longer as necessary as they were."[7] That Louise suffers from this psychic compulsion is clear when she begs him "never to abandon his mother for a girl friend or a wife." (93) She tells her son, "I am your mother, your best friend. I am part of you and you are part of me. Never forget that." (93) It is important for emotionally insecure parents to have someone who needs their attention, love, care, protection and support because it gives them the feeling of being powerful and important. It gives them a kind of status in a world where many forces conspire to make the individual feel helpless and impotent. Louise protects her son from everyone else in order to strengthen her own hold upon him.

Possessiveness on mother's part results in making Patrice hate all other relationships and become jealously possessive about his mother. His whole world centres around her. Intrusion by his step-father Lanz is disturbing for him. He hates Lanz because it is he who has taken away his mother, his world, from him. Now he is no longer welcome in her room. His mother's obvious delight in the company of Lanz makes him irritable and angry to the extent that he kills him. Throughout the novel Partice hates Lanz and not Louise. She is the strongest need in his subconscious mind and it is she whom he wants all to himself.

Another strange and disturbing aspect of this mother-child bond is that Louise displays no concern for the below average intellect of her son. Patrice is a body made to house a non-existent mind. She is rather ever eager not only to defend but also to glorify her son, supplying when necessary, the soul which was lacking. For Louise his stupid silence is indicative of his savouring some secret insight. If he keeps repeating a particular gesture it is because he is guided by an instinctive sense of his own beauty. A normal mother becomes apprehensive about the silences of a child when the age demands physical activity and curiosity on his part. But for Louise the strange silences and idiotic behaviour of Partice are the symptoms of some secret insight the child is gifted with and hence she does not question the intelligence of her ten-year-old Adonis. He speaks very little, but she attributes this speechlessness, "like the silence of gods, to unconcern." (16) She treats him like an exceptional being and carefully protects him from any feelings of deficiency and failure. He is her child-god and so the beautiful Beast wants nothing, it eats, sleeps, smiles and laughs when it sees others laughing. He discovers nothing in life, his mother's love, other's admiration, sister's hatred: "He was destined to know only about his beauty and this he discovered." (18) Full credit goes to his mother, who introduced him to vanity by placing him in front of mirrors to admire himself.

Personality traits of the parents go a long way in making them model parents, capable of instilling right values into the tender but all absorbing mind of a growing child. The very temperament of Louise makes her incapable of being a proper guide for her son. Being a vain and frivolous woman she teaches Patrice only to take interest in his own person, to make himself attractive, physically perfect and one teaches others what one knows. What adds to her shallowness is the fact that she wants to take her idiot son everywhere, even for a business deal, because without him she is shorn of both roots and flowers. Partice's beauty is to her but a reflection of her own. According to her there has never been a child like him. Blinded by his beauty she regards him to be a genius. When Isabelle starves her brother in their mother's absence, Louise is unable to guess what actually could have happened to her son. Her self-conceit makes her quite confident of the fact that nothing else but her absence has caused such great suffering to Patrice.

The inhibitive nature of the mother-child bond denies Patrice the oppotunity to develop any logical observation and analytical power but his instincts remain intact. Even in an emotionally disturbed state Patrice perceives Lanz as his most potent rival. At the first sight of Lanz, Patrice becomes suspicious of him. He does not know why he dislikes the intruder, but he instinctively feels threatened. The peculiar ties between Patrice and his mother do not provide an opportunity for the growth of his intellectual human attributes but the same do not, in any way, dilute the intensity of the animal ones. It is all the consequence of over-mothering or pampering by Louise. She could make him into whatever she wants, and this makes her feel more like a mother.

Pampering is almost always detrimental to the growth of a healthy personality and in addition to it, its sudden withdrawal usually leads to severe emotional dislocation. When Louise is out with Lanz, back home Patrice is furious, he breaks all the glasses there with his hands. He is bleeding profusely but is not aware of it. He is unable to understand what he is doing and why. He wants his mother back and in a fit of anger against Lanz he breaks all the glasses and hopes that his tantrums will force his mother to come back to him. Louise is also torn between two worlds. After Lanz's arrival she gives less of herself to Patrice than to her husband and whenever she reveals her desire to pay more attention to Patrice, Lanz interferes with cunning display of false tenderness. Patrice who hates his stepfather kills him in a moment of rage. And so strong is the infatuation between the mother and the son that Louise totally ignores the fact that Patrice has killed her husband. The event brings peace to Louise. She says, "Patrice, you are all I have left." (75)

The mother-daughter bond in the novel is again something unusual and unpalatable. It is characterized by emotional deprivation.

When there is mutual understanding between the child and its parents, and when channels of communication between them are open and functioning, many of the emotional shocks and disappointments that are inevitable part of growing up can be eased: "Most young people have a somewhat better relationship with their parents during this stage of development . . . but there are number of factors that can create or aggravate tensions. Some people are so sensitive about their inadequacies that they cannot discuss them with anyone, some parents are so critical that it is difficult for the young people to discuss anything with them," opines Lindgren. (133) The peculiar relationship between Louise and her daughter Isabelle can be explained in the light of this observation. Since Isabelle is not blessed with a beautiful face like Patrice, she is just an object of hatred and criticism for her mother who rates physical beauty above everything else. The daughter therefore suffers from a nagging sense of inferiority and tries to compensate for it by becoming violent, aggressive, and domineering. It is rightly argued by Kakar that it is "the mother who helps her infant learn to deal with anxiety without feelings of frustration and anger." (55) There is no such effort on Louise's part in this novel. In this bizarre world where beauty is the sole criterion for being loved even by one's parents, the ugly daughter gets alienated from her mother.

It is believed that daughters need mothers to train, protect and guide them. Without her mother's guidance Isabelle fails to internalize womanhood and ends up becoming cruel and ruthless at times. She starves her brother, plunges his face into boiling water, feels happy on seeing her mother suffering and dying and takes pleasure in burning all the farms of her mother. In this context Samuel Lowy makes an apt observation when he says, "In the world of its fantasies the hating person is able to multiply his attacks on the hated object and even to destroy it again and again, and from this point of view the satisfaction value of hatred is more extensive than that of a factual single attack." (11) Louise's discriminating attitude towards her daughter drains Isabelle of all tender feelings of love and trust. She is not able to overcome her mother's hatred for herself. It instills in her a strong feeling of jealousy and hatred and a deep sense of insecurity. A true human relationship can only be achieved through love, contact, relatedness but this kind of blessed set up is far from the lives of Louise and Isabelle. When she realizes that it is no more possible for her to live in this cruel loveless world she throws herself in front of a train leaving her ugly daughter alone in the same world in which she couldn't enjoy feelings of love and belongingness.

The mothers in *Mad Shadows* are strange from another perspective also. It is believed that strong maternal instincts give joy to a woman in bringing up her children but such feelings are absent in mothers in this novel. Both Louise and Isabelle hate their daughters because they are ugly. To a child his or her parents are role models; so Isabelle following her mother's footsteps finds nothing wrong in ill-treating her own daughter and leaving her alone in the end in this cruel world. Isabelle has been a rebel all through and according to Lindgren, "the rebellious person is also an immature person. He has difficulty in controlling his impulses and lacks a sense of reality and proportion when it comes to real or fancied wrong." (448) The parents present in front of their children a picture of world full of love, companionship and understanding. When they are deprived of such relationship in their childhood it becomes very difficult for the child to have a positive emotional interaction at any stage.

The mother who can overlook any fault in her son is unable to find any appreciable quality of head and heart in her daughter. She is extremely protective about the son but displays hardly any tender feelings for Isabelle. She is doomed to work all the time in the fields, suffer loneliness and neglect. No wonder she hates her mother and is jealous of her. Her mother loves her brother only because he is beautiful and hates her because she is ugly: "She knew that the woman's eyes, indeed her whole being, rested on this solitary and fragile beauty." (16) This leads Isabelle to destroy her brother's beauty. She plunges it into boiling water and transforms him from the adored son to the abandoned one. In the end Isabelle fearlessly admits that she is the one who disfigured Patrice and the reason behind it is the discriminatory attitude of the mother. Since her childhood she has seen her mother adoring Patrice for his beauty and hating her for being ugly: "Patrice, always Patrice! You never loved me and you never realized that your son was stupid that he was an idiot . . . nothing but a beautiful body. Not even a man, or a child, either. Your darling Patrice never had a mind. Did you think I had no feelings just because I was ugly?" (104) She also reveals that she hated her mother because the only thing she believed in was her own damnable beauty. She says, "How could anyone take pity on me when my own mother rejected me." (105) Isabelle has only hatred for her mother and nothing else. When she is dying Isabelle remarks scornfully, "She is wasting away. I have come just in time to see her struggle for life, she who has never known how to struggle but for herself." (120) Her hatred for her mother leads her to destroy all the farms of Louise but the thirst for destruction is not yet quenched. So she kills herself too.

The foregoing discussion leads one to conclude that for Marie-Claire Blais the filial relationship is not a mechanical one. It has deep roots and far reaching consequences. A harmonious mother-child bond is the basis of a wholesome personality. Socialization that ultimately leads one towards achieving integration and harmony at the social and personal levels takes place during the formative years of childhood when the child interacts most with the mother. Pampering and overprotection not only impede the normal social development of the child, they also prevent one from becoming a self-reliant spontaneous being. Emotional deprivation is equally injurious for proper personality development. Rejection and criticism by the mothering person result in breeding a feeling of insecurity and inferiority and a low self-esteem. A low self-esteem makes one hostile, aggressive and withdrawn and thus incapable of enjoying fulfilling human interaction.

NOTES

1. Graham A. Allan, *Sociology of Friendship and Kinship* (London: George Allen and Unwin, 1979), p. 31.
2. *Child Development* (New York: Rinehart and Winston, 1967), p. 314.
3. (Canada: McClelland and Stewart, 1959).
4. Sudhir Kakar, *The Inner Word* (New Delhi: Oxford University Press, 1981), p. 54.
5. *Man and His Fellowmen* (London: Kegan Paul, Trench, Trubner, 1953), p. 30.
6. Henry Clay Lindgren, *Psychology of Personal and Social Adjustment* (New York: American Book Company, 1959), p. 157.
7. Elton B. McNeill, *Psychology of Being Human* (New York: Confield Press), p. 154.

Impact of Media in Role-Modelling: A Study of Joan Barfoot's *Dancing in the Dark*

INDIRA BHATT

Describing the woman as she is required by man, the Bangladeshi poet Taslima Nasreen writes:

> She is dressed in red
> For red is a very bright colour, it draws attention easily. . . .
> Her face is painted,
> She is not enough, not complete with some colouring.[1]

Give her glamorous dress, ornaments and cosmetics. Drowned with the physical possessions, she will forget or wish to forget that they serve only to chain her to the traditional role-model. She will willingly accept the defined and destined role in the family and society and remain a doll-like object to please the man, her husband. Most women wouldn't want to have or to be anything else in life if they get the full attention of their men. And why not? Even to this day, both in the East and the West, the societal norms and women's magazines talk about and write about woman and her home and how to keep them clean and neat, trim and attractive. Day in and day out the newspapers, magazines, TV and radio talk about attractiveness of women with a result that they help create and keep the role-model of wifehood of generations when Eve had her hearth. The modern middle-class wife prefers for the peace of her home to live in the image of a perfect wife—the Sita image. Eve had chosen knowledge but Joan Barfoot's Edna in *Dancing in the Dark*[2] does wish to know and be unhappy. It appears that like the Indian wife, the Canadian middle-class woman too self-negating herself works towards a perfect body and perfect home in sparkling condition, thinking that this would please her husband and keep him attached to herself. But this dream is shattered, the bubble is burst and the safety and security of the home is exposed to the tempest outside. My attempt here is to examine what the impact of media is on Edna the protagonist of *Dancing in the Dark* and why she breaks out of her chosen cocoon to emerge a real individual.

Dancing in the Dark is a novel that portrays the dreams of a young pretty girl of twenty who considers marriage an investment and as with investment in the stock market it should bring return. Edna had invested herself—her sole possession in Harry: "I invested the goodness I had in Harry, and I did expect compounded goodness would be my return." (49)

Her mother had said whatever you do, comes back to you and Edna had believed this. Since she was afraid of the dreary prospect of taking up a job of teaching, she decides to marry Harry. Having determined to become a wife she follows what her mother's magazines said "show that you are interested." Her only ambition is to be safe, to be happy, to be wanted. As Patricia Spacks in *The Female Imagination* states: "A girl with an imagination larger than her opportunities must be particularly careful to control her actions, not to manifest too much, not to seem a lunatic. Vocation, what a person does in the world, represents literal social possibility."[3]

Edna's vocation is wifehood. She does not want to become somebody, nor does she want to do anything else. To her there is no difference between being and doing, liking and loving. Hers is a very limited vision of life. Her responses to life too are limited to self-contempt and terror of remaining a lonely person. She jumps at the first opportunity to make life a life for Harry with all his conditions and promises. It is Harry who knows what he wants for himself as well as for her. Though often he inquires of her as to what she really wants in life, and tries to explain the difference between doing and feeling, he is satisfied that Edna does not want much from him, from life and that he is free to pursue whatever he wishes to. It is enough for her to look after the Home and Harry: "All I ever wanted was to make a good home." (145) With an assurance from Harry, "The house is great, and of course you've made it a place to be proud of," (145) a magazine would have come and taken photographs, would have called it a typical middle-class house, a neat, clean and sparkling house, but to Edna, "it was more to me, the place, the *haven*, where our lives were led, disregarding Harry's life outside." (15) She feels that she is called to perfection in making herself indispensable and absolute. Marriage to her becomes a vocation. She is frightened to cross the threshold of the perfect home and face the realities of the outer world. To keep herself safe and secure, she carefully builds the walls of safety: "I thought all that pudding, all the layers of soft warmth behind the walls would keep me safe." (169) Little does she know that what keeps her safe inside, can also prevent the light of reality to penetrate her life and her truth of life. Nor does she know that "It can be destroyed in a phone call, a sentence, a moment." (168)

All this Edna has absorbed from magazines which are easily available at the super market. The magazines said: "Rate your marriage—how close are you really? or the women in his office," (93) and they had quizzes which Edna finds irresistible: "When your husband comes home from work, do you greet him" (93) and scored well on all the quizzes, knew all the answers from the magazines, how to be more attractive for your man and how to be sure he'll always come home. Joan Barfoot vividly gives the details of what a gullible housewife believes in, from her reading of women's magazines owned by men. They always talk about fashions in dress and food, woman's body and her attractiveness to men but rarely prepare her to face the harsh realities of the world beyond her marriage. They, perhaps not fully conscious of what they are doing, play the role of keeping women ignorant and vulnerable. Accordingly, Edna is happy and satisfied with her role of a perfect traditional housewife.

It is only on her fortieth birthday that Edna suddenly realizes that her life of twenty years of marriage had no meaning:

> One ought to have things in place. One ought to be able to say I have done that, and I will do this . . . but for me? If one does the same thing over and over again, each time properly, each time to the best of one's ability, still what one seems to have is a handful of endless identical tasks. It's not like getting anywhere. (141)
>
> She is stuck with a thought, not a blow: this is nothing: This is not anything at all. (142)

Yet she is reluctant to risk emotional exposure. She is afraid of being hurt and has full faith in her Harry who is almost like a God to her. She does not discuss frankly her doubts with Harry even when he keeps on asking her. The novelist presents a crystal clear picture of a woman without confidence, a woman who does not open up and talk about her fears to her husband, a woman who only thinks of her safety, and yet a woman who has an absolute faith in her husband. Though she has no secrets from him except her half hour in the afternoon when her daily routine work is over, the half hour when she is important to herself:

> I sang for my family and danced in front of Harry's friends, sometimes on a small club stage. Wherever, they looked and admired. I was *someone,* I was anyone: from Streisand to Baez I could claim anyone's voice I chose, for my own small neat body. . . . Most often I placed him [Harry] in the audience, where he sat watching proudly and with amazement, like the others, sometimes I found myself smiling. The trick has always been to keep the *eyes closed.* . . . It was a shock to see my clean cool living room when I was sweating from the dance inside. . . . It was just an old *familiar dream* that gave me, for a little time, my old *familiar second* life. It was enough, I always knew I wouldn't like it to be real, all those people staring, and certainly knew that the life I had was the one I wanted. (91)

It is a dream of being somebody important, at the centre of the stage, and not on the periphery. It is a dream she cherished since her student days, always having kept a painting of a dancing girl. But she thinks that she does not have the gift of dancing. She envies her sister Stella who could do what she wanted and knew what she wanted from life, who could defy the world and say "no." Edna is a quiet and shy girl and thinks that she could never realize her dream, that it would always remain her secret dream and would never become real. She considers herself weak and untalented, having no other choice. So she considers her secret half hour spent dreaming and longing a flaw since, then, she is someone else forgetting her vocation being a perfect wife.

In her effort to keep Harry comfortable, she has moulded herself to his requirements. Yet she finds that he wants something more from her. She queries herself: "What did I do wrong? What were you looking for? What more could I have done?" (97) and that "My magazines, the ones I liked and was *raised on,* made it seem so clear. If one did this that would result. Did I not follow the instruction carefully enough?" (96) In spite of all this and her devotion to him, she finds that Harry had changed. He had broken his promise, his faith and betrayed her. A mere phone call from a friend and her dream house of perfection is broken, a home that she had so carefully and lovingly built, she is shocked to see that twenty years of her happy life could be shattered by phone calls. Struck with a bolt from the blue she is unable to comprehend his affair.

Had she discussed the problem with Harry, maybe her life would have been different. Now in the hospital she feels the rage and thinks of "driving a bulldozer to that house and smash it into splinters." (97)

For she finds that her house was built on false promises though most of her life with Harry was happy. Analyzing her plight, she feels: "Poor Harry, to have been loved with such a grip. To have carried my small weight upon his back for so many years. No wonder he began to stoop," (168) and gives him the benefit of doubt, though she wonders about his part, "a whim, a desire, a selfishness and a lie." The shock numbs her and when she receives the second phone call from Harry informing her of his stay away from her, she knows that she has been blind and deaf and dumb all her life, not to realize that walls of safety could obstruct the truth of life. She feels like a nun who worships her God and finds herself rejected by him. She equates Harry to God. The novelist uses the metaphor of convent, nuns and God to focus on the purity and sacredness of home life, sacrifices and surrender to God the husband to vividly describe the helpless Edna and her terrifying loneliness. What Edna could not visualize is the anger that the saintly persons feel: "Would they reach for knives and kill God?"

Both Edna and Harry take too much for granted. Harry's affair is simply a leap from this trusted taken-for-granted base. A woman does not like to be touched by a man who loves someone else. Nor does she like to touch a person she does not love. As Taslima Nasreen puts it in "Women Can't":

> Any man can get heated
> By suddenly opening up any woman from
> top to bottom . . .
> Only animals and men can
> Touch a body of flesh
> Without love

> *Women can't. . . .*
> women cannot caress skin without love
> Those who can, let them.[4]

Edna cannot accept Harry's caresses. The whole purpose of her life is shattered. She could not follow Stella's example and gather the broken pieces of her life to create a new design of life. Suddenly she finds herself on a wrong path leading nowhere. She cannot let Harry escape the consequences of his betrayal. Like Clytemnestra she too must kill, she finds herself taking a kitchen knife and cutting Harry to pieces.

While recounting her life faithfully in the hospital, she feels free and light. All her life she had controlled her feelings but now:

> I find I am dancing
> with my eyes open . . . and
> If I step on my own toes
> or fall down, it does not hurt,
> it is not dangerous. (182)

Having become free from her self-imposed bondage she determines to dance without fear: "The freedom to tomorrow, eyes open, watching the people watching." She is confident and fearless now that she has broken the magic circle of marriage and thinks of tomorrow, the new start in life.

The novelist has painted a wonderful picture of a woman and her fears, her limited world and her terrors of the bigger world. It is interesting to note that on one hand women are struggling to find space for themselves in the male-dominated world and on the other hand the images of fabulously fit women, fashions, cosmetic industries and media-instructions push them to become and remain merely the objects of male attention and desire. Barfoot portrays a character commonly found all over the world, anywhere, any time, who is victimized not only by the societal norms but also by the male-dominated industries, without ever realizing how she is led into the darkness of oppression. It is an unfair battle of a leaf against the wind. The image of leaf is very suggestive. The leaf keeps fighting this unfair and futile battle, so too a woman must fight her battles even through darkness dancing with eyes open. It is a remarkable awakening of a new consciousness that breaks the fetters of fear and slavery of role-model of a perfect wife. The novelist portrays the revelations of hidden areas of the self moving from the status quo to the inner independence accepting the dangers of reality and achieving real selfhood.

NOTES

1. Taslima Nasreen "The Wheel" in *Infinite Variety,* ed. Firdous Azim and Niaz Zaman (Dhaka, Bangladesh: University Press, 1994), p. 307.
2. Joan Barfoot, *Dancing in the Dark* (Canada: Macmillan Paperbacks, 1988).
3. Patricia Spacks, *The Female Imagination* (London: George Allen and Unwin, 1976), p. 229.
4. Taslima Nasreen, "Women Can't" in *Infinite Variety*, p. 306.

Childhood and the Family Reverie: A Study of Native Life in Beatrice Culleton's *In Search of April Raintree*

N. KALAAMANI

When George Ryga's *The Ecstasy of Rita Joe* premiered at Vancouver playhouse on Nov. 23, 1967, it veritably punctured an euphoria of a complacent white Canadian psyche and an indigenous cultural history was swept into the limelight. This awakening on the one hand became instrumental in displacing the widespread, unsympathetic accommodating attitude of the white settlers towards the natives, and on the other, harbingered a plethora of creative works chronicling native Indian life and culture. The mid-seventies of the twentieth century when the *Literary History of Canada* (1976) spoke of the "historical absence of an Indian presence in Canadian Literature" it simultaneously ushered in a reactionary move that brought the native literature into the literary milieu of Canada. In the spring in 1974, native publications have been so considerable that literary surveys quickly observed, "Indians are, this season, an even hotter topic than oil."

Primarily biographical, this aboriginal literature was the pulse of the post-colonial phase in Canada, a revisionist perspective, which had brought the "outsider" inside, the peripheral to the centre-stage. The deregionalized deracinated aborigine was no longer the marginalized man and writers began to disenchant fellow natives about the white man's superiority. Quite ironically, for the whites too, the Indians were no longer the savage antagonists, coloured foils against whom their own cultural standards had been gauged, but a people whose cultural history was their nation's indigenous past and heritage.

The reversion of priorities impregnated a literary environment when the native writer found it imperative to take up the task of regenerating his community. With this objective in mind, he essayed to dismantle the complexes of years of denigration and self-denigration of his race. Consequently the writers desperately rummaged for a lost ground, and struggled for the resurgence of the indigenous culture. Every attempt at revival was counterbalanced with the defiance of the colonial imposition. Acculturation apart, more articulate discourse began to untaint the stigma of ethnicity, and define for the aborigine, a new cultural contour, to make it worthy of respect in the eyes of the world by giving it a new focus and identity. Echoing many a third world writer in this vein in Canada, ethnic writing found its own voice. Like their Australian counterparts Thomas Keneally, Xavier Herbert, F.B. Vickers, Randolph Stow and Patrick White, Canadian writers Margaret Laurence, Rudy Wiebe, Yres Therianit, Edith Sharp and Tomson Highway dwelt elaborately on the native themes and struggles. Cultural collisions in Canada however hardly ever turned militant.

Want of an organized mass movement in protest, lack of efficient leaders to monitor protest activities, with the exception of a few like Riel, Tecumesh etc. and want of substantial issues that could demand attention are reasons too obvious why native stand was not emphatic in Canada. After Ryga, however, writers emerged on the forefront focussing the eyes of the world upon the racial and social injustice that natives were subjected to. Ethnic issues perpetrating the world were already the grave concern of the day with the third world writers raising their voices in protest against white imperialism. Since most of the writings are investigations into primitive societies, an analysis of a native work could succinctly illustrate how they were pining in the throes of a hegemonic suffocation.

In the works of, for instance Lee Maracle, Jeanette Armstrong, Maria Campbell or Beatrice Culleton, one could cognize "the emergence of a literature which will be the underpinning of a newly conceived Aboriginal heritage. This is a heritage which has always been there, but which is now both traditional and mixed with the traumatic circumstances of the struggle of a people to find or assert their own unique identity and have that identity recognised by others."[1]

Beatrice Culleton's *In Search of April Raintree,* like Maria Campbell's *Half-breed* records a society whose ills are irrevocable. The Métis people are half-breeds and they are repugnant and obnoxious to the whites. A Métis Indian herself, Beatrice Culleton recounts native life in all its primitive harshness in this novel. To be a native was a banality. Shame, humiliation, hunger, separation from homes, deprivation were their maladies for which there was no relief. Most traumatic of all their experiences were those of childhood.

Childhood is a vital stage in everyman's life. In Métis societies, children are most sullied. The emotional, mental upheavals of Métis children often end in death. Not only Beatrice Culleton, but all writers chronicling the decadence of Indians seldom fail to touch upon the barbarity and slaughter of the innocent Indian children in the hands of the whites. For instance, F.R. Scott describes the residential school for boys at Fort Providence as a "firetrap mental goal" which mirrors the spiritual imprisonment of an entire people. In *House of Whale* Macewen catalogues the destructive malignant forces of the city (which is referred to as the house of whale) that bring about frustration, despair and violence in the young boy Lucas George until ultimately he is cast into a prison cell 'a cage' for "the biggest bird of all." George Ryga's plays have insistently dwelt on images of the Indian existing within a prison created by a white society. *Indian* depicts a young boy locked up by a white farmer in an attempt to threaten the boy's uncle. In *The Ecstasy of Rita Joe* scenes are repeatedly set in courtrooms and jails. The city to Rita is itself a maze-like prison. Jaimie in this play despairs in his search for an Indian identity: "Teach me who I really am you've taken that away! Give me back the real me so I can live like a man."[3] Desperation, death, separation from parents, life in foster homes form the gamut of the Métis childhood.

Recurrent images of children dying abound the works. Al Purdy's poem "The Children" depicts Indian boys in Churchill, Manitoba enduring lives filled with desperation, death. In the play *Lament for Harmonica* (1958), Gwen Ringwood records the death of an infant son and the subsequent deterioration of a young mother with alcoholism and prostitution.

Separation of children from their parental homes is a recurrent motif in native writings. The separation may be due to disease, death, or due to neglect of parents. Tom Wayman's song: "I wish I was an Eagle" (the 2nd part of the Kumsheen Trilogy) finds the accidental death of a young Indian boy. Garner's "One-Two-Three Little Indians" describes the death of the Algongian protagonist's infant son, who dies of pneumonia. Alan Fry's documentary novel *How a People Die* (1970) uses the death of an Indian child to depict poverty and despair on a pacific coast reservation. Sometimes it is not death, but separation that finds the children in foster-homes, children yearning for families, yearning for parental love and affection. Life in foster homes is the most pernicious of the maladies that beset Métis children. Their life-in-death problematic is well exemplified in the lives of two Métis Indian children in Culleton's *In Search of April Raintree.*

April and Cheryl Raintree are two young children who grow up into girlhood bearing the stigma of ethnicity. How they withstand the onslaught of a society that is keen in undoing them forms the crux of the novel. One sister believes that she can gain social identity by racial denial. The other believes that she has to bear the burden of her ethnicity. The novel probes into the psyche of two sisters for whom the term "Indian" connoted two different things. The trauma of upheavals in their lives due to family break-ups, displacements, settlements in foster homes shatter their dreams of a family and the identity crisis ensues. *In Search of April Raintree* could be read as a domestic drama depicting the ignominy in the lives of the two sisters who are endlessly battered by a heartless society; the novel adduces the cultural malaise of a social system where institutions like home, school, foster-home etc. become scaffolderies where native children are psychologically beheaded. And the family which is the locus of security and identity becomes symbol of degeneration, disintegration, disillusionment. In the novel the separation of the two children April and Cheryl is brought about due to the alcoholic addiction of parents. They are always tipsy 'drinking medicine' as they dupe their children. The drinking parties they throw are nightmarish experiences for the children; drinking sprees mean gatherings at home when strange people come and a lot of yelling, fighting, sex and brutalism take place. The trepidated children go into hiding, lost, frightened and insecure. However the children wonder why after taking much medicine their mother still feels unwell. The parties at home front become more frequent and the situation chaotic until one morning the people from welfare societies come in an attempt to retrieve the children from their parents. This is one of the heart-rending episodes of the novel. April and Cheryl yearn for parental protection as the welfare society gets ready to take them away. Half happy, half dismayed, the vanquished alcoholics await the inevitable. 'We came home,' says April

> and there were some cars in front of our house. One had flashing red lights on it and I know it was a police car. When we entered the house, Mom was sitting at the table, openly weeping right in front of all these people. There were empty medicine bottles on the small counter at the table, but I couldn't figure out why the four people were there. (15)

The children conjecture that these people have come to take them away from home and they are to be separated from their parents. Their suspicions confirm when Mrs. Grey, the social worker gestures them towards her. Her attempts at friendly persuasion do not prevail with the children. April, angry and hurt, queries in distaste:

> "Why is Mom crying? Did you hurt her?"
>
> "No dear, your mother is ill and she won't be able to take care of you anymore. Would you like to go for a car-ride?" (16)

Tantalizing though the car-ride was, the children refuse. Surely if the mother is unwell, the father can take care: "We can stay with Daddy. He will take care of us. You can go away now." (16) But Mrs. Grey only responds "I'm afraid not honey." Alarmed at the arrangements being made to take them away, the children desperately cling to their father. "I was hoping Dad would walk in and he would make them all go away. He would make everything right. But nothing happened." Feeling lost, they yearningly look at their mother. Only amidst much sobbing, she directs them to go away:

> I kind of know that she was really saying good-bye to us but I was determined that we were not going to be taken away. I clung to my Mom as tight as I could. They wouldn't be able to pull me away from her and then they would leave. I expected Mom to do the same. But she didn't. She pushed me away. Into their grasping hands. I couldn't believe it. Frantically I screamed. Mommy, please don't make us go. Mom, don't. (17)

Clinging to the mother will make them go away is the child's logic. Attempts being futile, she tries another strategy:

> I tried hard to put everything into my voice sure that they

> would all come to their senses and leave us be. There were a lot of grown-up things I didn't understand that day. My mother should have fought with her life to keep us with her. Instead she handed us over. It didn't make any sense to me. (17)

This was the grand finale of life at home. The children lose their ground of security, love and parental guidance. Separation from their homes marks the beginning of a life of mental turmoils. Unstability of lives at foster-homes is the signia of their existentialistic rootlessness. The angst and the loneliness the children suffer separated from families and from each other is the microcosm of the mounting feeling of alienation in the so-called white man's land. With the anticolonial protest also rose their quest for identity. In fact, as one of the critics aptly puts it, the native's quest for identity was not a pursuit of the narcissistic self but a search for self respect as a native citizen of a free country.

In the lives of these two children who grow up in different foster homes, the identity crisis assumes diverse propensities. April contemplates how her race has been instrumental in her disruption, whilst Cheryl, for whom the parents were lost prior to her picturization of a home life, begins to rumble for her roots, familial and racial.

Lost to each other, such was their life in foster homes, the sisters had two or three occasions to meet in a year, when the welfare societies arranged family get togethers. These were the silver streaks in the lives of the sisters when they could meet each other and sometimes their parents and exchange news. On one such instance, their father and mother not being present, the children discuss Riel, the revolutionary hero. It was April's birthday and Cheryl with much thoughtfulness had bought her a book on Riel. The carefully chosen present however did not delight April. It was utterly distasteful to her:

> 'A book about Louis Riel?' I said and crinkled my nose in distaste. I knew all about Riel. He was a rebel who had been hanged for treason. Worse, he had been a crazy half-breed. I had learnt about his folly in history. Also, I had read about Indians and the various methods of tortures they had put the missionaries through. No wonder they were known as savages. So anything to do with the Indians, I despised. And here, I was supposed to be part Indian. I remember how relieved I was

> that no one in my class knew of my heritage when we were going through that period in Canadian history. (44)

So April only shrugs her shoulder in response in sheer repulsion of her race: "Well, I wasn't going to live like a half-breed. When I got from being a foster child, then I would live just like a real white person." Being a half-breed, to April, only meant "being poor and dirty, it meant being ugly and stupid. It meant living off white people. And giving your children to white people to look after. It meant having to take all the crap the white people gave." (49) She dreams of inheriting a white culture, spiting her own.

Throughout April takes dexterous care to conceal her racial roots. With companions and neighbours, why even at her marriage she is exceedingly alert. For fear that her name may betray her ethnicity she changes her family name from Raintree into Raintry as the latter sounds Irish. All her endeavours are to relieve herself of the racial burden. In fact, her very marriage with Bob, she hopes could be an antidote to her racial imbalances, her poverty, humiliation and suffering. The concept of living in a mansion, like a white man meant much more than the marriage itself, so much so that when the marriage fails, April is still cheerful because she's given a mansion to live in and a large sum of money. Ideologically and practically her position is directly in opposition to Cheryl's.

The note of opposition between the two sisters, which anticipates the later division that ensues between them is established in the reaction to the book. For Cheryl, this book on Riel was an invaluable treasure. Riel was a fascinating revolutionary Métis hero. And she was proud to share this identity. When she presents the book to April, she loftily claims: "He is a Métis like us," and innocent of April's reaction, continues: "Mrs. McAdams says we should be proud of our heritage. You know what that means? It means we are part Indian and part white. I wish we were whole Indians." (45) Championing the cause of the Métis takes root in her life-blood. To realize the native heritage in toto was young Cheryl's strongest urge. An incident in school will elucidate how Cheryl's crusade against racism had already commenced:

> That morning, her teacher had been reading to the class how the Indians scalped, tortured and massacred brave white explorers and missionaries. Cheryl's anger began to build. All of

> a sudden she . . . loudly exclaimed, "This is all a bunch of lies."
>
> "I am going to pretend I didn't hear that," the teacher had said calmly. "Then I'll say it again. I'm not going to learn this garbage about Indian people." Cheryl had said louder feeling she couldn't back down. Everyone else had looked at her as the teacher came and stood by her desk. "They are not lies; this is history. These things happened whether you like it or not." "If this is history, how come so many tribes wiped out? How come they haven't got their land anymore? How come their food supplies were wiped out? Lies! Lies! Lies! your history books don't say how the white people destroyed the Indian way of life. That's all you white people do is to teach a bunch of lies to cover your own tracks!" (57)

Cheryl attacks her teacher who is a white. The fire of fury in her heart against the impostors rages and eventually finds a vent when April declares her intention of marrying a white. For a long time the hiatus between them had been widening. April fears her social identity so much that she begins to cut off all association with her sister. She ceases writing to her and prevents her from coming to meet her. Cheryl's last straw of familial ties snaps when April announces she is going to marry a white man. She feels abandoned, betrayed, stranded. With a vengeance she delves deeper into her ancestral roots pecking nostalgically into her past, she uncovers her history. Her bitterness and resentment at April become a wall of separation from her sister. And the family disintegration has gone full circle.

She abhors her sister first for abandoning her, and second for her seemingly morale life and her double standards. The novel's turning point is Cheryl's hospitalization. April tries to talk Cheryl into normalcy but her sister feels provoked: "Don't lay that crap on me, big sister. You turned your back on me a long time ago. You think I don't know why you married Bob? It was to get away from me, that's why. I'll bet you wished you were an only child. I bet you wished I was dead." (192-93) She had gauged April's mind. All her anger against the whites now gets focussed on April and she lashes endlessly against her. She openly criticizes April's marriage with Bob: "Your kind makes me sick. Big white snobs who think they're the superior race. Your white governments, your white churches, sitting back in idle rich comfort, preaching what ought to be but making sure it isn't." (197) She sneers, remonstrates with sickening disgust at her sister: "You're a snob. You have double-standards. You were so shocked when they said I was a hooker." (197) She is not merely a snob, worse than that, a prostitute: "You prostituted yourself when you took Bob's money, that's how. You never loved the man. You loved his money. You figured out you were going to be Miss High Society. But you figured wrong." (197)

She wants to scandalize April, startling her out of her smug white complacency. This is one way of having her vengeance served. She lays threadbare her own attempts to uncover her past, her essays to trace her father, mother, racial past and vehemently glorifies the fact that she not only discovered them, but how she found that they were only gutter creatures; the reason why they took to alcoholism, in order to forget the fact that they were only gutter creatures. She also discloses the fact that she had begun to share the Métis identity by taking to drinking. The charge is not complete. "But that's not all," she says, she talks of her mother and their baby sister Anna and how her mother committed suicide by jumping off the Louise Bridge.

This was Cheryl's attempt to cream April with her past, which she wanted to escape from. How she succumbed to these gutter creatures and herself became a gutter creature she elaborates: "They were bums, you know. Both of them. Bums. Boozers. Gutter creatures. Dad took all the money from me. He didn't know where it came from. He didn't care where it came from. Mark Desoto." (198-99) And Mark Desoto, her fiancé was not an industrialist or moneylender he was only another gutter creature. Jack of all trades, "drug pusher, bootlegger, stealing, breaking and entering, pimping if it was illegal, he was in it. And guess who was right there in it with him? Your little sister, Cheryl Raintree. It was not merely a disclosure. It was a total identification partly in fulfilment of her goals, and partly in defiance of April.

This was just before the suicide which Cheryl attempts. Cheryl's death makes profound inroads into April's own identity crisis. Her identity questions have already begun to torment her when she is mistaken for Cheryl and is gang-raped. Cheryl's death takes her on to a journey into herself and the search which she has till then been camouflaging now assumes new significance.

Cheryl's death, like the death of the Indian in almost all the native works, is the cultural death after a struggle for survival. Finding a family is finding an ancestry, a heritage, an identity. In Cheryl's death, April finds her roots. The novel thus does not end on a note of despair. Cheryl leaves behind her son Henry Lee, who becomes the survivor of the Raintree family. April's last notes become affirmative: "But for Henry Lee and me, there would be a tomorrow. And it would be better. I would strive for it. For my sister and her son. For my parents. For my people." (228) Unlike *Rita Joe,* where the native had no promise of a future, *In Search of April Raintree* offers a new hope for the old race. Cheryl does not die an infant's death. Her life signifies the struggle of a race for identity. Like Hemingway's old man Santiago, though external forces overpower her, she wages her battle single-handed in the hope that she will win one day even if she will have to die.

In Mort Forer's *The Humback* (1969), the story is set in the backdrop of a Métis settlement in north eastern Manitoba. Here the constant disappearance or death of Toinette's children mirrors the fate of all the Humback inhabitants; poised between the city and the bush, the Métis of the settlement constantly risk disappearance into either world, leaving scant trace of their existence. However, as in *April Raintree,* the novel does not portray a bleak future for the Indians. If the children's death suggests the over-riding threat to the whole settlement, Toinette also insists on the child as a symbol of endurance and hope.

Cheryl's child Henry Lee, as Toinette remarks, becomes now the living symbol of endurance and hope; and as she says everytime something dies there should be something new to take its place. Cheryl's is a phoenixian death. It is affirmative. The suggestion of a family integration is a cultural hope of survival.

NOTES

1. Ronald M. Berndt, "Opening Address," *Aboriginal Writing Today,* ed. Jack Davis and Bob Hedge (Canberra: Australian Institute of Aboriginal Studies, 1985), pp. 7-10.
2. Beatrice Culleton, *In Search of April Raintree* (Toronto: OUP, 1987).
3. George Ryga, *The Ecstasy of Rita Joe, Modern Canadian Plays,* ed. Jerry Wasserman (Toronto: OUP, 1989).

Edibility and Ambiguity in Margaret Atwood's *The Edible Woman*

N. RAMA DEVI

The title of the novel suggests that the food metaphor plays a dominant part in the evocation of the meaning of the novel and also that more than food gets eaten in a capitalist and patriarchal society dominated by conspicuous consumption, rationality and industrialism where there is no place for the attitudes, desires, beliefs and opinions expressed by the females, the central figures of Margaret Atwood's fiction.

As is the case with Atwood's other heroines, Marian McAlpin, the heroine of *The Edible Woman* is also a sensitive, self-reflective and finely articulate female. She uses quite an artful language, to voice forth the changes that take place in her attitudes and feelings, as she journeys through her various associations with several male and female friends and arrives at ways of understanding as to what it means to be a woman. Though the narrative language abounds in various symbols and metaphors, it is the food metaphor which is the chief vehicle that serves to put forward the feminist tendencies of the heroine that help her protest against the dehumanizing tendencies of the society and save herself by rejecting her inauthentic self.

The novel introduces us to the protagonist, Marian McAlpin, a fairly sensible, intelligent young woman, decently liberal in her views and somewhat defensive about her own individuality and her responsibility to others. She is employed in the Seymour Surveys Company, a market research group. She shares an apartment with Ainsley Tewce and the relationship between them is purely non-obligatory. On weekends, she occupies herself with Peter Wollander, a lawyer, and the relationship is a non-interfering one, based on non-expectations for the future. It suited both because Marian chose not to be close to anyone and because Peter sees marriage as male capitulation and capture. Further Marian has no really strong views on anything. Though she perceives the hypocrisy and unreality of much of society, she accepts it:

> Her acceptance of the consumer-consumed syndrome as the basis of society seems to stem from her own distance from it, and from a feeling of ineffectuality on her own part. . . . Marian is an instinctive victim never naming her hunters, but knowing who and what they are just the same.[1]

Her feeling of ineffectiveness makes her think that she has no power to confront and overcome the sources of her oppression, whether they are people like Peter or institutions. Peter, who at the beginning of the novel is found lamenting over the marriage of the last of his bachelor friends, later proposes to Marian just because it suits him and his values which are well synchronized with those of the plastic society he serves. He rationalizes his sudden surrender to marriage by saying:

> A fellow can't keep running around indefinitely. It'll be a lot better in the long run for my practice too, the clients like to know you've got a wife, people get suspicious of a single man after a certain age, they start thinking you're a queer or something. . . . And there is one thing about you, Marian, I know I can always depend on you . . . you're such a sensible girl.[2]

Peter considers Marian a sensible girl because she leaves all the major and minor decisions to him. Marian, on the other hand, agrees to the marriage as she sees marriage as a matter of convenience and inevitability, especially after the trauma she undergoes when she hears about the pension plan in her office. Given her insights, her constant paranoia, her inner doubts and defensiveness, it is not surprising that she considers marriage as a means of total concealment. It is when she is about to take this extreme step that her body intervenes and confronts her with the reality of the situation. It makes her realize that marriage to Peter means more than protection, that it means death—a form of socially acceptable suicide. The rebellion is carried on through the "body language" in which the body makes it impossible for Marian to eat one thing after the other and it is in this sense that the significance of the food metaphor can be felt.

The first symptoms of anorexia (loss of appetite) are seen in Marian immediately after she agrees to the marriage proposal made by Peter. When she goes to a restaurant along with her colleagues who are all spinsters, she finds it difficult to eat: "Marian was surprised at herself. She had been dying to go for lunch, she had been starving, and now she wasn't even hungry." (114)

First, her body refuses anything that may at one time have been alive. It begins with meat when she goes to dinner with Peter:

> Watching him operating on the steak like that, carving a straight slice and then dividing it into neat cubes, made her think of the diagram of the planned cow at the front of one of her cookbooks; the cow with lines on it and labels to show you from which part of the cow all the different cuts were taken. . . . She could see rows of butchers somewhere in a large room, a butcher school, sitting at tables . . . cutting out steaks . . .
>
> She looked down at her own half-eaten steak and suddenly saw it as a hunk of muscle. Blood Red. Part of a real cow that once moved and ate and was killed. . . . She set down her knife and fork. (155)

After this, one after the other like a pork chop, the planned cow, the planned sheep are crossed out of her list of eatables:

> Whatever it was that had been making these decisions, not her mind certainly, rejected anything that had an indication of bone or tendon or fibre . . . she had been afraid to try chicken, she had been fond of it once, but it came with an unpleasantly complete skeletal structure, and the skin, she predicted, would be too much like an arm with goose bumps. (156-57)

For protein variety and energy, for sometime, she relies on omelettes, peanuts and cheese, which also slowly, she finds impossible to eat as she identifies herself with these things also:

> The next morning . . . when she opened her soft-boiled egg and saw the yolk looking up at her with its one significant and accusing yellow eye, she found her mouth closing together like a frightened sea-anemone. It's living; it's alive, the muscles in

> her throat said, and tightened. She pushed the dish away. (165)

This makes her stick on to "Salads" and vitamin pills for some time. But when she loses appetite for vegetables also, her panic is clearly evident:

> She was watching her own hands and the peeler and the curl of crisp orange skin. She became aware of the carrot. It's a root, she thought, it grows in the ground and sends up leaves. Then they come along and dig it up, maybe it even makes a sound, a scream too low for us to hear, but it doesn't die right away, it keeps on living, right now it's still alive . . .
>
> She thought she felt it twist in her hands. She dropped it on the table. Oh, no, she said, almost crying. Not this too. (183)

Thus identifying herself with lower forms of life, she refuses to eat, which she equates with preying upon—first steak and all meats, then eggs, then carrots. She reaches a stage when she is unable to destroy the lowest form of life, mould. She finds herself unable to clean the used vessels and the kitchen sink. As Peter begins to gain control over her in every aspect, her identifications with the hunted and the consumed reaches the precipitation point. She comes to the realization that she is powerless to control her own life. Marian's horror at the act of consuming flesh coincides with her alienation and detachment from the society. She becomes a passive figure, just watching the society with shocking clarity and not playing any active role. She comes to view "eating" as a violent action concealed behind the social facade of dining which also reminds us of the sacrifice of the victim in the Moose Beer ads. The cook book description of preparing turtle soup suggests to Marian 'the deaths of early Christian martyrs':

> You were supposed to keep your live turtle in a cardboard box or other cage for about a week, loving it and feeding it hamburger to rid it of its impurities. Then just as it was beginning to trust you and perhaps follow you around the kitchen . . . you put it into a cauldron of cold water . . . and then brought it slowly to the boil. The whole procedure was reminiscent of the deaths of early Christian martyrs. What fiendishness went

> on in kitchens across the country in the name of providing food. (159)

In terms of the ever-present food metaphor, Peter is a master-chef, and Marian is in grave danger of becoming puff pastry. He subtly prepares her for the different fillings he will demand of her for his cultured palate. George Woodcock has rightly described the novel as a "novel about emotional cannibalism,"[3] noting the predatory nature of human beings and the necessity to maintain the distances and defences between them in the human society.

We, then, see Marian's revulsion spreading "from the things eaten and the act of eating to the body which lives by ingesting and regurgitation."[4] She begins to view even the women of Seymour Surveys as they celebrate her engagement with detachment: "What peculiar creatures they were; and the continual flux between the outside and the inside, taking things in, giving them out, chewing words, potato-chips, burps, grease hair, babies, milk, excrement, cookies, vomit, coffee, tomato-juice, blood, tea, sweat, liquor, tears and garbage." (171-72) Later she discovers that she too is "one of them." And her dream of being trapped in the supermarket at closing time and found in the morning in a coma, surrounded by overflowing carts suggests both her sense of claustrophobia within, and her identification with, a consumer society where life preys upon life. The idea of consumerism is again in terms of the food metaphors and metaphors of the body—human or animal—in decay.

As the impending engagement party approaches, Marian becomes more and more aware of her loss of free will and choice. She finds herself lost and she wants to know what she was becoming and what direction she was going to take. Waking up one morning she finds herself changed and wants to clarify with others like Clara and Peter as to what kind of abnormality had crept into her.

In Chapter 24, Marian's presence in the beauty parlour reminds one of the preparation of animals for the sacrifice. She becomes an object. Her hair is decorated "like a cake something to be carefully iced and ornamented."[5] (214) Later when she gazes into the mirror and sees not herself but the beautiful Egyptian mummy, an iced, frozen, ornamental life—form devoid of life—whose open eyes reveal a "serene vacancy." "Marian stared into the Egyptian-lidded and out-lined and thickly fringed eyes of a person she had never seen before." (228) She begins to fear more and more of divided self, self annihilation, and lack of identity at the engagement party.

In the party, Marian congratulates herself prematurely on having evoked from Peter the image of domesticated male, and begins to dream in Peter's bedroom: "She opened a door to the right and went in. There was Peter, forty-five and balding . . . beside a barbecue with a long fork in his hand. He was wearing a white chef's apron . . . but she wasn't there and the discovery chilled her." (250) She was panic-stricken and when Peter pursues her with a camera in hand to capture her picture she gets hysterical and runs away to Duncan hoping to regain control of herself.

Then comes Marian's act of liberation, through the most crucial image of the novel, the cake-woman or the edible woman. Marian takes all pains to make a cake-woman and presents it before Peter to be eaten. The cake-woman is a symbolic representation of the woman. That is what Peter really wants Marian to be. When he refuses to eat the cake, the cake-woman, and is horrified at seeing it, it is clear that he does not understand Marian. But what triumphs is Marian's sense of self-determination, her recognition that she was being consumed by Peter and her desire to remain intact as a person. Once Peter leaves her apartment and her life, her body returns to normal metabolism, as she eats the cake herself. With her new consciousness she has a new perspective. She is no longer a status symbol for Peter, once the transference of victim-identity she has projected out of food disappears. When Duncan later visits her, she offers the remaining cake to him, which he eats. But much should not be read into this as Duncan is not going to be the substitute for Peter. While Peter is similar to a cannibal, Duncan is "a more insidious kind of parasite, a lamprey batteing on her [Marian's] compassion to feed his monstrous self pity."[6]

This is the end of *The Edible Woman,* which sounds rather ambivalent. Though the consumer society gulps up, Marian has realigned her body with her head. Marian's release is immediate. No longer isolated and alien, Marian has rejoined society. In her newly found state of freedom, she is prepared to take an active role in her life, find a new home, a new job and presumably, a new boy friend which is suggestive of the ambiguity behind the ending of the novel. About the ending, Alan Dawe says, "ambiguous but somehow triumphant"[7] or rather it is triumphant because of its ambiguity all through.

The entire book is full of contrasts which are manifested as the choices with which Marian is confronted. She must be either a victor or a victim, either consumer or consumed. This seems to be confirmed by the technique adopted by the novelist i.e., the three-part structure as an "I" in Part I. In Part II, the "I" is replaced by the "she," as Marian ostensibly becomes the packaged product of a male-dominated, corporate society that thrives on consumerism and its stereotypes. In Part III the first person voice returns as Marian rejects her role as victim, transcends her role as product, and consumes her disembodied self as she confirms her new identity. This is suggested by her consumption of the cake-woman at a crucial point of the novel.

As Robert Lecker suggests, Marian, in Part II stops eating for two reasons: (a) her job with an advertising research agency has led her to reject the artificial forms of sustenance provided by an artificial society, and (b) she equates the consumption of food with her feeling that she has been assimilated and exploited as a female object.[8] Still, the ending of the novel depicts Marian partaking in eating which was originally seen as taboo. Moreover, by offering the cake to Peter and Duncan and by eating it herself she re-enacts her "female as food" role. But it is Duncan who pinpoints the irony, her fate, when he says "you're back to so called reality, you're a consumer," (287) which suggests that Marian's plight is not resolved and that the plot of *The Edible Woman* is metaphorically circular, as the author herself has remarked.

In refusing to eat, Marian refuses to be labelled as the victim of a system which treats people as consumer products. But as her anorexia intensifies, she finds herself withdrawing from meat, eggs and vegetables and finally relies on vitamin pills and thus the boundary between the natural and synthetic begins to disintegrate. Marian's rejection of food points out, paradoxically enough, that in order to survive one must starve and that by starving one can survive. Her non-eating thus turns into a metaphor of sustenance. Her rejection is also suggestive of her rejection of a culture which tends to exploit women and treat them as edible objects. It is her refusal to eat, once again, which leads to her discovery of the "natural," real and untainted female self.

Once she comes to an awareness of her real self, she rejects both Peter and Duncan in the hope that she will be forced to become productive by relying on herself. So she is led back to the super-market and back to her kitchen to create the cake which symbolizes the artificiality of her existence which, in turn, is destroyed when she consumes it. By this act of eating it she also reaffirms the fact that she still thrives on artifice, i.e., she continues to be sustained by the symbol of all that she once was. Much of the ambivalence in the novel results from what Atwood seems intent on suggesting, i.e., that people aren't what they really think they are, and that "everything that rises must eventually converge."[9]

The Edible Woman is viewed often as a contemporary comedy of manners—as a satire on Modern Society, which in the final analysis offers a depressing vision of life—depicting men as propagators and victims of corruption, vice and lust. Man, getting caught in this web, deludes himself into believing that his own debased or immoral view does participate in a comedy of manners which comments on a world where men and women are mere faceless non-entities and where the search for true identity only leads to a "sinking feeling."

NOTES

1. Sheila Page, "Supermarket Survival: A Critical Analysis of Margaret Atwood's *The Edible Woman*," *Sphinx*, vol. I, Winter 1984, pp. 9-10.
2. Margaret Atwood, *The Edible Woman* (USA: Fawcett Popular Library Printing, 1976), p. 91.
3. George Woodcock, "Margaret Atwood," *The Literary Half-Yearly*, Vol. XIII, No. 2, July 1972, p. 237.
4. Catherine McLay, "The Dark Voyage: *The Edible Woman* as Romance," in *The Art of Margaret Atwood: Essays in Criticism*, ed. Arnold E. Davidson and Cathy N. Davidson (Toronto: House of Anansi Press, 1981), p. 133.
5. Robert Lecker, "Janus through the Looking Glass: Atwood's First Three Novels," *The Art of Margaret Atwood*, p. 178.
6. George Woodcock, p. 237.
7. Robert Lecker, p. 179.
8. *Ibid.*, p. 185.

Margaret Atwood's *The Edible Woman*: An Expression of Feminine Sensibility

A. HARIPRASANNA

I cannot go on
sharing his nightmares
My own are becoming clearer.

The status of woman has constantly been changing, yet it cannot be said that her condition has improved much. Her image also is constantly changing, often to suit the changing needs of man. Woman and her images are moulded, reshaped and reoriented by man and for man.[1]

It is this awareness of their condition and treatment meted out to them that made the women writers take up the question of "female identity in a male-dominated society." What is she? and where is she getting to? They are essentially involved with such a crucial problem as this: how society sees women, how women see themselves and how they should direct their lives and thoughts.[2]

Precisely, it is the self-same theme that captured the imagination of Margaret Atwood. She takes up for exploration the theme of women's place in society, particularly in a male-dominated society in her novel *The Edible Woman*. The novel, "proto-feminist"[3] in attitude, was written in the 60s and could be said to be a voyage depicting Marianne's self-discovery.

Part and parcel of a "consumer society,"[4] Marian is faced with a choice of being "edible" to her husband and remaining single as an individual and asserting herself, chooses the latter and thus refuses to be an edible woman.

But the choices available to her are limited. She has to confront several issues crucial to her. "What does it mean to be a woman, what is her situation, and what constitutes femininity?"[5]

"Through a series of haunting images, a sequence of dream-like hallucinations which flicker through the mind"[6] of Marian, the novel presents a kaleidoscopic picture of her life. To make the picture more real Marian is presented as "a perfect foil to her friends." Wherein, owing to her coming into contact with them she learns immensely of women's problems.

The dealing as it is with the patriarchal society which has become synonymous with consumersim (of women especially), the novel presents "symbolic cannibalism" of women. The novel proves once for all that financial independence is no independence at all. The awareness of being subjugated and victimized has to come from within the self of an individual. This is exactly what the novel depicts—the reasons for the suppression of women within and without marriage.

The Edible Woman[7] is a quest for self-identity by Marian, the protagonist. Facing an identity-crisis she is confronted with various alternatives. The first phase of the problem Marian has to face and overcome is at her work place. The company Marian works for has a highly stratified, three-tiered hierarchic structure. The top floor is occupied by men and is not accessible to her. The bottom is managed mostly by old housewives and she does not wish to go there: "On the floor above are the executives and the psychologists referred to as men upstairs, since they are all men. . . . Below us are the machines—mimeo machines." The prospect of getting grooved into the fixed middle-point of the office structure for the whole of her life, with a pension at the end of her tenure of job, makes her feel that in front of her was a "self . . . waiting, performed, a self who had worked during innumerable years for Seymour Surveys and was now receiving her reward." (27)

This disturbing awareness is the direct result of a technologically advanced society (a culture-specific phenomenon) which by its very advancement forces individuals into are fabricated roles, and is therefore of a general nature. "What then could I expect to turn into a Seymour Surveys? I couldn't become a machine person or one of the questionnaire-marking ladies, as that would be a step down." (20) Marian's crisis, however, acquires a feminine colouration when she looks for alternatives to her present situation. These alternatives are represented in her office colleagues Eurney, Lucie and Millie, her friend Clara and her husband Joe, Peter and Ainsley her flatmate.[8]

A pro-feminist to the letter, Ainsley has strong views about the male-dominated 'consumer' society. That she becomes a victim of the self-same society is one of the ironies of fate. Ainsley though against marriage does not deny motherhood. She does want to get pregnant. For she would like a child of her own. She thinks that motherhood satisfies one's "deepest femininity" (41) and "every woman should have at least one baby. . . . It's even more important than sex." (40) And she is absolutely certain that "the thing that ruins families these days is the husbands." (40) Wanting children "by choice"[9] rather than as a natural consequence of a happy relationship in a marriage, she looks out for a perfect male specimen to father her child and finds one in Len, thus partially fulfilling her dream. It does not take her long to realize that such a role as she has chosen for herself would be a difficult one to perform in the patriarchal society and she changes her views regarding matrimony and accordingly gets married to provide the infant a father. Marian, repulsed by Ainsley's cold-blooded attitude to men and marriage thinks it is all wrong: "I knew Ainsley was wrong, but she sounded so rational. I thought I'd better go to bed before she had convinced me against my better judgement." (43)

Clara and Joe present Marian with another alternative—a different facet altogether of love and marriage. Theirs is a fairly good marriage with three children—Clara is quite content to remain within the bounds of family. But Marian is not unaware of Joe's condescending attitude towards women. "He tends any way to think of all unmarried girls as easily victimized and needing protection." (131) Clara, impractical and non-assertive as she is, tends to be rather leaning on Joe and "lets herself be treated like a thing" (38) much to Ainsley's annoyance. In this regard Marian agrees with Ainsley, for it becomes clear to them that "the power of the wife declines as the number of children grows"[10] and Clara "wasn't able to control the more mundane aspects of life, like money or getting to lectures on time . . . her own body seemed beyond her, going in its own way without reference to any direction of hers." (35) Even though Clara does not admit it to herself this seems to be perfectly true, for, the children are unplanned: "Clara greeted her first pregnancy with astonishment that such a thing could happen to her, and her second with dismay; now during her third, she had subsided into a grim but inert fatalism" (36) thus unwittingly becoming a pawn in the marriage game.

Choices and alternatives presented by her friends apart, Marian also feels outraged by the attitude adopted by Seymour Surveys towards its women employees. The Manager, Mrs. Bogue regards the very acts of marriage and pregnancy as offensive and disloyal to the company: "Mrs. Dodge in Kamloops will have to be removed. She's pregnant." (24) Such discrimination against women arouses in Marian the righteous indignation. While conducting a market research survey Marian interviews a man who feels "you ought to be at home with some big strong man to take care of you" (48)—a comment which enrages her justifiably.

Marian refuses to accept the alternatives given to her in Ainsley and Clara. She seeks something different from life. She rather hopes that she would be able to fulfil this yearning for a better life with Peter. She thinks that "Peter is an ideal choice. He's attractive and he's bound to be successful." (102) He seems to be a godsend to relieve her from her monotonous life at Seymour Surveys—"a rescuer from chaos, a provider of stability." (89) Despite her dreams as to their future, she also has her own doubts regarding Peter. Disturbed on occasions with his casual attitude towards sex and general behaviour, she feels at times, that "he was treating her as a stage-prop; silent but solid, a two-dimensional outline." (71) But she is able to forget all her doubts and misgivings in his arms.

Peter in his turn is drawn to Marian because she is unlike the other women of his acquaintance: undemanding and non-aggressive "a girl who wouldn't try to take over his life." (61) When he proposes to her he gives out his reason as to Marian's suitability as a wife: "I know I can always depend on you. Most women are pretty scatter-brained but you're such a sensible girl. You may not have known this but I've always thought that's first thing to look for when it comes to choosing a wife." (89) In other words, Peter is trying to fit Marian into a "conventionalized, even stereotyped image of a woman passive and dependent."[11]

Marian accepted the proposal of Peter and in spite of her unease at the acceptance, tries to defend her choice: "I'd always assumed through high school and college that I was going to marry someone eventually and have children, everyone does. . . . I've never been silly about marriage the way Ainsley is. . . . She's against it on principle, and life isn't by principles but by adjustments. As Peter says, you can't continue to run around indefinitely; people who aren't married get funny in middle age, embittered or addled or something. . . . But although I'm sure it was in the back of my mind I hadn't consciously expected it to happen so soon or quite the way it did." (102) It is clear that Marian is just echoing Peter's words that "she has ceased to be her true being."[12] Here Marian is accepting the role that is traditionally foisted upon women. That "Marriage is the destiny traditionally offered to woman by society. . . . The celibate [single] woman is explained and defined with reference to marriage whether she is frustrated, rebellious, or even indifferent in regard to that institution."[13] It is only after the acceptance of the marriage proposal that she is assailed by serious doubts as to whether she made the right choice. Her relationship with Peter seems to have undergone a sea-change and Marian realizes that "she had let herself be sold as some kind of a desirable commodity."[14] She fails to identify the real Peter underneath all that sophistication and doubts her understanding of his true self. Disliking strongly Peter's manipulation of herself, she identifies him with an anonymous caller who introduced himself to ladies as a seller of underwear, but whose real identity was not known to anybody: "This was his true self, the core of his personality, the central Peter who had been occupying her mind more and more lately. Perhaps this was what lay under the surfaces, that secret identity which in spite of her many guesses and attempts and half-guesses she was aware she had still not uncovered: he was really the Underwear Man." (118)

Nauseated by Peter's hunting activities Marian goes off non-vegetarian food. Soon she finds it difficult to eat anything at all. The more uncertain her relationship with Peter, the more disturbed she becomes and her mental strain weans her away from food and she feels more and more reluctant to eat anything. She fears for her sanity and thinks if things go at the same rate soon she would be requiring the services of a psychiatrist, feeling she is becoming mentally unstable. But both Peter and Clara assure her that "she is wonderfully normal," and tell her it is nothing more than bridal nerves. She remains unconvinced and is afraid that she is "coming apart layer by layer like a piece of cardboard in a gutter puddle." (218)

The unreality of her situation becomes more evident to her when she agrees to play the part of a meek and submissive fiancé as dictated by Peter. She decks herself out in all her finery but when she looks up in the mirror she fails to see the rightness of it, as she is unable to recognize the true Marian behind the glittering facade. Nothing seems to be real anymore: "What was it that lay beneath the surface these pieces were floating on, holding them together? She held both of her naked arms out towards the mirror. They were the only portion of her flesh that was without a cloth or nylon or leather or varnish covering, but . . . even they looked fake, like soft, pinkish—white rubber or plastic, boneless, flexible." (229) As the party progresses and Peter clicks away with his camera she realizes that "once he pulled the trigger, she would be stopped, fixed indissolubly in that gesture." (245) It dawns on her that she is nothing but a saleable commodity wrapped up as a wife. She at once grasps that Peter manipulated her cleverly and made her a puppet in his hands.

She recognizes her loss of identity and her "edibility" to Peter. Her sense of victimization becomes acute after she comes across Joe discussing the after-effects of university education on women. He says: "She gets the idea she has a mind, her professors pay attention to what she has to say, they treat her like a thinking human being; when she gets married, her core gets invaded. Her core . . . the centre of her personality, the thing she has built up, her image of herself. . . . Her feminine role and her core are really in opposition, her feminine role demands passivity from her." (235) The conversation provides Marian with a flash of insight. She realizes what married life with Peter would be. She perceives that as Peter's wife she would be expected to don the mantle of a conventional woman, assuming the role of a meek and docile woman; dependent on her husband, allowing him to devour her slowly and relishingly.

Although Marian refuses to be an "edible woman" for Peter by running away from him, yet she falls a victim to male-dominance in the person of Duncan. He seduces her feigning ignorance and helplessness. Later on it occurs to Marian that she has allowed the men in her life to use and consume her, thus actually helping the process of victimization. This new awareness provides her a renewed strength and purpose in life.

After she returns to her place, Marian bakes a cake in her own image. Atwood herself says that by doing so Marian is trying to depict: "an action, a preposterous one in a way, as all the pieces of symbolism in a realistic context are, but what she is obviously making is a substitute of herself."[15] Marian admits that "the price of this version was testing the other one." (271) She offers the cake to Peter who is affronted at the very sight of it. Denying the passive role as his fiancé she tells him: "You've been trying to assimilate me. But I've made you a substitute, something you'll like much better. This is what you really wanted all along." (271) Marian eats the cake with relish. "Liberated of the false notion of having an existence in which she is some kind of appetizing food, she begins to enjoy taking food."[16]

Marian's baking of the cake and eating it could be said to be a gesture of defiance, a way of saying no to a system that defines women as commodity and devours them.[17] It also seems a reflection, a way of seeing herself in a mirror, and it expresses a truth not before perceived.[18] Further it signifies her recognition and rejection of the former compliant self, culminating in her new ability to respond to her own inner feelings.[19]

Marian is also able to destroy the society's synthetic stereotype of femininity through the ingenuous mirroring device of the cake and free herself to realize her own true identity.[20] Apart from this the act signifies the celebration of Marian's new freedom and even rebirth,[21] making her "a whole person" again.

Thus *The Edible Woman* "a convincing narrative of personal growth" shows how female passivity and submersion in the traditional wife and mother roles can pose a serious threat to the very survival of the self,[22] for Marian after being battered in body and psyche, finally passes into a state of raised consciousness. She comes to think of herself in the first person singular and acquires a confident voice of her own[23]: "In Atwood's own words, the novel makes a negative statement about society. . . . The complications are resolved, but not in a way that affirms the social order."[24]

NOTES

1. Sunaina Singh, "Margaret Atwood's *Surfacing*," *Indian Journal of American Studies*, vol. 13, no. 2 (July 1983), p. 189.
2. *Ibid.*
3. Margaret Atwood, "An Introduction to *The Edible Woman*," *Selected Critical Prose* (Toronto: Anansi, 1982), p. 370.
4. John Lauber, "Alice in Consumer-Land: The Self-Discovery of Marian MacAlpin," *The Canadian Novel: Here and Now*, ed.

John Moss (Toronto: N.C. Press, 1978), p. 20.
5. T.N. Dhar, "Raised Feminine Consciousness in *The Edible Woman*," *Feminism and Recent Fiction in English*, ed. Sushila Singh (New Delhi: Prestige, 1991), p. 269.
6. T.D. MacLulich, "Atwood's Adult Fairy Tale: Levi-Strauss, Bettelheim and *The Edible Woman*," *Essays in Canadian Writing* (1970), p. 116.
7. (Toronto: McClelland and Stewart, 1973).
8. Dhar, pp. 269-70.
9. *Ibid.*, p. 271.
10. David Miller, "Dominance and the Working Wife," *Social Forces*, 36 (May 1958), pp. 342-47.
11. Dhar, p. 272.
12. *Ibid.*
13. Simone de Beauvoir, *The Second Sex*.
14. Dhar, p. 273.
15. Graeme Gibson, "Margaret Atwood," *Eleven Canadian Novelists* (Toronto: Anansi, 1973), p. 25.
16. Dhar, p. 276.
17. Gayle Green, "Margaret Atwood's *The Edible Woman*: Rebelling against the System," *Margaret Atwood: Reflection and Reality* (Edinburgh: Fan American, 1987), p. 117.
18. Barbara Hill Rigney, *Margaret Atwood* (Ottowa: Barman and Noble, 1987), p. 34.
19. Jayne Patterson, "The Taming of Externàls: A Linguistic Study of Character Transformation in Margaret Atwood's *The Edible Woman*," *Studies in Canadian Literature*, 7 (1982), p. 152.
20. Nora Foster Stovel, "Reflections in Mirror Images: Doubles and Identity in the Novels of Margaret Atwood," *Essays on Canadian Literature*, 33 (1986), p. 53.
21. Catherine McLay, "The Dark Voyage: *The Edible Woman* as Romance," *The Art of Margaret Atwood: Essays in Criticism*, ed. Arnold E. Davidson and Cathy N. Davidson (Toronto: House of Anansi Press, 1981), p. 138.
22. J. Brooks Brouson, "The Anxiety of Being Influenced: Reading and Responsibility to Atwood's *The Edible Woman*," *Style*, p. 23.
23. Dhar, p. 269.
24. Linda Sandler, "Interview with Margaret Atwood," 41 (Jan. 1977), pp. 13-14.

Pen as a "Weapon" in Margaret Atwood's *Bodily Harm*

M. PRABHAKAR

> Woman must put herself into the text—as into the world and into history—by her own movement. Helena Cixous

Bodily Harm is Margaret Atwood's best known feminist text to date. It was written after the women's liberation movement. In the 1970s women were very hopeful and optimistic and they felt that they could change the society for the better. But their protest which was geared towards the restitution of rights for women failed to produce the desired results in the 80s. Atwood is critical of the facile optimism of the post-feminist era concerning the state of women's emancipation. She comments: "It would be a mistake to assume that everything has changed . . . the goals of the feminist movement have not been achieved, and those who claim we're living in a post-feminist era are either sadly mistaken or tired of thinking about the same subject."[1] This paper seeks to discuss Atwood's *Bodily Harm* from the point of view of feminist consciousness in the post-feminist era. Renata Wilford, the "camera-narrator"[2] of *Bodily Harm,* is a Canadian free-lance journalist as well as a "Life-Tourist" writer. She uses "pen" as a "weapon" to write her travelogue, "Bodily Harm." Rennie's travelogue addresses itself to the nature of violence and victimization of women. She writes the travelogue with a sense of commitment to expose the wickedness of men on the one hand and the brutality of the state on the other. She uses her pen as "weapon" to let the world know how the female body is sought to be abused, mutilated and destroyed in prison cells.

II

To comprehend the progression of Renata Wilford's career as a free-lance journalist and a "Life-Tourist" writer, it is important to consider her early life in the small town of Griswold, Ontario. Rennie is the child of an irresponsible man who has abandoned his family for a mistress in Toronto. She is brought up in an unhealthy and joyless environment in Griswold by her grandparents. For Rennie, her grandparents' place is "a subground, something that can't be seen but is nevertheless there, full of gritty old rocks and buried stumps, worms and bones."[3] (18)

Rennie's impressionistic years of childhood are suppressed and spoiled by her grandmother's traditional approach. She detests the servile existence in Griswold and leaves the place in order to lead a life of freedom in Toronto. Griswold forms the background to her career of free-lance journalism as well as her travelogue.

Rennie begins her adult life in Toronto as a versatile writer. She gets commissioned to write articles for *Pandora*, a woman-oriented magazine and for *Visor*, a male-oriented journal. These two offer her enough scope to write about both men and women.

In the course of writing a piece called "The Young and the Solvent" for *Visor*, Rennie comes in contact with Jack who works as a designer of appearances for a packaging company. Rennie is of the view that she is a product of the post-feminist era. She seems to be over-confident that she can stand upto any crisis situation without any harm either to her body or her psyche. But little does she realize that Jack is an exploiter. In spite of all her care and intelligence, she allows herself to be sucked into the evil designs of Jack. He uses all his tricks to use and pack her just as he does things. Later on, she realizes that his interest in her is limited to the gratification of his carnal desires. Her relationship with Jack remains as if it were a "newly renovated house" (102) without strong bonds.

Jack feels ill-at-ease in the company of Rennie following her mastectomy. He imagines the scar on her breast as "the kiss of death on her." (201) Jack abandons Rennie feeling that life is not enjoyable with a diseased woman. Rennie regrets that she has allowed herself to be used by Jack as a commodity—a kind of "raw-material." Thus, Rennie's maiden encounter in love with Jack ends abruptly leaving her bruised and battered physically and emotionally.

Later on, she gets involved in love with Paul because of his impressive manners and ideals. She feels that Paul is a good substitute to Jack, her first lover, who turns out to be an exploiter and to Jack, her first lover, who turns out to be an exploiter and seducer. She hopes against hope that she might be able to live with him while keeping her "options" open. She is of the view that she might be able to strike a meaningful relationship with him. Unlike Jack, Paul does not hate or abandon Rennie on the grounds of the scar on her body. She thinks that he has some sense of compassion for her damaged body. She is involved in bouts of sex with him for a brief spell.

The age-old maxim, familiarity breeds contempt, seems to influence both Paul and Rennie. Very soon, she realizes that he is an immature person interested in sporting and wielding a gun needlessly. She begins to detest him because she is scared of the very sight of the gun. She is gradually disillusioned with him. This marks yet another meaningless relationship with Paul. She feels that involvement in love affairs is "like running barefoot along a street covered with broken bottles." (102) She realizes her female passivity and her inability to establish meaningful relationships with any one of her male associates. She feels a sense of urgency to run away from all her meaningless and loveless involvements with all men.

III

Rennie's association with Jocasta, a feminist activist, raises her consciousness of herself and helps her understand better the villainous attitude and victimizing nature of the male world towards women. She is convinced that women's liberation continues to be a distant dream and a lot has to be done to realize the desired goals. Jocasta's assessment of man-woman relationship illuminates Rennie's thinking. She begins to assess all her love relationships from a fresh perspective. For Rennie, Jocasta represents a complete and complex socio-gender system. Under the influence of Jocasta she publishes an article entitled, "Burned Out" on the alleged death of the women's movement. In this piece, Rennie reasons out why and under what circumstances women take to odd, mean and degrading vocations like "bitching" and "trashing." (93)

Rennie takes to writing as a serious and full-time occupation. She does a piece on pornography as an art form from the "woman's angle" for *Visor.* She interviews Frank, an artist, who depicts pornography as an art form. She views life-sized mannequin tables and tions. She realizes how art is abused to depict women as ugly creatures meant for violence.

The article on pornography takes Rennie to visit the Toronto policeman's pornography museum along with Jocasta. She is horrified by the sight of nude film clips, of women meant for display and exhibition at the museum. Naked forms of women in different postures of brutality are displayed.

Some of the films project women copulating with animals leading to the mutilation of their bodies. The museum films also include women's nipples being chopped off and a "couple of sex-and-death pieces." (210) The purpose of all these ugly and horrible films seems to display bodies of women as maps of violence. Looking at the films Rennie thought that such things could not be real and "it was all done with ketchup." (210)

The most horrifying of all the film clips is a scene in which "the head of a rat" (210) moves in and out of a woman's vagina. Rennie is appalled by this sight and her detachment is completely shattered. This seems to have been "deliberately contrived by a film-maker for sexual titillation which indicates the utter depths of human depravity and cruelty."[4] It points out the abuse of woman in the so-called civilized countries which are primitive as far as brutality of a woman's body is concerned.

Rennie realizes that women are stripped of their identity and they are reduced to raw-materials. She also feels that men destroy women's individuality behind a mask of anonymous authority and power. Rennie realizes that she too is part of the "raw-material."

IV

Rennie is commissioned to do a travel piece for *Visor* and it takes her to the Caribbean island. She carries a camera bag which symbolizes her tourist vision and identity. Rennie travels around the Caribbean island for the next six days meeting people. She lives in the real world. She finds her tragedy reflected in the tragedy of mute and innocent masses all over the world. She discovers that all human principles and issues like democracy, liberalism, individual dignity and even love are used as pretexts to get "rid of people you don't like."

Rennie detects that the voters' list contains dead people's names while many living people's names are excluded. Floods are

Rennie detects that the voters' list contains dead people's names while many living people's names are excluded. Floods are like a boon to the rulers because these fetch charity and aid which are used for purchasing votes. Thus, the political scene on the island has no room for love, decency and humanity. Women are treated as non-entities. They are tortured and even sliced off into pieces. So Rennie discovers different victims in the Caribbean island. She understands that women are not different from common people because both of them are powerless and hence are abused. Rennie's travel piece expands and extends the implications of the term "woman" to cover all the exploited and abused people in the world.

Rennie finds out that women are still where they were a century ago. The much spoken freedom and identity of women are only delusions. She realizes that people enjoy torturing women. She recognizes that the Caribbean is essentially as bad as Canada, the representative of the civilized world. Rennie points out that women everywhere are abused just as the helpless poor. In this way, she equates women with the poor throughout the world.

Rennie visits women prisoners in the Caribbean prison along with Dr. Minnow who is known for his rebellion against the tyranny of the government. Rennie is accused of massive involvement in the island's current revolution and in the political affairs. Following an outbreak of violent disturbances on the island, Rennie is arrested. She is accused of being an outraged tourist. She suffers incarceration for about two weeks in a Central American prison where she comes in contact with Lora Lucas, a fellow prisoner.

In her travelogue, Rennie includes the tales which Lora narrates in the prison. Lora's tales of woe and brutality completely shatter Rennie's over-confidence in women's liberation. Lora narrates the story of her "non-violent" rape by her vicious stepfather with whom she used to live in a cellar. She leads a life of terror under the gross exploitation of her stepfather. Ultimately, she stabs him as he tries to rape her and leaves the place for good.

Following her escape from home, she is hired to work on a boat. Lora's experience at this place of work turns out to be worse still. She is shocked to know that all the men around expect her to sleep with them. Either she has to comply with them or to lose the job. The very assumption that a woman is meant for rent smacks of male arrogance towards women. The tales of Lora convince Rennie pathetic tales of Lora's experiences in Canada and in the Caribbean shock Rennie's feminist sensibility.

Rennie watches from the prison cell, with impotent rage the barbaric killings of people who oppose the ruler. Rennie is a witness to some riots in the prison cells following which the male prisoners have been tortured and their heads shaved off with bayonets.

Yet another victim Rennie finds in the prison is an islander, a deaf and dumb man whom once she sees in the street being beaten by the police. He is brought to the prison in a bad shape. He is a crusader for human rights and civil liberties. He represents "the vast mass of people in the world crippled by poverty whom ignorance and political tyranny have deprived of their capacity to proclaim the suffering and injustice of their plight."[5]

Rennie recollects the ugly, obscene, and nauseating film clips. She thought it was a kind of "ketchup." She finds such horrible deeds enacted in the prison cell. Rennie discovers that woman is at the mercy of a whole host of oppressors in any society. She witnesses how Lora very reluctantly obliges the prison guards for sex in return for news about prince of peace, her lover. Lora is sexually assaulted and beaten, mutilated and killed by the very custodians of society, namely policemen. Rennie, the naive heroine is finally radicalized. Henceforth, Rennie proclaims that detachment, neutrality, and non-involvement are no longer possible to think in terms of some kind of positive action against atrocities on women.

The sight of the neglected and uncared dead body of Lora touches the very core of Rennie's being. She feels a sense of empathy with her. Lora's face is not "a face any more, it's a bruise, blood is still oozing from the cuts . . . the mouth looks like a piece of fruit that's been run over by a car, pulp . . . it's the face of a stranger, someone without a name, the word *Lora* has come unhooked and is hovering in the air, a part from this ruin . . . face off with, all the cloth in this room is filthy, sceptic, except her hands . . . there's no such thing as a faceless stranger, every face is someone's it has a name." (298-99) Rennie feels, touches and finally licks the dead face of Lora as the animals do to their newly born offspring. This is how she identifies herself with the tragedy of Lora. Feeling the hand of Lora, Rennie imagines the possible resurrection of the dead. She mutters: "something will move and live again, something will get born." (299) This, precisely, is the feminist consciousness of the hand of Lora, Rennie imagines the possible resurrection of the dead. She mutters: "something will move and live again, something will get born." (299) This, precisely, is the feminist consciousness of Rennie. Rennie is committed to immortalize Lora in the form of a book she wants to do as per Lora's death wish. Lora tells Rennie: "The story of my life, you could put it in a book." (270)

V

Rennie and Lora in their prison cells symbolize how women in all walks of life are vicitimized and oppressed by male power and authority. The brutality done to Lora is the real "bodily harm" which surpasses both in agony and shock the partial mastectomy done to Rennie. The brutal and heartless mutilation of Lora is symbolic of the limited gender-specific role of women in society. It finally dawns on Rennie that cancer or partial mastectomy of her breast has no significance and it is no more than a minor accident of her life.

Rennie feels an enlightenment in her. She refuses to be a victim although she has "her scar, her disability, her nibbled flesh, the little teeth marks on her." (284) Rennie's body which has been maimed, dismembered, altered and fragmented symbolizes the crippled human beings all over the world. Rennie realizes that human malice is as dangerous as cancer. As Dorothy Jones says: "Fear of death by a disease like cancer is weighed against those threats to life which result from human malice—poverty, malnutrition and political violence."[6]

Rennie tries to figure out the "bodily harm" done to Lora and other modes of harm which might be done to other bodies in future. She says: "This is what will happen." (293) In her travel piece, Rennie encompasses a reality of "bodily harm" which merges past-present-future.

Rennie asserts that "bodily harm" is everywhere—both inside and outside of the prison, both in civilized and uncivilized countries, and both in political and personal fields. Thus there are no fixed hard boundaries to "bodily harm." Free-lance journalists like Rennie never leave the prison cells as the rulers will ensure her continued imprisonment.

Rennie is set free at the instance of a Canadian diplomat. However, she continues to be a living witness to "the variously hued

Rennie rejects her submissive role as a woman. She is prepared to speak out the truth, the disturbing truth about all those exploited people and women in particular. She becomes subversive and bold enough to narrate and publish her experiences in the form of a travelogue called "Bodily Harm." She discovers her identity through her newly assumed "subversive role" as a free-lance journalist.

Rennie uses her pen as a "weapon" to depict her experiences in her travelogue. She takes pledge to devote her life in the service of the weak and women. According to Helena Cixous, Rennie puts "herself into the text—as into the world and into history—by her own movement." "Bodily Harm" is what Rennie has reported to the world as her novel.

The name "Renata Wilford" implies "born again."[8] She takes in her strides all her ugly and unpleasant encounters of her life. In this process, she is born anew and lives in the present with a meaningful message for the future. In her new role as a committed writer, she uses pen as a "weapon" to expose the cruelty and brutalities on the weak and women. She also looks forward to a day of better and healthy relationships between men and women.

NOTES

1. Margaret Atwood, "Introduction to *The Edible Woman,*" *The Second Words: Selected Critical Prose* (Toronto: Anansi, 1982), p. 370.
2. Sharon R. Wilson, "Turning Life into Popular Art: *Bodily Harm*'s Life-Tourist," *Studies in Canadian Literature*, X, 1 (1985), p. 137.
3. Margaret Atwood, *Bodily Harm* (Toronto: McClelland and Stewart, 1981).
4. Dorothy Jones, "Waiting for the Rescue: A Discussion of Margaret Atwood's *Bodily Harm,*" *Kunapipi,* VI, 3 (1984), p. 96.
5. *Ibid.*, pp. 96-97.
6. *Ibid.*, pp. 86-87.
7. Wilson, p. 144.
8. Ildiko De Pappa Carrington, "Another Symbolic Descent," *Essays on Canadian Writing,* 26 (1983), pp. 61-62.

6. *Ibid.*, pp. 86-87.
7. Wilson, p. 144.
8. Ildiko De Pappa Carrington, "Another Symbolic Descent," *Essays on Canadian Writing,* 26 (1983), pp. 61-62.

Creating Female Space in Patriarchal/ (Colonial) Power Structures: A Study of Margaret Atwood's *The Handmaid's Tale*

CHRISTINE GOMEZ

Patriarchy and colonialism are both power structures which operate on similar principles. Colonialism may well be seen as a paradigm of patriarchy in feminist literary criticism. This is because gender relations provide the "blueprint for all other power relationships" and are "the model for power relations between generations, socio-economic classes, relations, racial and ethnic groups as well as between imperial powers and their colonies."[1]

Both patriarchy and colonialism involve relationships of domination and suppression, assumed superiority and imposed inferiority, where the dominated is forced to take up the oppressed, exploited victim position. In both, the dominant party makes the laws for its own benefit and advantage, to be conformed to by the dominated group, offering reward for conformity and punishment for non-conformity. Just as colonialism maintains, underlines and emphasizes the difference between the native and the coloniser, patriarchy promotes and stresses the difference between women and men.

Both in patriarchy and colonialism, various subversive tactics may be resorted to by the dominated group—open rebellion, secret revolt, formation of defiant groups, outward submission accompanied by a slow carving out of inner independent space, acts of subversion and sabotage and the creation of free space through written or oral language composition.

According to Northrop Frye, Canada is "the only country left in the world which is a pure colony, colonial in psychology, as well as mercantile economics."[2] Margaret Atwood says, "Canada as a whole is a victim or an 'oppressed minority' or 'exploited,' a colony for someone else's profit."[3] Just as colonial power-structures seem to be built into the collective unconscious of Canada, patriarchal power-structures too have left their impact on the female psyche. A sensitive and consciously self-aware writer like Atwood exposes these power-structures and their effects on both those who exercise power and those who are subjected to it. While colonial domination is a recurrent theme with the Canadian male writer, women writers may see colonialism as a metaphor of the gender power-struggle. In Linda Hutcheon's opinion, "In all her writing, Atwood shows herself to be the tireless explorer and exposer of cultural cliches and stereotypes, in particular of those that affect women."[4] In *The Handmaid's Tale*, "the colonies" are mentioned, in a purely negative sense, as a symbol of exploitation, isolation and alienation, where people are used as objects or functions. Given a choice, the characters in the novel prefer not to go to the colonies, where the sole occupation seems to be cleaning up "toxic dumps and radiation spills,"[5] or burning dead bodies. They prefer to stay in Gilead, though it reveals the negative characteristics of a colony—domination and suppression—as applied to gender.

Many novels of Atwood deal with women's experience in a male-dominated culture. They present women caught in oppressive stereotypes from which some women struggle to create a female space for themselves. This may be done through autonomy of thought, through self-definition and self-reconstruction of one's own history (her story?), through creative composition, oral or written, through bonding among women and through a refusal to take up the victim position or the role of subjugation. This paper examines *The Handmaid's Tale* thematically and structurally, to explore how female space is wrenched out of patriarchal power-structures.

At the thematic level, the novel carries patriarchal power to its logical and nightmarish extreme and shows how women live in such a situation and create female space for themselves through various strategies. An example of post-modernist fabulation, the novel is set in the future, in the Republic of Gilead, which occupies part of the territory of what was once the USA. Gilead is a repressive, fundamentalist theocracy which interprets the Bible literally. In the hands of the tyrannical rulers of Gilead, who are exaggerated versions of the worst elements of the early Puritans and the later Mormons, the Bible becomes a patriarchal narrative, which uses religion to ensure the subjugation of women.

Gilead is a highly alienating structure of society, especially for women. Women are prohibited from communicating with one another, under the 'Divide and Rule' policy of patriarchy. Women are separated according to their functions, as Wives, Marthas (housekeepers), Handmaids (child-bearers), Aunts (disciplinarians), and Jezebels (prostitutes), and kept in segregation. Marthas are forbidden to become friendly with Handmaids; Wives regard Handmaids with hostility and envy; Aunts are used to oppress Handmaids; and Handmaids are not supposed to talk with each other. There is constant invigilation to prevent the forging of relationships among women. Women however overcome the externally imposed interpersonal alienation and reach out to one another secretly. The bonding among women and the slow forging of a caring sisterhood is a strategy by which female space is acquired in the novel. As Olivia Frey points out, "The ethic of care and relationships is most commonly at the centre of women's lives; it provides us with 'space' to think differently, another model for doing things."[6] Despite the strict regimentation at their training centre, the Handmaids communicate with one another through whispers, lipreading and touch, while lying flat, each in her own bed. (14) The protagonist manages to communicate with her former friend Moira who also arrives at the same training centre. Later too the Handmaids Offred and Ofglen discover joyfully that they were both 'non-believers.' The discovery makes Offred delirious with joy. (177) Despite the ban on all communication between the Handmaids and the Marthas, one of the housekeepers, Cora, develops a liking for Offred and is even willing to lie for her once. For Offred, that is a triumph in itself, a subversive carving out of female space. "It pleased me that she was willing to lie for me, even in such a small thing, even for her own advantage. It was a link between us." (160) When Offred first arrived at Serena's house as a Handmaid, she had wanted to turn her into an older sister, a motherly figure, someone who would understand and protect her. (25-26) But Serena, the Wife, was hostile at first, though she later offers to help Offred and arranges clandestine meetings between Offred and Nick and gets a photograph of Offred's daughter to be seen by her. Serena's offer of a cigarette to Offred, (216) Rita's gift of an ice cube to her (219) and Offred's compliments to Rita on her vegetable-carving (219) for the dinner-table, all are examples of the growing goodwill among the women in Gilead, under restricted circumstances.

In Gilead, women are alienated from their own bodies by the elaborate clothes that have to be worn by them at all times, covering them fully in many layers. The Handmaid's clothes are specially designed to hide bodily contours and the wings and veils are meant to prevent her "from seeing and also from being seen." (18) She is not even allowed to bathe by herself. Around her ovulation time, on the night before the "Ceremony," she is given a bath by a Martha. After the bath, she waits for the Ceremony, feeling completely dehumanized—"I wait, washed, brushed, fed, like a prize pig." (79)

Gileadean women are alienated from the universe around them by the severe restriction on their freedom of movement. They are forbidden to read and write, for that is a man's prerogative in Gilead. By thus being denied self-expression through writing and speaking and being denied perception of reality around them through reading, they are isolated from the world around them. However they try to keep in touch with the world through furtive reading, whenever possible and through a secret exchange of oral information with one another.

When Gilead first came into being, the very first step of the new regime had been to freeze women's credit cards and bank accounts and take away their jobs and property rights, thus destroying their financial independence, which is the primary requisite in any true liberation of women. With the loss of her job, the protagonist had felt stripped of her independence and individuality, perceiving herself as a doll-wife, her husband's possession. (191)

A deliberate and systematic attempt is made in Gilead to obliterate all sense of individuality and identity in women, by taking away their names from them. The Aunts are given the names of popular brands of cake-mixes and cosmetics. The Handmaids lose their original individuating name. A Handmaid's name indicates merely the male to whom she is assigned. The name "Offred" is composed of the preposition 'of,' indicating possession and the name of her Commander. It is a Gileadean variation of the contemporary patronymic "Mrs. Fred."

The destruction of the individual name is part of the attempt to destroy the past and force woman to live in the present moment alone, in a two-dimensional existence. But Offred carves a free space for herself in her flashbacks, contrasting the past free and casual style of life with the present regimentation, the past friendship with other women like Moira and her own mother and the present enforced isolation. She often recalls the views and actions of her mother, a militant feminist who believed that "A man is just a woman's strategy for making other women" (130-31) and spoke of "networking" or forging ties with other women. She often recalls vignettes of her life with her husband Luke and their daughter, perhaps to convince herself of the objective reality of the former state of affairs before Gilead. As narrator, Offred apologizes for her frequent flashbacks, "You'll have to forgive me. I'm a refugee from the past and like other refugees I go over the customs and habits of being I've left or been forced to leave behind me." (239)

Gilead's aim is the total annihilation of Woman as a person. Offred discovers that even the memory of her has been erased from her daughter's mind, as if she had never existed: "I have been obliterated for her . . . you can see it in her eyes; I am not there . . . I can't bear it, to have been erased like that." (240) Her 'Being-for-others' has been destroyed. The Gileadean Handmaids discover that one way of creating female space is by assiduously affirming one's own 'being-for-others' and reciprocally doing it for others too. During the shopping trips, they show their recognition of each other: "I see several women I recognize, exchange with them the infinitesimal nods with which we show each other we are known at least to someone, we still exist." (295)

The separation of women according to their functions in Gilead, promotes their fragmentation. The Wives are mainly decorative in functions and are dressed in blue. The middle-aged housekeepers, called Marthas, are dressed in green. When they become weak and sick and cease working, they are deported to the Colonies. The Handmaids, dressed in red, are young women in their twenties or thirties and serve as child-bearers to elderly childless Commanders. The Biblical precedent of Hagar, Bilhah and Zilpah, who served Abraham and Jocob as handmaids were quoted in support of the practice. Prostitution continued in Gilead, though its presence was assiduously denied by the Establishment. These women were dressed in feathers and sequins and the system of prostitution was justified as being dictated to by Nature: "Nature demands variety for men. It stands to reason, it's part of the procreational strategy." (249) Of all these functional roles assigned to women in Gilead, the Handmaid's role was the most dehumanized. Handmaids were valued only as walking wombs, for their child-bearing function, annihilating all other personal traits. They are a "national resource," (75) "containers," (107) "two-legged wombs," "sacred vessels, ambulatory chalices." (146) In the case of most of the Handmaids, Gilead succeeds in reducing woman's perception of herself as a mere function. Offred experiences anguished disappointment at the onset of menstruation because of her failure to conceive: "I have failed once again to fulfil the expectations of others, which have become my own." (83) She herself thinks of herself only as a womb, i.e. only in the child-bearing context and regards herself as a failure when that function is not fulfilled.

In the separation of women into functions, Wives become ornaments. Serena Joy's way of creating female space in this context is through gardening. This is a device resorted to by many Wives in Gilead, reminding one of Alice Walker's discovery about her mother's garden[7]: "Many of the Wives have such gardens, it's something for them to order and maintain and care for." (22) That it is a subversive device and a symbol is made clear. "There is something subversive about this garden of Serena's, a sense of buried things bursting upwards, wordlessly into the light, as if to point, to say: whatever is silenced, will clamour to be heard, though silently." (161)

In Gilead, only the women of the poorer classes, called Econowives, wearing striped dresses in red, blue and green, were not separated into functions: "They have to do everything, if they can," (34) i.e. wiving, housekeeping and child-bearing. This is looked down upon as an existence that is inferior to the fragmented, functionalized one of the Wives, Marthas and Handmaids.

The Gileadean social structure with its focus on child-bearing is imagined to be devised because of the decline in Caucasian birth-rates, due to a conglomeration of causes in our own age—widespread birthcontrol measures, R-strain syphilis, the AIDS epidemic, widespread birth disorders like stillbirths, miscarriages and genetic deformities due to nuclear plant accidents, shutdowns, sabotage, leakage from chemical and biological warfare, stockpiles and toxic waste disposal sites and uncontrolled use of chemical insecticides, herbicides and sprays. (316-17)

The Aunts in Gilead are rigid, middle-aged women who have

internalized patriarchal values and are used to impose them on other women. The basic principle of colonialism, "Control of the indigenous by members of their own group" (320) is adapted in Gilead to the control of women, for it is believed that "The best and most cost-effective way to control women for reproductive and other purposes was through women themselves." (320)

Suicide is one of the ways in which the women in Gilead attempt escape from their intolerable oppression. Offred's predecessor had hanged herself from the light fixture. The Gilead administration therefore takes preventive measures to block this particular escape-route. In the Handmaid's room, "They've removed anything you could tie a rope to." (17) In the bathroom razors are removed: framed pictures have no glass and the window-pane-glass is shatterproof so that there is no "cutting edge." (18)

Escape through physical flight is another possibility, though the chances of success are almost nil. Despite deterrent screening of news-items showing the capture and punishment of fugitives, (93) Moira and later Offred attempt escape via the "underground Femaleroad" of "Frailroad" (313) to Canada and thence to England or elsewhere.

There are other ways of manoeuvring for female space in Gilead. Moira adopts defiance and rebellion. Ofglen joins a subversive group with the password 'Mayday' and indulges in sabotage activities. Playing games with Man in a show of acquiescence or compromise, but with the ulterior motive of wheedling privileges out of patriarchy is yet another subversive method of creating female space. In return for clandestinely playing Scrabble with her Commander, Offred gets precious hand-lotion for her face and hands. But more valuable than that is the intangible gain that she is no longer just an object to him after that: "To him I'm no longer merely a usable body." (172)

Thus, in this novel, the child-bearing function of woman is isolated, exaggerated and focussed on in the Handmaid, who begins just as an isolated function, but imperceptibly evolves into a person, wrenching female breathing space in a patriarchal power-structure. At the thematic, plot and character level, various strategies are employed, by the women in the novel, to create female space—bonding with other women and forging a sisterhood, defiance, sabotage, compromise, maintaining autonomy of thought, holding on to the objective reality of the past through flashbacks, keeping the oral reconstruction of one's own history, physical flight and as a last resort, suicide.

At the structural level, *The Handmaid's Tale* may be viewed as Atwood's strategy for creating female space out of patriarchal structures. Atwood achieves her purpose through the novel's structure, the narrative mode of oral reconstruction, the use of language and imagery and through ambivalence. Placing the novel in the future is itself a structural strategy by which contemporary patriarchal tyranny is viewed with detachment through the distancing of time and also by the device of exaggeration.

The novel chooses patriarchal narrative structures as its basic framework and then subverts them, thus creating female space. Chaucer's *Canterbury Tales* and the Biblical narrative in *Genesis* concerning Patriarchs like Abraham, Isaac and Jacob provide the base of the novel. But the patriarchal method of child-production through the impregnation of Handmaids is debunked in the novel and shown to be highly alienating to the women concerned. The pun on "Tale" and "Tail" in the title *The Handmaid's Tale* with its sexual innuendo burlesques the Chaucerian original intentionally.

The Handmaid's Tale is not presented as history or his story, i.e. a story from a man's point of view, but as Her Story, the story of Offred, narrated by herself orally. The narration is made off and on, not chronologically, into a recording machine and preserved in tapes. Annis Pratt's generalization about women's fiction could perhaps be applied to Offred's narrative: "Women's fiction manifests alienation from normal concepts of time and space precisely because the presentation of time by persons on the margins of day-to-day life inevitably deviates from ordinary chronology."[8]

Though "goddesses like Sarasvati in India, Brigid in Britain and Nidaba in Sumer were credited with the invention of the alphabet and the creation of language and writing,"[9] women in general are connected with the oral tradition and language. The entire novel, *The Handmaid's Tale*, except for the Epilogue, is supposed to be orally narrated by Offred. The oral element of the narration is often emphasized: "It's also a story I'm telling in my head as I go along. *Tell*, rather than write, because I have nothing to write with and writing is in any case forbidden." (49)

The importance of the oral tradition among women is indirectly suggested in the novel by the manner in which Moira's story is pieced together from what others have said, a story passed from woman to woman, by word of mouth: "Part of it I can fill in myself, part of it I heard from Alma, who heard it from Dolores, who heard it from Janine. Janine heard it from Aunt Lydia." (139) This is not gossip. The reason for the spread of Moira's story was that Moira's daring escape served as a positive role model for all Handmaids: "Moira was our fantasy. We hugged her to us. She was with us in secret, a giggle." (143) When Offred records Moira's story on tape it becomes the oral narration of an oral narrative, and her purpose is to keep Moira alive, in and through the narrative: "I've tried to make it sound as much like her as I can. It's a way of keeping her alive." (256) In a way, narration confirms existence.

For Offred, narrating her own story validates existence and makes her exist, in a certain sense: "I don't want to be telling this story." "I don't have to tell it. I don't have to tell anything to myself or to anyone else. I could just sit here peacefully. I could withdraw. It's possible to go so far in, so far down and back, they could never get you out." (237) And yet she does not do so. She tells her story to herself lying on her bed and later to another on tape. She prefers telling the story to just sitting there "peacefully" in a catatonic trance. Offred might almost claim, "I narrate and therefore I am."

Atwood frequently reminds the reader that the narrative is an oral reconstruction by Offred, after the events, and as such, can only be an approximation to reality at several removes and never the actual happening itself. Of course this is true of all narration and all history too, though one does not think of it as such: "It's impossible to say a thing exactly the way it was, because what you say can never be exact, you always have to leave something out, there are too many parts, riders cross currents, nuances." (144) Sometimes later reflections are superimposed on the reconstruction of the original event. Thus "in fact, I don't think about anything of the kind and put it in only afterwards. Maybe I should have thought about that at the time, but I didn't. As I said, this is a reconstruction." (150) Sometimes three or four different versions of an event are given in the reconstruction and it is futile for the reader to grope for what 'really' happened. The author conveys the idea that all narration, both in real life and in fiction is only an oral reconstruction. And there will be always difficulty in achieving accuracy and strict veracity in it and it will be almost impossible to recapture in words all that had happened at a particular moment. After giving an account of her first rendezvous with Nick, (273) Offred adds, "I made that up. It did not happen that way. Here is what happened." But again on page 275 she says, "It didn't happen that way either," and adds, "All I can hope for is a reconstruction." The point that emerges most clearly from the various discussions on oral reconstruction in this novel is that all narrative and all history can only be a reconstruction from a particular point of view and a particular perspective. History has indeed been *his* story, the male perspective.

According to Offred, the reconstruction of one's own life as a story gives a sense of control over the events in the story and hence a sense of control over one's own life: "I would like to believe this is a story I'm telling." "If it's a story I'm telling, then I have control over the ending. Then there will be an ending, to the story, and real life will come after it. I can pick up where I left off." (49) Yet at the same time she also realizes her own lack of control over the story that she tells.

Another advantage of oral narration as perceived by Offred is that it presupposes the objective reality of a listener, outside oneself and the possibility of communication, even one-way communication, with this listener: "But if it's a story, even in my head, I must be telling it to someone. You don't tell a story only to yourself. There's always someone else." (49) A narrator implies the presence of a listener: "By telling you anything at all, I'm at least believing in you, I believe you're there. I believe you into being. Because I'm telling you this story, I *will* your existence. I tell, therefore you are." (279) Offred's above statement, modelled on Descartes, might as well be taken as the credo of every feminist writer who *wills* into existence her own audience of committed and enlightened readers.

Narrating a story thus becomes an effective strategy of acquiring female space for oneself and others in a patriarchal universe. In the discussion centring on the oral reconstruction method of narration, the novel borders on metafiction, fiction about the narration of fiction.

Language has always been acknowledged as a powerful and perhaps the only weapon at the disposal of those under subjection. Caliban had realized this too. A strategy by which those under subjection try to create space for themselves is by using language to debunk the wielders of power. This is the motivation behind all ironic fables and satiric narratives which are obliquely directed at the powers that be, whether the power is colonial or patriarchal.

Offred expresses this realization: "There is something powerful in the whispering of obscenity about those in power. There's something delightful about it; it deflates them, reduces them to the common denominator where they can be dealt with." (254)

In the hands of Atwood, language becomes a powerful weapon to wrench female space within the existing structures. She exposes the shortcomings of conventional patriarchal language and the encoded sexism in it. For example after declaring, "The Marthas are not supposed to fraternize with us," (21) Offred adds, "There was no corresponding word that meant to behave like a sister," though one may coin "Sororize." While the word 'fraternize' exists, which means 'to behave like a brother,' there is no corresponding word for women. It was as if language, in collusion with patriarchy, conspired to deny sisterhood to women.

Sometimes Atwood takes up a traditionally used phrase and turns it inside out like a cheveril glove. For example, on the night of the ceremony, the Commander takes up the Bible to read to the household. "We are expectant. Here comes our bedtime story," (98) comments Offred, evoking a picture of childhood innocence. But the tone is deceptive. The Biblical story of Rachel and Bilha is meant to justify the use of handmaids in bed to produce children to aging childless commanders. The phrase "bedtime story" becomes ambiguous. It is a story of the bedding of the Biblical handmaid and precedes the bedding of the Gileadean handmaid. Sometimes traditional linguistic structures of patriarchal origin, like proverbs, are taken and fractured and idioms are twisted out of shape: "Waste not want not. I am not being wasted. Why do I want?" (17) The proverb in the active voice, 'waste not' is twisted out of shape by being cast in the passive voice as "I am not being wasted." Offred often plays language games by which perhaps Atwood tries to breathe new life into the existing fossilized patriarchal language: "I sit in the chair and think about the word chair. It can also mean the leader of a meeting. It can also mean a mode of execution. It is the first syllable in charity. It is the French word for flesh. None of these facts has any connection with the others." (120) Similar games occur on pages 182 and 236. The perception of the simultaneous coexistence of plural meanings in a particular word may perhaps be related to the feminist rejection of the either/or binary opposition which typifies patriarchal discourse. Elsewhere, Offred imagines three possibilities about her husband Luke—that he is dead, that he is captured and alive, that he has escaped and is well: "The things I believe can't all be true, though one of them must be. But I believe in all of them, all three versions of Luke, at one and the same time. This contradictory way of believing seems to me right now, the only way I can believe anything." (116) This pluralism in belief is reflected in the multiple layers of language perceived by Offred. Atwood, like Dorothy Richardson, Virginia Woolf and Alice Walker, is seen to be a bold experimenter in "feminine prose,"[10] "a woman's sentence"[11] and "Womanist prose."[12]

The novel reveals a skilled use of images, metaphors and symbols to convey the chosen themes. The Ibsenite image of a doll is used often to convey a woman's estrangement in an alienating environment: "I thought I was sounding like that, voice of a monotone, voice of a doll." (26) "Without a word she swivels, as if she is voice-activated, as if she's on little oiled wheels, as if she's on top of a music box." (53) The rug on the floor of the handmaid's room, made of braided rags becomes a metaphor of the occupant who struggles to make something meaningful of her life, like the Black foremothers and their patchwork quilts, as perceived Alice Walker.[13]

The novel concludes with an Epilogue, supposedly placed about 200 years after Offred. The Epilogue presents the male point of view of the woman's story, which had formed the main narrative. This becomes the frame or perspective against which the novel acquires depth. There is much ambivalence in the Epilogue. The Epilogue gives clues and hints regarding the main story, in case the reader has missed them and yet it laughs at critical interpretations of the story by posterity. Professor James Darcy Pieixoto might be seen as exhibiting scholarly objectivity when he says about Gilead, "Our job is not to censure but to understand" (315) and yet it is possible to view him[14] as an insensitive M.C.P. who has grossly misunderstood Offred's narrative and the relationship between the sexes in Gilead.

There is also ambivalence of another kind in this novel. There are moments when feminism itself seems to be viewed ambivalently and a woman's culture is seen to be not an unmixed blessing. This is seen, for example, in chapter 21, in the description of the natural childbirth, in which Wives, Aunts and Handmaids, all participate. Offred apostrophizes her feminist mother in imagination: "Mother, I think, wherever you may be, can you hear me? You wanted a woman's culture. Well, now there is one. It isn't what you meant, but it exists. Be thankful for small mercies." (137) Perhaps it is such ambivalence and irony that distinguish the artist from the partisan. Perhaps the underlying message of the novel is that anything carried to an extreme, has potential evil in it, whether it is patriarchal tyranny or Feminism or religious fundamentalism in interpreting the Bible literally.

NOTES

1. Jean Lipman-Blumen, *Gender Roles and Power* (New Jersey: Prentice Hall, 1984), p. 5.
2. Northrop Frye, *The Bush Garden: Essays on the Canadian Imagination* (Canada: Anansi Press, 1971), p. iii.
3. Margaret Atwood, *Survival*, p. 35.
4. Linda Hutcheon "Afterword" in Margaret Atwood, *The Edible Woman* (Toronto: The New Canadian Library, 1969), p. 313.
5. Margaret Atwood, *The Handmaid's Tale* (Toronto: McClelland and Stewart, 1985), p. 260.
6. Olivia Frey, "Beyond Literary Darwinism: Women's Voices and Critical Discourse," *College English*, Vol. 52, No. 5, Sept. 1990, p. 523.
7. Alice Walker, *In Search of Our Mother's Gardens, Womanist Prose* (New York: Harcourt Brace Jovanovich), pp. 241-43.
8. Annis Pratt, *Archetyppal Patterns in Women's Fiction* (Bloomington: Indiana University Press, 1981), p. 11.
9. *Ibid.*
10. Dorothy Richardson, *Pilgrimage* (London: Dent, 1938), p. 9.
11. Virginia Woolf, "Romance of the Heart," A Review of *Revolving Lights* by Dorothy Richardson, in *The Nation and the Athenaeum, Literary Supplement*, May 19, 1923, p. 229.
12. Alice Walker, *In Search of Our Mother's Gardens*.
13. *Ibid.*, p. 239.
14. As done by Carol A. Senf, "The Tenant of Wildfell Hall: Narrative Stances and Questions of Gender," *College English*, Vol. 52, No. 4, April 1990, pp. 448-49.

A Violin in the Void: The Voice of the Narrator in Zamiatin's *We* and Atwood's *The Handmaid's Tale*

VIMALA RAMA RAO

Margaret Atwood's *The Handmaid's Tale*[1] and Eugene Zamiatin's *We*[2] are both set in futuristic distopias, politically totalitarian regimes in which the individual identity is obliterated under the banner of the collective good. But the novel as a genre has always been an individual creation and in fact, both these novels are cast in the form of a personalized utterance which would have no forum in the fictional worlds wherein they take birth. The voice of the narrator in both novels is a "Violin in the Void," to use a resonant phrase of Vladimir Nabokov.

Zamiatin's *We* has for its locale a country called the United State and Atwood's *Tale* divulges its location only in the thirty-seventh chapter of the novel. Up to that point the action could have taken place anywhere in Christendom. The strictly regimented life of the inmates of the place recalls Solzhenitsyn's Ivan Denisovich's routine. Ivan goes out to work; the protagonist of Zamiatin's *We,* D-503, has his work too, he is the builder of the great machine Integral. These men, for all the regimentation and the mindless monotony of their lives have the dignity of their work, however subordinated it may be to a collective design. In the case of the heroine-narrator of the *Tale*, work is not hers to do. All women in the reproductive age-group have been rounded up and kept in communal Houses manned by Aunts and Commanders and watched over by Eyes and waited upon by Marthas. Their sole function is to produce children. They have been reduced to one biological function, reproduction; motherhood divested of dignity, privacy, poetry and grotesquely linked to the strategies of survival. While all the positives of a normal life have been erased in this state, evidently the negatives are not. The Commanders are the studs of this animal farm and they service all the females under their command. Such arrangements are not unknown in history, for example, the harems of Oriental potentates have had a similar structure. But a special feature of this place is its Biblical structure superimposed upon a totalitarian design. The various service points of the camp such as the grocery and the fish-mart all have names like 'Loaves and Fishes' and 'All Flesh.' The Biblical resonance is carried over into sexual transactions also. One of the epigraphs of the book reads:

> "And she said, Behold my maid Bilhah, go in unto her; and she shall bear upon my knees, that I may also have children by her." Genesis, 30:13.

This notion of a woman bearing children through her handmaid is given a ritual enactment in this place. The wife of the Commander is very much present, obscenely implicated in the ceremonial stud performance of the Commander with the Handmaid. All erotic and personal elements are banned from the transaction and the deed is done in stark obedience to the Will of the State.

The central episode of the novel is the subversion of this officially required impersonality between the members of the House. Offred, the narrator, finds herself preferred by the Commander and involved in an intrigue. Once in a while, when his wife is safely elsewhere, the Commander sends for Offred to come to his study. Offred, whose very name is made up of her official subservience to him (Of+Fred) wonders what he could want of her, perhaps something kinky and perverted. She is right, this man to whom she is a bonded slave sexually, wants to do something forbidden with her, play Scrabble. Under the perverted circumstances where sexual congress between a man and several women is enforced and regimented, playing Scrabble has all the excitement of a forbidden pleasure. So also the notion of meeting a Handmaid under circumstances other than those designed for procreation. Offred and her Commander meet several times in the greatest secrecy and do many forbidden things together; he lets her look at a magazine; she reads Dickens in his room; he gets her some hand-lotion (Handmaids had to live in a cosmetic-less state of simplicity) and finally even takes her out one night. The outing is to a kind of playboy club, the sort of thing supposedly rooted out of the theocratic State. The Commander attempts to commit sex with Offred under these rather romantic circumstances. But Offred's training has been too thorough for her to relish it. Or perhaps, she is not corrupted and nullified enough by the State to enjoy something merely because it is forbidden. A Handmaid, in other words a bonded slave, she still retains enough individuality to choose her pleasures, even though choice really does not seem to exist. The play-boy club incident where she does not fall in with the Commander's wishes is an instance of her continuing to exercise an option, an assertion of individuality.

When the Commander in the new-found intimacy of Scrabble and reading asks Offred what she wants, she answers: I would like to know. The Commander smuggles her out so that she could know at least a fraction of what goes on. Unfortunately what she learns of the leisure pastimes of the Gileadian elite is not very edifying; the Commanders take their pleasure in a sort of club to find relaxation from their regular duties as uxorious studs by proxy. Offred learns other things as well, but without the Commander's connivance but with that of his wife; she has a brief interlude of love with Nick, the Commander's driver. The wife who is the Rachel of the novel (the Biblical original who conceived the notion of begetting by proxy) believes that if she is to bear children, the biblical arrangement is not good enough but a further refinement is necessary. It is not enough for a Rachel to have her obliging Bilhah but a counterpart of Bilhah has to be found for her barren husband also. The choice is Nick, who is not averse to Offred, for aversion is a free man's prerogative and Nick lives in Gilead where all rights have been abolished to accommodate one paramount duty which is to be fruitful and multiply. Offred's interlude with a man with procreative potential takes on other dimensions; it acquires, under the circumstances, a tinge of romance. The curious, pathetic thing about it is that even in Gilead, under the bestial conditions of breeding in captivity a human relationship sprouts, though Nick makes a joke of the dehumanized, clinical need that brings Offred to him, the necessity to prove herself fertile so that she may not be classified as dispensable and shipped off to the colonies. This link with Nick also provides Offred with her final escape from Gilead though it is not clear whereto.

The principle around which the worlds in which Offred and D-503 live are built, is that freedom and happiness are mutually incompatible, a theoretical position most forcefully articulated by the

Grand Inquisitor in Dostoevsky's *The Brothers Karamazov*. His argument is that men are congenitally incapable of using their freedom for constructive ends and only make themselves unhappy by the abuse of freedom and that most people yearn only for materialistic happiness and eagerly surrender their difficult freedom in exchange. When Zamiatin wrote *We* in 1920, he adopted this creed to the needs of a modern technocratic State. In the United State, every conceivable need of a human being is taken care of governmentally, not forgetting the need for "personal hours." All that one has to do is to fill in a form with the identity number and address of the chosen one and if it pleases the Bureau of the Guardians, that citizen will be assigned for the personal hour to the requester. D-503 finds himself assigned to I-330 on a particular day when actually he had been booked by another number. He makes a choice and tells himself: "Let the situation solve itself mechanically; I would send her a copy of the official communication." (49) A perfect instance to vindicate the Grand Inquisitor's argument; not for D-503 the creator of the Integral the mundane problem of fending off one woman while spending the personal hour with another. The State takes care of such things for their valued mathematician as for all other citizens. The narrator, D-503 has at the beginning of his story, a quotation from the State newspaper: "Your mission is to subjugate to the grateful yoke or reason the unknown beings who live on other planets, and who are perhaps still in the primitive stage of freedom. If they will not understand that we are bringing them a mathematically faultless happiness, our duty will be to force them to be happy. But before we take up arms, we shall try the power of words." (3) Everyone who feels capable is required to write treatises, poems, manifestoes, odes and other compositions on the greatness and beauty of the United State. D-503, a mathematician, intends to record only "the things I see, the things I think, or to be more exact, the things we think" therefore his narration is entitled *We*. He believes that as the records are a derivative of life in the United State, it will be a poem in itself despite his limitations.

As it happens, as the narration proceeds it imperceptibly begins to acquire the lineaments of a personal creation and not that of the derivative of the State. Its presence makes itself felt in Record Seven: "I really feel there in the brain some foreign body like an eyelash in the eye." (31) The sense of a self, individuality, is severely dealt with by the State. A poet who suddenly went crazy and said "I am a genius! and I am above the law" (41) received death sentence put into verse. D-503 says: "Fortunately the antediluvian time of those Shakespeares and Dostoyevskys (or what were their names?) is past." (41) But he says it in a voice "deliberately loud."

The eyelash was the tip of an iceberg, the self that D-503 sees as his other, hairy-ape self, or the instinctual self the State had virtually obliterated. As a citizen is obliged to, he goes to the Medical Bureau and pours out his troubles. And the doctor accurately diagnoses it: "Yes, it is too bad. Apparently a soul has formed in you." (84) He is informed that it is incurable, the only recourse being surgery; by extirpating the center for fancy in the brain, a person's life is saved for the State. In fact he is not the only one who seems to be thus afflicted, the Medical Bureau fears that there may be an epidemic unless dealt with promptly. At the end of the novel the narrator is fully restored to health. The woman I-330 who was responsible for the narrator's growing sense of self was a revolutionary who had planned to overthrow the regime by taking over the Integral. Another woman O-90 conceives a child by D-503 even though she knows that "private children" are not allowed and a defaulter is liable to Death Sentence. The two selves of the narrator struggle within him, the planned takeover of the Integral misfires. I-330 thinks that he betrayed them. He is operated upon, the center of fancy is removed from the brain and the next day he watches I-330 being tortured and led to her execution without emotion.

Both Zamiatin's and Atwood's fictions operate within certain literary conventions, the most important among them being the fiction that these narrations were not written as fiction but as something else, for example a diary or a record. This evidently is a necessary device because given the particular worlds of the two novels, fiction-writing is not a likely activity. A totalitarian state is not the ambience in which a novel focusing attention on emotions, feelings and actions other than state-approved ones can be shown as being written. Not that this has not been done. Writers in Eastern Europe have invented various ruses by which there is a coded message imbedded which the cogniscenti understand. An outstanding example of this is Mikhail Bulgakov's *Master and Margarita.*

What *We* and *The Handmaid's Tale* have in common is that the mainspring of the two narrations can be likened to violins in the void, that is, the main action centers around the normal human need for love and affection. When that is seen as subversive, as deviant behaviour from the desirable state of being a non-person, the expression of that state of being, a normal person's ordinary emotions appearing to be extraordinary even to himself or herself, there the narration begins. *The Handmaid's Tale* begins with matter-of-fact descriptions of the camp where she lives. It gathers momentum from the time Offred begins to want to assert her self, however marginally; that self which asserts itself even under the most adverse conditions and demands expression even if it is on to mute white paper or a cassette (modern day variants on Cervantes's Cid Hamete Benengeli's note books) which may never be read or heard. In other words, these two violins play in a void but recorded within the framework of a fiction attain the resonance of a melody that is no less sweet for being heard.

NOTES

1. (London: Virago, 1987).
2. Trans. Gregory Zilboorg (New York: E.P. Dutton, 1952).

Articulating Silence: Margaret Atwood's *The Handmaid's Tale*

MADHUMALATI ADHIKARI

Margaret Atwood believes that the silencing of woman, the thematics of victimization, functions not only through patriarchal attitudes but also through woman's conscious or unconscious complexity in the matter. She insists that to combat it, "Recognize the source of oppression, express anger, suggest ways for change. What she can't do is write as a *fully* liberated individual-as-woman-in society. . . . Three attributes that power-mad regimes cannot tolerate [are] a human imagination . . . the power to communicate, and hope."[1] The scheme of depriving woman of imagination, the power of communication and hope, is stringently, viciously and deliberately carried on by patriarchy. The creative female artist to rediscover the strangled voice, to articulate woman's silent discourse, to decipher the coded language, to demystify and deconstruct the myths, to liberate the imagination of woman, uses a double-voiced narrative strategy that camouflages the harsh undertones with an innocent exterior. She often resorts to "silence, euphemism, circumlocution"[2] with great success to articulate woman's oppression, marginalized status, exploitation and political domination. Paradoxically, her silence is very vocal.

Atwood's dystopian novel *The Handmaid's Tale*[3] imitates the epistolary form with a slight difference: it is recorded and not written, a cumbersome exercise in twentieth century with all technical amenities at our command. Writing or recording, both a form of speech, is denied to our protagonist in the theocratic society of Gilead, situated in South Dakota, US, established by the religious fanatics. The protagonist's 'own story' recalled from memory is transcribed by Professor Pieixoto (another Quixote?) an activist. (313) It cannot be the authentic version, yet it reaches us. Maybe controlled and altered by patriarchy but surely an approximation and reconstruction of her version. The suppression of her individuality by curbing her liberty of thought, action and speech, an imposition of homogeneous order on heterogeneous reality, aborts. The Professor bewails the loss of the Commander's computerized information but he forgets (Atwood does not) that a female is specifically debarred access to this kind of intelligence. Offred's power of word triumphs despite the barriers constructed by time and man. This paper would investigate and interpret, the means and methods of articulating woman's silence.

In *Survival,* Atwood had "hinted" that the quotations at the beginning of each chapter have been "chosen with care,"[4] in *Surfacing,* the protagonist's journey towards self-discovery is hinted; and it would be no exaggeration to assert that *The Handmaid's Tale* is also loaded with clues. The dedication, the epigraphs and the careful selection of names and words and images are the tools in the artist's hands to convey truths that may be otherwise unspeakable. Mary Webster a witch, whom Atwood considers her ancestor, though was found not-guilty by the jury, yet the mob-justice as in the 'Salvagings' section, had beaten and buried her alive which is "a form of licensed reprisal of ritualized victimization."[5] With recurring pictures of witch hunting, the novel is dedicated to her and Perry Miller, Atwood's teacher who instilled in her that the study of any written material was necessary to discover the pattern of development of any country. Atwood presents a modern form of woman hunting that aims at subjugating woman's power that is her fertility. And then, the epigraph from Genesis 30:1-3 not only suggests patriarchal manipulation to instill in woman a sense of unworthiness sans motherhood but also points out the complexity of woman in subordinating other women and advocating self-effacement. The quotation from Swift prepares us for Swiftian satire that would conceal the harsh truths of the Sufi proverb. Atwood's strategy is made amply clear.

The Handmaid's Tale narrates the 'tale' of a quasi-military Republic that chiefly concentrates on human reproduction, as a combination of chemical pollution, an epidemic of veneral diseases (maybe AIDS) and radiation has brought about a sudden drop in the fertility rate of women. Offred the protagonist, now the handmaid of Commander Fred, was picked up as she along with her husband and daughter was attempting to escape from this country. Her husband is probably dead and the daughter quite possibly is in one of the Morality schools and is being adequately trained either to become the wife of some unknown Angel or to serve a Commander as a future handmaid. In either case, her womb is to be colonized. Like Rennie, the central character in *Bodily Harm,* Offred is placed in Red Centre for training. Such "speculative literature"[6] as Atwood defines it, is built up from the experiences of past and present and extended to the future.

Initially, Atwood articulates silence by carefully selecting symbolic and meaningful names of places, characters, objects and coins new words to signify special ceremonies. 'Gilead' in Hebrew means the 'Hall of Witness' and the novel is nothing but a fiction about or witness of history. Since it is a 'tale' of the present century, it cannot be ignored or disbelieved. Everything happens in Gilead and ironically, it presents the picture that Jeremiah prophesied for its biblical namesake: 'Is there no balm in Gilead; is there no physician there? why then is not the health of the daughter of my people recovered?' (Jeremiah 8:22) There is no answer. The health—physical and emotional—of the daughters of Gilead is really in jeopardy. Transferred from one household to another for sexual exploitation, their final destiny is either the disintegrating madness of Janine or the self-slaughter of Ofglen or a permanent banishment to the polluted colonies for total decomposition. One cannot question the scenario as Atwood rightly comments in *Quill and Quire*: "There is nothing in the book that hasn't already happened."[7] Offred, Ofwarren and Ofglen are appropriately re-named; their personal identities effected as they are now the material possession of the Commanders: either Fred or Warren or Glen. The guards known as the Guardians, the spies renamed as Eyes, spy on each other and everyone. In fact, the truth is revealed by Offred's comment on Ofglen, her shopping companion, "she is my spy as I am hers." (29) It refreshes our memory of KGB or CIA. Through circumlocution, Atwood makes us conscious of the mutually distrustful atmosphere.

Lyle Koehler in *A Search for Power* mentions that Hetty Shepard (1677) recounts in her diary about her aunt Lydia and other women of the family who made her feel "guilty" because she loved "dresses," "merriment" and had "independent thoughts."[8] By christening the most autocratic aunt as Lydia, Atwood conveys the image of thought controlling matrons, who are present not to protect their nieces from sexual exploitations but to expose them to physical abuses through the 'Ceremony' when the Commander in the presence of his wife attempts to impregnate the handmaid. A shocking instance of forcible control of the womb.

The ethos of the handmaid's world is domestic and they are segregated from all male contact. The Commander is the exception to the rule. In Gilead, we have Atwood's eternal analogy: male versus female. The women are divided into different classes with specific uniform: the Commander's wife wears a blue dress; the aunts sport army uniforms; the Ecowives (the working class) have red, green and blue striped outfits; Marthas, the housemaids have green garments and the handmaids drape themselves in red gowns with nun-like white head-gears. They are cloistered but act like mistresses. Offred considers herself, "a distorted shadow, a parody of something, some fairytale figure in Red cloak [A Red Riding Hood?] descending towards a moment of carelessness that is the same as danger. A sister dipped in blood." (19) Red is the colour of death, fertility and martyrdom. Atwood conveys these ideas simultaneously. The Commander's wife renamed Serena Joy, once known as Pam on Television, neither has serenity nor joy; her name is a misnomer. Despite her apparent high status in society, she too has been robbed of her identity and judged worthless, "damaged, defective" (213) because of her infertility. Atwood not only gives intimations of woman's obliteration, debasement and humiliation but also intentionally follows the tradition of Puritanic New England that named its daughters to reflect feminine destiny: Silence, Fear, Patience, Prudence, Fruitful, etc.[9] The Commander's car, black and sinister looking is named 'Whirlwind' and interestingly Jeremiah 4:13 reads, 'his chariot shall be as a whirlwind.' Thus the car becomes a symbol of destruction.

Offred in her autobiography *The Handmaid's Tale,* "sets before us . . . her desperate struggle to reconstruct her being across an all but unbridgeable, violent severing of time before and after the imposition of Gilead. To do this she must insist upon her own script, in a world where her voice has been erased and her role in life rescripted for her by others, where her meaning, use and plot are totally controlled by other interest and forces."[10] Despite the call of authority to forget, to be silent and thus remain effaced, pilotless, Offred's response is defiant; her scripting of the self through memory and language proclaims the defeat of Gilead's monologistic authoritarian discourse. In this venture, Atwood is the fountainhead of all activity. Every action of Offred like having a physical relationship with Nick, every symbol like playing of the scrabble, every image like that of the wall, Square, Church, Shops, the use of Bilhah's myth, the hint of chosen words like 'Ceremony,' 'Salvagings' and 'Partcicution' etc. demonstrates a poet's control of structures, symbols and words. Like Morrison, Atwood is more a poet than a fiction writer and her initial orientation as a poet has enriched her style. Her protagonist, explicitly and more often implicitly, sings her music that is perfectly audible and comprehensible to the discerning ear. "*The Handmaid's Tale* though written in the tight-lipped minimalist style that has become an Atwood trademark, conceals an ultimate insight that is far more complex and illusive."[11]

Like a traditional epistolary writer Offred reminds us, "This is a reconstruction. All of it is a reconstruction." Later, the professor's comments, "There is a certain reflective quality about the narrative that would to my mind rule out synchronicity" and "It has a whiff of emotion recollected if not in tranquillity, atleast *post facto*," (315) are a deliberate attempt to silence woman's voice as excessively emotional and thus not trustworthy enough for attention. This is an old strategy of male authority (See *Meridian, The Color Purple, Sula, Beloved, Wide Sargasso Sea, That Long Silence, Where Shall We Go This Summer?* etc.) The gymnasium once a place of dance, music and sports, now is turned into a training centre controlled by unsexed (metaphorically) aunts with cattle prods hanging from their belts. The so-called Angels stand outside "the chain link fence topped with barbed wire" (12) that subtly documents the altered conditions in the Republic where all humane and liberal qualities have disappeared. Atwood "knows the strength of language and its vulnerability. . . . Such is the case in Gilead and Offred's narrative. . . . It stands as a proof that true language means survival."[12] Offred is aware that the fruition of the survival-wish is possible only through a communication with the outer world that is debarred to her and thus regrets: "If only we could talk to them [Angels]. . . . We still had our bodies." (13) The power of the body language is also seized from the handmaid; they have been successfully segregated from the opposite sex. Only minor liberties, with a silent permission from the abused wives like accepting the advances of the doctor (71) or cooperating with the stud duty of Nick (313) can be enjoyed. Despite being constantly warned against the evils of talking and advantages of silence, the handmaids communicate, in different ways and defy the vigilance of aunts: "We learnt to whisper almost without sound. In the semi-darkness we could stretch our arms, when the aunts were not looking and touch each other's hands across space. We learned to lip read. . . . In this way we exchanged names from bed to bed: Alma, Janine, Dolores, Moira, June." (13) These soldiers of revolution, apparently passive, voiceless, erased, circumscribed, assert their identity by exhuming their names from the pit of obscurity with the help of a new mode of speech. Their new code language is carried to the other with the movement of silent lips, looks, smiles, whistles, and winks (18) or Ofglen's "May Day" message or Moira's conversation with Offred through the "wooden holes" in the "wooden stalls." (83) "Whatever is silenced will clamour to be heard, though silently," (161) comments Offred and her statement is accurate.

Offred's room is a transit camp, a prison cell; the use of mirrors, glass windowpanes, hooks have been dispensed with for safety purposes and also for dispossessing woman of her identity: "Time here is measured by bells, as once in nunneries." (18) To overcome the feeling of isolation, Offred loves to gossip with the Marthas who despite their confined existence, know and pass the message from house to house: "Stillborn, it was. Dr. stabbed her with a knitting needle, right in the belly. Jealousy, it must have been. . . . Or, tantalizingly, it was toilet cleaner she used. . . . Must've been that drunk; but they found her out all right." (21) Each reported act is an articulation of revolt. Our protagonist loves to 'fraternize' with the Marthas but is shocked to realize that the oppressor's language has no "corresponding word that meant to behave like sister." (21) The patriarchal language banishes woman from such healthy relationships. It is the result of an age-old fear of "Woman's Power." The handmaids are denied the opportunity to create: woman's significant claim to creation, child-bearing, is controlled by the fundamentalist theocracy. The Commander's wife is more fortunate; she can knit scarves for Angels; weave elaborate designs of 'fir trees' (reaching for the sky) or 'eagles' (soaring heaven-ward in their free flight) or 'boy and girl' motifs (an obsession and a reminder of the infertility plus inadequacy), 'a form of procreation.' (22) Offred's conjecture is that they are not sent to the Angels but "unravelled and turned back into balls of yarn, to be knitted again in their turn." (23) The condition of both the victims is palpable and pathetic. One is reminded of Celie's passive and meaningless existence in *The Color Purple*,[13] till she learns to exist symbolically through the physical act of stitching pants. The aunts insist that the handmaids have "a position of honour." (23) Can it be true? Can a victim claim to have honour? No. But very soon, Offred the powerless, is empowered by her intellectual competence; she begins to win the wordgame of scrabble. Her communicatory skill becomes multi-dimensional. In contrast, Serena Joy's language degenerates into contextless expressions. Her proud assertion about her husband, "till death do us part" (26) is meaningless. Though she voices the precepts of the founding fathers yet her speech is really silent. Offred often pretends like Celie, "I am a tree" (28) but this ossification is an intelligent strategy to transcribe the inner feelings into an explicit expression.

In Offred's room, the previous occupant had stealthily scratched a coded message in a cupboard: "*Nolite te bastardes carborundorum*" (let not the bastards crush you). The language is foreign to her yet the message is carried, "It pleases me to ponder this message. It pleases me to think that I am communicating with her. . . . They give me a small joy." (62) Despite the restrictions and the impossibility of the situation, Offred communicates with the unknown inscriber and demolishes the barriers of death. The speech of the oppressed metamorphoses into a rallying cry for liberty. Her subsequent plunge into a life-redeeming relationship with Nick is the vindication of her sacrifice.

Orwell had perceived that the state's control over the individual's thought could be carried out by a standardization and impoverishment of the language. Atwood accepting the power of the same strategy makes her rebels exploit the multi-dimensionality and ambiguity of language that cannot be controlled by the state. The handmaids use orthodox language quoted from the Bible. The standard address is, 'Blessed be the fruit' and the accepted response is, 'May the Lord open' or 'Praise be' yet (29); much is unofficially communicated through these hackneyed phrases. Men and women are equally muted in the Republic but they speak with their eyes. Speaking is dangerous; silence is also dangerous at times. Offred realizes the delicate situation and thus to the query of the tourist, "Are you happy?" (39) Offred's ironic reply is, "yes we are very happy. Because sometime it's as dangerous not to speak." (30)

Routine shopping takes the handmaids to the "wall" (The Berlin Wall?). Six bodies with covered heads hang from the hooks (like pigs). Their death is the symbol of injustice, tyranny and defiance. That may be the precise reason, why despite their reduced circumstances, a blot of blood on the sack where there should be the mouth, there is "a shape of a smile," (46) the smile of defiance. "What we are supposed to feel towards these bodies is hatred and scorn. This isn't what I feel." (47) The explicit message of fear is translated into a call for insurgency. Ofglen's suicide to safe-guard the identity and the secrets of the resistance group is a coded message for the friends and a challenge for the religious authoritarianism.

Offred reiterates that she is narrating a story: "It is also a story, I'm telling in my head" (51); "I wish this story were different. I wish it were more civilized"; "I'm sorry there is so much pain in the story"; "This is the story then." (278) Story-telling presupposes the presence of speech, a speaker and an audience. Offred's speech despite the indoctrination and regimentation is untainted, authentic and perfectly communicable.

Atwood concentrates on the problem of woman's survival in a hostile male-dominated world through her refusal to be a silent victim. Offred lives through her memory and the game of scrabble. Ironically, the path of emancipation is paved by the victimizer. In contrast, Serena Joy a fervent speaker on Television, "is now become speechless." (56) But the physical act of speechlessness is often not an indicator of the person's silence. The embittered wife's "resentment," "jealousy" and "hatred" are surely transmitted to Offred though overt speech is dispensed with. Aunt Lydia had warned her, "It is not the husbands you have to watch out for . . . it is the wives." (56) The tangible animosity between the wife and the mistress is relayed effortlessly and is not walled by silence.

Juxtaposing of the past and the present through Offred's memory, is a mode of locution to offer universal accounts of woman's subjugation through the ages that has been magnified manifold in Gilead. Women are indoctrinated through recorded messages: "Blessed are the meek, Blessed are the silent." (100) Woman's mission of life is framed in rigid words. "Oh God obliterate me. Make me fruitful. Mortify my flesh that I may be multiplied. Let me be fulfilled." (204) Handmaids have kneeling cushions with 'faith' embroidered on it but cushions with 'Hope' and 'Chastity' are suggestively missing. Through perceptual objects, conceptual messages are decoded. Quite often, Nick an emissary, creates potent body language even though maids are reserved for commanders: "We are for breeding purposes . . . we are two legged wombs . . . sacred vessels, ambulatory chalices." (146) Nick the liberating agent of Offred, also becomes the instrument to reach her to the world of books, knowledge, power: "room full of books no locks in plain view, no boxes." (147) Her final escape is aided by him; he also returns her confiscated identity: "He calls me by my real name. Why should this mean anything?" (302) It does. The suspended question evokes response from the reader, a communication and a strategy to demolish the tyranny of silence.

The game of scrabble, a symbol of reading, writing and knowledge, is forbidden for women: "Now it's forbidden for us. Now it's dangerous. Now it's indecent." (149) Instead of indulging in some perverted sexual act, the commander's request to play the game is so unexpected and ludicrous to Offred that she cannot but break into laughter. The fear of being condemned for an "emotion inappropriate to the occasion," (156) turns out to be the restraining agent. The laughter boiling inside her is a speech that declares the laugher's humanity, autonomy, an undermining of the person's authority at whom laughter is directed and an independent mode of perceiving reality. The Commander's reduced status encourages her to read an old issue of *Vogue*, (165) a symbol of female selfhood and its articulation banned by the draconian phallocentric culture of Gilead. Her subsequent demand for hand-lotion, a signifier of her identity and an externalization of her crushed desires, is an offshoot of the reviving fearless attitude. An access to the world of knowledge, the resurrection of the self, blends and transforms into a language of sympathy. Her inner voice stoned to unconsciousness is rejuvenated and thus her attitude towards Serena Joy softens: "I also felt guilty about her. I feel I was an intruder." (170) The awakening of the humanistic attitude articulates different emotions through a different language.

The suppression of the legitimate, natural voice, an abnormal arrangement, anticipates volcanic vibrations and eruption. Offred-Nick relationship, unarticulated, carried out under the cover of darkness, is one such explosion that voices their physical and emotional needs, exploitations and suppressions. The protagonist's rising confidence and her gradual acclimatization to the new ethos, makes her almost voluble in her demand, "I would like to know. . . .

Whatever there is to know" (198) and 'knowing' more often than not, ensures future communication that she passes to the resistance group through "clipped whispers. . . . It is more like a telegram, a verbal semaphore. Amputated speech." (209) Yet speech it is and not silence..

Speech flows more freely in the community of woman. The community of woman can be successfully formed in the fictional world of Toni Morrison, Alice Walker or Margaret Atwood. In Offred's world Marthas indulge in gossips, Aunts confide in Janine about Moira's whereabouts. Serena Joy while maintaining the communication gap with Offred, suggests that she could have a child through "someone we trust" (213) and Offred interprets it "She does want that baby." (214) Serena Joy's conversation is circumlocutory yet the correct meaning is construed; the purpose of speech is fulfilled.

In dystopian novels, it is customary to fabricate new words with a view to convey certain ideas precisely and concisely. Atwood follows the convention by formulating words like: "Unwoman" (barren and ideological female offenders), "Unbaby" (abnormal baby), "Prayvaganza" (an extravaganza of mass wedding conducted by males), "Salvagings" (a doomed place for Unwoman), "Partcicution" (the execution of male offenders through the participation of women by way of lynching), "Ceremony" (the ceremony of impregnation carried out by the Commander), etc. In all these words woman's marginalized existence is suggested. "Let the woman learn in silence with all subjection" (233) prays the Commander in the "Prayvaganza." Silence is the eternal Mantra for women. In Gilead, the act of silencing is carried on, a little beyond the realm of women; Angels, Guardians, Doctors do not speak openly but surreptitiously. The punishment for the crimes is challenged with a collective roar that takes the shape of an "outbreak of similar crimes." (286) Very aptly Offred says: "The crimes of others are a secret language among us. Through them we show ourselves what we might be capable of after all." (286) "Partcicution" though a savage act, is a "steam valve for the female elements in Gilead" (320); it is an expression of collective female resentment.

The knowledge of her predecessor's and Ofglen's suicide brings home the hard facts of a woman's life to Offred, that this might be her destiny as well. The voice from the other world is heard quite distinctly: "I am tired of keeping silent. . . . I want it finished." (302)

Thus Atwood reaffirms that our ancestors communicate with us. This faith is also carried on in African culture. It is an assertion of the fact that this word cannot be silenced. Her last cryptic words recorded on the tape are, "And so I step up, into the *darkness within;* or else the light." (307, emphasis added) Her choice of words emphasizes hope: light after darkness.

Atwood like Morrison takes risk with language. She establishes a link between one's physical self and the developing psyche. Pecola in *The Bluest Eye* searches for spiritual beauty through physical beauty and Offred perceives the external phenomena, searches within and communicates her feelings, emotions through simple words, ironical statements, laughter, specific acts, coded messages, body language and even through silence. The tale is often narrated by an extraordinary juxtaposing of ideas which in themselves are extremely communicative. The first act of conquest by patriarchy is through a strangulation of the female voice, a recurrent theme in Atwood's poetry/fiction. In "Circe/Mud," a poem in *You Are Happy* (1974), Circe is initially the christening authority on the island but later, Odysseus defeats her and steals her words; she spends her days "collecting the few muted syllables left over." She asks Odysseus, "When you leave will you give me back the words?"

The same problem confronts Offred. Muted economically, emotionally and literally, she must recreate herself, learn to speak afresh. The vanquisher's language insists on regimentation of emotion and speech, "We smile too, we are one smile." (130) They are turned into 'missing persons,' deserted rooms where things once happened and now nothing does. Fortunately for the reader, the orchestra of voices rising from the recorded story defeats this nothingness.

By weaving the myth of Heloise and Abelard into the fabric of the story, Atwood projects Offred-Luke relationship and concretizes Offred's thoughts into speech. Heloise-like, she refuses to believe that Luke is dead and this very irrationality sustains her. Her frequent forays into the past keep the past alive that the regime wishes to wipe off; it is rescripted by her. Her individual memory redefines intimate relationships, historical moments and woman's repressive and regressive roles in society. She is scorched but not burnt and thus she neither turns insane like Jean Rhys's protagonist in *Wide Sargasso Sea* nor opts for self-annihilation like Kate Chopin's heroine in *The Awakening.* The walling of one avenue inevitably leads to a new one. In fact, every object, concrete or otherwise, generates a new discourse, a conscious ordering of things, a coherency that acts as a defence mechanism against the chaos of thoughts which in itself is a fragmenting and disrupting agency. Offred's speech about the real value of woman and how she is valued by those about her, is too powerful to be buried. This is the reason, why some two centuries later, Offred's voice is exhumed. Atwood the feminist, has triumphed in restoring the gift of speech to the defeated, debased and oppressed woman. The myth of the muted woman implicit in Alice Walker's *Meridian* has been inverted and Atwood's Offred, a "talking woman," has "the cause and will and strength and means" to articulate silence.

NOTES

1. Margaret Atwood, *Second Words: Selected Critical Prose* (Toronto: Anansi, 1982), pp. 145 and 397.
2. Elaine Showalter, ed., *The New Feminist Criticism* (New York: Pantheon, 1985), p. 255.
3. (Toronto: McClelland and Stewart, 1985), p. 255.
4. Margaret Atwood, *Survival: A Thematic Guide to Canadian Literature* (Toronto: Anansi, 1972), p. 13.
5. Mark Evans "Versions of History: *The Handmaid's Tale* and Dedicatees," *Margaret Atwood: Writing and Subjectivity,* ed. Colin Nicholson (Edinburgh: St. Martin's Press, 1994), p. 180.
6. Margaret Atwood, "Interview, Author Margaret Atwood on *The Handmaid's Tale," WAMU*, 88, 5FM, 5 March 1986.
7. "Margaret Atwood, Interview," *Quill and Quire,* 51, No. 9 (Sept. 1985), p. 66.
8. (Urbana: University of Illinois Press, 1980), p. 60.
9. *Ibid.*, p. 29.
10. Sherrill Grace, "Gender as Genre: Atwood's Autobiographical 'I,'" in Colin Nicholson, p. 196.
11. W.J. Keith, "Apocalyptic Imagination: Notes on Atwood's *The Handmaid's Tale* and Findley's *Not Wanted on the Voyage," Essays on Canadian Writings,* No. 35, Winter 1987, p. 124.
12. Mary Pinard, "A Cautionary Tale," *New Directions for Women,* Vol. 15, No. 3, May-June 1986, p. 15.
13. Alice Walker, *The Color Purple* (NY: Washington Square Press, 1982).

Language as "Subversive-Weapon" in Margaret Atwood's *The Handmaid's Tale*

M. PRABHAKAR

The Handmaid's Tale[1] is Margaret Atwood's international award-winning best seller. It is a critique of female brutalization articulated in *Bodily Harm*. This paper seeks to discuss Atwood's *The Handmaid's Tale* from the point of view of feminist consciousness. *The Handmaid's Tale* is a cautionary and poignant tale that dramatizes a futuristic, bleak, totalitarian society where women are denied the basic rights. The novel is a kind of anti-utopia of the not-too-distant future as reflected through the voice of Offred, a Handmaid, one of the victims in the theocracy.

Offred, the protagonist in *The Handmaid's Tale* escapes from the Republic of Gilead to the Underground Female road to tell her tale of victimization. Freedom of speech is a capital offence in Gilead. She uses "language" as a means of communication to unlock her inner feelings and bitter experiences as well as a "subversive-weapon" to tell her tale. Her tale addresses itself to the marginalization of women. She tells her tale with a sense of commitment to expose how dignity and autonomy of women are negated by anarchic and repressive societies like the Republc of Gilead. She also suggests the ways and means to surmount the barriers to woman's individuality and autonomy.

The manuscript of *The Handmaid's Tale* is a reconstruction from voice recordings of Offred on cassette tapes. Offred uses language to demolish absolute authority of the Republic of Gilead. She rebels against male hegemony on the one hand and cruelty of the state on the other.

II

To comprehend the tale of Offred, a Handmaid, it is important to evaluate the background that has led to the establishment of the class of handmaids in Gilead. The Republic of Gilead is governed by a Fundamentalist Christian theocracy. The so-called church-state regime, Gilead legitimizes and enforces the class of Handmaids out of the dire necessity to overcome a fertility crisis among the ruling elite. Duc to AIDS, Syphilis and environmental toxics, many of them are sterile, their wives barren and the children mostly wretched mutants called "unbabies." Thus, the birthrate, which is dangerously low among the ruling elite has led to establish the class of Handmaids, whose "domestic" duties form a degraded, obscene version of the "flurry of sexual activity."

Bible is used by the regime as authority for their laws. The polygamy of the Old Testament provides them with the sanction of Handmaids. They regard themselves as latter-day Jacobs and use their Handmaids in a similar way in this new Gilead. In this way the Republic of Gilead justifies its "sexist policies with the socio-biological theory of natural pologamy and legitimizes its racist and sexist policies as having biblical precedent."[2]

III

Offred, the narrator of *The Handmaid's Tale*, is one of the several "Handmaids" who, because of their "viable ovaries" (135) are to be recruited for "breeding purposes" of the "Commanders of the Faith" who are childless as a result of their wives' infertility. The Republic of Gilead is openly misogynistic, in both its theory and practice. The state reduces the Handmaids to the slavery status of being mere "breeders." As Offred says: "We are two-legged wombs, that's all: sacred vessels, ambulatory chalices." (128) If the Handmaid becomes pregnant, the child she bears will be regarded as that of the Commander and his wife. After the delivery the Handmaid has to surrender the child to her mistress. So the Handmaid must act as surrogate mother and bear a child for the aging Commander with the collusion of his barren wife by a literal enactment of the device invented by Rachel in the Bible. In this way the Handmaid is desexed and dehumanized.

The Handmaid is proclaimed an Unwoman if she does not succeed by the end of her third two-year posting. The dire alternative for her is the punishment of banishing to the Colonies, where women clean up radioactive waste as slave labourers. Thus, the dictates of state policy in Gilead relegate sex to a saleable commodity exchanged for mere minimal survival. In contrast male sterility in Gilead is unthinkable. As Offred says, "There are only women who are fruitful and women who are barren, that's the law." (57) So, women are judged by double standards of morality in respect of infertility.

Moreover, the state cancels the original names of the Handmaids in order to erase their former identity and labels them according to the names of their Commanders. It is metaphoric of the silencing of women that has given them names by the state. Hence "Offred" the narrator's relational naming is not a name but a tag that she wears to signify that she is the Handmaid "of Fred." As Offred says: "My name isn't Offred, I have another name, which nobody uses now because it's forbidden . . . name is like your telephone number, useful only to others." (79-80) Similarly other Handmaids' names are Ofglen, Ofwayne, Ofwarren. They are doomed to wear the scarlet robes signifying their adultery.

In addition to the Handmaids, the Republic of Gilead offers its own state-sponsored brand of sex prostitutes called the Jezebels whose sole function is to entertain foreign delegations. The Aunts, the policewomen of Gilead, who are clad in paramilitary Khaki, train the Handmaids. Thus women are completely controlled by men and are arranged in a hierarchy of value in Gilead. Therefore, Offred's *The Handmaid's Tale* posits a "future culture in which such feminist dreams have been replaced by fundamentalist patriarchy that divides women into rigid categories based on function."[3]

IV

Offred, the Handmaid, in her "reduced circumstances" (99) obeys "ritualized subjugation" to the ruling elite because she knows what the statement "Give me children, or else . . . die" (Genesis) means. She is compelled to discharge her duties as a Handmaid knowing fully well the consequences. Under the pressure of terrifying alternatives, Offred feels: "I resign my body freely, to the uses of others. They can do what they like with me. I am abject." (268) Offred is forced into pregnancy tests every month. The doctor who examines Offred and other Handmaids periodically for signs of pregnancy never even sees their faces. The Commanders who attempt to impregnate them once a month, are indifferent to their appearances. As appearance is unimportant for them, the Handmaids are not given face cream. Their bath is regulated by others. Their eating of food is not chosen by them. They are fed only with what the authorities regard as healthy food. For minor offences like reading, their arms and legs which are seen as inessential for reproduction, are ruthlessly chopped off.

As part of their "re-education" in submission, Offred and other Handmaids are made to watch pornography films from the seventies and eighties in which women appear in various attitudes of submission, brutalization, and grotesque mutilation. To keep obedient to the regime, the Handmaids are ordered to listen and utter the prayers which Soul Scroll machines say while printing them. The Handmaids are also taught by the "Aunts," the thought-police of Gilead, to walk with their heads bent down low. So silence and powerlessness go together in the lives of Offred and other Handmaids.

Their predicament lucidly illustrates Simone de Beauvoir's assertion in *The Second Sex* about man's marginalization of women. This view corroborates Michel Foucault's observation about the "power-sex"[4] correlative. According to this observation, the regime assigns roles to Handmaids, and decrees after social, religious, and cosmic concepts convenient to the interests and desires of the ruling elite. Consequently, Offred, the narrator-protagonist becomes the victim of a prohibition ordinance of sex in the Republic of Gilead. Offred feels the indignity and terror of living under a futuristic regime contrólled by Christian fundamentalists. She is aware of her present reality which is oppressive denying her individuality, nurturance and autonomy. Her life turns into a painfully prolonged prison term.

V

According to Offred, language in the Republic of Gilead is officially forbidden because the ruling class recognizes the power of words as weapons that can free the people from bondage. In Gilead only the ruling class has access to books. As part of the training, the Handmaids are required to recite the Biblical injunctions which are distorted to reinforce their submissiveness. Biblical and Marxist teachings are blended and distorted in the effort to brainwash the Handmaids: "*From each*, says the slogan, *according to her ability;* to each *according to his needs*. We recited that, three times, after dessert. It was from the Bible, or so they said St. Paul again, in Acts." (111) Offred's ironic comment, "or so they said" casts doubt on the authority of the statement, and forces us to note also the use of the pronouns "her" and "his" as yet another evidence of the oppression of women in Gilead. So Offred questions the authority of patriarchal language which comes from the reservoir of male discourse. Women in Gilead are denied books, paper, pens and even scrabble is a clandestine activity. The shops are identified by pictures rather than by names: "they decided that even the names of shops were too much temptation for us." (24) Thus, words are themselves forbidden in a society governed by The Word.

Offred attacks Biblical language, the language of patriarchy more subtly. She refers to the Bible as an "incendiary device" (82) because, like other weapons, it is available only to the ruling-class men in Gilead. Offred attempts her own version of the Lord's Prayer, but finally concludes, "I feel as if I'm talking to a wall." (183) She experiences the hollowness of the concepts of home and family in Gilead by word associations. She thinks: "The Commander is the head of the household. The house is what he holds. To have and to hold, till death do us part. The hold of a ship. Hollow." (77) She regards the evening Bible-readings as her bedtime stories.

VI

Offred begins to break the slavery syndrome by transgressing the uniforms of Gilead. She steals into her Commander's study to play illicit games of scrabble and discovers that there can be freedom even within the prison house of language. She is able to ask the Commander questions, to criticize and even to condescend to him. She gives him an insight into the real living conditions and situation of Handmaids. Offred imagines stabbing the Commander when he asks her to kiss him. She says: "I think about the blood coming out of him, hot as soup, sexual, over my hand." (131) She realizes the power of "pen." As she says: "The pen between my fingers is sensuous, alive almost, I can feel its power, the power of the words it contains. . . . Just holding it is envy. I envy the Commander his pen. It's one more thing I would like to steal." (174)

Offred, who witnesses the bloody "Salvagings," the ritual

slaughter and dismemberment of women, begins to feel shock, outrage, nausea and considers them as barbarous. She is alert and seems to be put in jeopardy. She feels her stay as if it were a jail sentence and she should like to scratch marks on the wall. She is filled with lassitude in Gilead. She would like to repent, abdicate, renounce and sacrifice her life in Gilead. She feels her body no longer suited for pleasure. She does not wish to be a doll hung up on the wall. She occupies herself with nostalgic memories of her husband and daughter, and strongly desires to escape from her present claustrophobic environment. She is not even free to die in Gilead. Ultimately, Offred decides to end up by hanging: "I could noose the bedsheet round my neck, hook myself up in the closet, throw my weight forward, choke myself off," (274) but she considers suicide an idle thing, a timid action. Offred has much patience and disbelief for rumours: "I become the earth I set my ear against, for rumours of the future." (69) The cushion on which the word "Faith" (274) is embroidered is an image that reveals Offred's profound faith in her life as a woman. Although she lives in the man's tyrannical world in Gilead, she feels a sense of pride for having been born a woman. As Offred says: "Oh God, king of the universe, thank you for not creating me a man." (182)

Offred recalls her visceral connections to the husband and daughter from whom she has been so abruptly separated. She mourns a holistic love for them:

> Nobody dies from lack of sex. It's lack of love we die from. There's nobody here I can love, all the people I could love are dead or elsewhere . . . where they are or what their names are now? They might as well be nowhere, as I am for them. I too am a missing person. From time to time I can see their faces, against the dark, flickering like the images of saints. . . . I can conjure them. (97)

In this way, Offred endorses a genuine and holistic love for her husband and daughter. She hopes she will receive a message that keeps her alive.

Offred's gradual development of feminist consciousness toward initiating risky but assertive schemes, breaks completely the slavery syndrome. As Offred says: "I'm tired of this melodrama, I'm tired of keeping silent." (275) It is through Nick, the Commander's chauffeur, Offred associates with underground network which shifts her from "being a helpless victim to being a sly, subversive survivor."[5] Ultimately Offred is rescued by Nick, the Private Eye and the Underground May day resistance group who have come in the "black van." Nick calls her by her real name and says: "It's May day. Go with them." (275)

VII

Offred's *The Handmaid's Tale* conducts us on a miniature tour of the Republic of Gilead. Because language in Gilead is officially denied, Offred, the Handmaid escapes along with the Underground May day resistance group to the Underground Female road to tell her tale. She tells most of her tale in the present tense, giving it the immediacy of direct experience. Offred's voice on cassette tapes serves as a record of an emergence from silence.

Offred is initially silenced by Gileadean culture, but she eventually works her way to freedom through language. The very thing that is denied Offred—the freedom to speak up, speak out, be heard—becomes the medium through which she defines herself. Offred realizes the centrality of language to the process of self-realization and the struggle for equality. Language—the ability to speak, to tell one's own story—is at the heart of Offred. So language is initially an intimidating silence for Offred but ultimately she could convert it into a liberating phenomenon. Language enables Offred to survive in Gilead and to raise her voice against the sexual oppression of the patriarchal society.

Therefore, Offred uses "language" as a "subversive-weapon" in her tale with a sense of commitment to demolish the totalitarian society in the so-called church state regime, Gilead. She condemns Gilead for "its intolerant, prescriptive set of values that projects a tunnel vision on reality and eliminates human volition."[6] She rejects male misogynous mentality of the totalitarian society. In short, she raises her voice against the marginalization of women in anarchic or repressive societies.

Offred's *The Handmaid's Tale* is a challenge to traditional values. It is also a recognition that the structures that cause and perpetuate women's oppression are arbitrary. Therefore, any kind of oppression is subject to change. In this way Offred tells us in her cautionary tale something we need to know about the human capacity for survival which is a canonization of feminism.

NOTES

1. Margaret Atwood, *The Handmaid's Tale* (Toronto: McClellend and Stewart-Bantam, 1986).
2. Coomi S. Vevaina, "Wastelanders in This New Gilead: An Analysis of Margaret Atwood's *The Handmaid's Tale*," *Ambivalence: Studies in Canadian Literature,* ed. Om. P. Juneja and Chandra Mohan (New Delhi: Allied, 1990), p. 224.
3. Nancy A. Walker, *Feminist Alternatives: Irony and Fantasy in the Contemporary Novel by Women* (Jackson: Univ. Press of Mississippi, 1990), p. 69.
4. Michel Foucault, *The History of Sexuality: An Introduction,* trans. Robert Hurley (1978; rpt. New York: Vintage, 1980), Vol. I, p. 84.
5. Amin Malak, "Margaret Atwood's *The Handmaid's Tale* and the Dystopian Tradition," *Canadian Literature,* No. 112, (Spring 1987), p. 13.
6. *Ibid.*

Cat's Eye: Margaret Atwood's Portrait of the Artist as a Woman and a Survivor

URBASHI BARAT

Cat's Eye, Margaret Atwood's latest novel, is a Bildungsroman that in its exploration of what she believes is the central concern of both women's writing and Canadian literature—survival—reiterates the importance of the universal quest for self-realization and self-expression. In early Bildungsromans written by women, the female protagonist discovered herself and her place only in marriage and submission to patriarchal norms, and thus grew "down" rather than "up," as Annis Pratt puts it[1]; it is only in the twentieth century that a feminine counterpart to the male version of "the epic theme of the individual's growth into life and love" has begun to emerge, as women project into their fiction their belief that "the experience of a young girl may stand as a paradigm for that of the whole human race every bit as much as the boy's can."[2]

The choice of the Bildungsroman form to embody the quest for identity and autonomy is of course an obvious one for any writer, especially for one so committed to the fundamental feminist issue of the victimization and marginalization endemic in a society dominated by struggles for power. Perhaps Atwood's proximity as a student at Harvard to the noted Victorianist and fellow-Canadian, Jerome H. Buckley, may also have had something to do with her proclivity for the form; Buckley is after all the author of the definitive work on the modern Bildungsroman, *Season of Youth.* Atwood's Bildungsromans, moreover, identify the quest for selfhood with the artist's for artistic integrity, and thus belong also to that subdivision of the Bildungsroman tradition, the Künstlerroman, which deals with the development of the artist and which has been popular in Western fiction ever since Goethe's *Wilhelm Meister.* Both her Bildungsromans follow the characteristic

Künstlerroman pattern of the sensitive young protagonist struggling against an unsympathetic environment in her bid to fulfil her destiny as a creative artist and discover her personhood, and realizing that they are ultimately identical goals.

Atwood's first Künstlerroman, *Lady Oracle*, analyzes the relationship of popular women's fiction to the actual lives of women through the quest of the narrator-protagonist, Joan Foster, a writer of Gothic romances. As the novelist told Joyce Carol Oates shortly after *Lady Oracle* was published, "The hypothesis of the book, insofar as there is one, is: what happens to someone who lives in the 'real' world but does it as though this 'other' world is the real one?"[3] This question regarding the connection between life and art is one of the fundamental themes of the Künstlerroman, one which *Cat's Eye*, too, explores in its examination of the growth and development of the woman-as-artist/artist-as-woman in a society where both these roles are marginalized. The conflict between the person, the artist and the social environment is after all particularly acute for the woman, for whom the quest for selfhood itself is problematic: the female protagonist of the Künstlerroman has almost invariably had to choose between her artistic instincts and patriarchal norms of femininity, and in communicating her confrontation with these usually opposing forces she has also revealed the relationship between the artist and society.

Thus, as long ago as 1807, Corinne in Madame de Stael's *Corinne* was, like the archetypal Künstlerroman protagonist, a highly sensitive person whose very sensitivity alienated her from a philistine society, and whose realization of her artistic integrity was achieved with her discovery that true art is generated only through this same heightened awareness and responsiveness to experience: but she was also a woman, and had to agonize, further, over the great divide between the claims of her selfhood and her creativity on the one hand and the expectations of society from women on the other. Similarly, George Sand's *Consuelo* (1844) explores the characteristic Künstlerroman themes of the conflict between time and timelessness and the suffering through which alone art is born; but it also underlines the gulf between conventional views about women and the quest for freedom that she must somehow bridge. The woman in the twentieth-century Künstlerroman continues to face the same situation. Esther in Sylvia Plath's *The Bell Jar* soon realizes that her social role as a woman will inevitably destroy both her creativity and her selfhood: "So I began to think that maybe it was true that when you were married and had children it was like being brainwashed, and afterward you went about numb as a slave in some private, totalitarian state."[4]

The experience of the artist-narrator of *Cat's Eye*[5] is not very different. Elaine Risley tries constantly to achieve androgyny and social approval, but there is a continual struggle between her awareness of her selfhood and her need to conform to societal expectations. Like her predecessor, Joan Foster of *Lady Oracle,* she becomes a willing accomplice in her own victimization, and her passivity—a quality important, paradoxically, to the artist, who must first suffer in order to create—is also a part of her acceptance of patriarchal attitudes to gender roles. Hence her participation in the power games of her childhood, in which she is almost invariably victim but against which she dare not complain because she feels that "it would be the greatest, the irreparable sin [note the religious terminology]. If I tell I will be cast outside for ever," and because she believes that acquiescence is necessary to "belonging": "They are my friends, my girl friends, my best friends. I have never had any friends before and I'm terrified of losing them. I want to please." (126) This longing to be accepted by the dominant culture translates itself into her joining in someone else's victimization. Thus her concurrence in her art teacher's sexual exploitation of herself leads her to a betrayal of her femininity in her betrayal of Susie, Josef Hrbik's first mistress; her attempt to be "one of the boys," in popular parlance, prevents her from feeling any sense of solidarity with women artists, even when she joins a feminist group. Even with them she sees herself

> standing outside a closed door while decisions are being made, disapproving judgments are being pronounced, inside, about me. At the same time I want to please [note the repetition of this phrase].
>
> Sisterhood is a difficult concept for me, I tell myself, because I never had a sister. Brotherhood is not. (361)

Elaine tries to compromise all the time. When her first husband, a fellow painter whom she had married because he had offered her equality and comradeship, now resents her working at night—the only time she has to herself as mother and housewife—because it disturbs his sleep, she realizes that he would even prefer her to stop painting because "He thinks they [her paintings] are irrelevant. In his mind, what I paint is lumped in with the women who paint flowers. *Lumped* is the word." (362) Her frustration turns her into the archetypal 'mad wife' of women's fiction,[6] and she attempts suicide, like Plath's Esther, for, as Pratt describes the characteristic nineteenth-century female Bildungsroman protagonist,

> Every element of her desired world—freedom to come and go, allegiance to nature, meaningful work, exercise of the intellect, and use of her own erotic capabilities—inevitably clashes with patriarchal norms. Attempts to develop independence are met with limitation and immurement, training in menial and frustrating tasks, restrictions of the intellect (lest she perceive her status too clearly), and limitation of erotic activity.[7]

Since for Atwood "fiction is one of the few forms left through which we may examine our society not in its particular but in its typical aspects,"[8] her novels suggest that this betrayal of selfhood and of humanity is a part of patriarchal/imperialistic conditioning. Elaine's desire to please, to be accepted, is thus the mark of a larger dehumanization of a society which rejects anyone who does not belong to the dominant culture: a world which is threatening to self-destruct, through war, through environmental pollution, through any form of selfish exploitation that everyone is guilty of and that everyone will suffer from. That is why Elaine is both colluder and victim, and sees herself in Cordelia, her friend, tormentor and fellow-victim: "Because in some way we changed places, and I've forgotten when." (239) Hence, too, the images of death and dying, dirt, decay and desolation as the only physical realities of existence, and the continued references to wars: "Somehow the war never ended after all, it just broke up into pieces and got scattered, it gets in everywhere, you can't shut it out. Killing is endless now, it's an industry, there's money in it, and the good side and the bad side are pretty hard to tell apart." (330) If death is the inevitable end of life, it is human beings who have made the living world the centre of a poisoned existence, as Elaine's father and brother point out in a series of choric comments on relationships in the novel. Where the artist-narrator of *Surfacing* could turn to nature and the green world to transform herself, in *Cat's Eye* "eventually there's nothing that you can put into your mouth without tasting the death in it." (426)

Yet Elaine survives, and finds authenticity. The very fact that this is a middle-aged woman telling her story from childhood to the present—not, as in the conventional Bildungsroman/Künstlerroman, to the time the protagonist discovers where his or her selfhood lies (witness *David Copperfield, The Way of All Flesh, A Portrait of the Artist as a Young Man*, *Sons and Lovers, The Bell Jar)*—a story that includes, moreover, her daughters, is itself a promise and an indication of feminine and human survival. Elaine may be an established artist, but she resents being considered an institution, static, belonging to a past; she thinks of herself as constantly evolving, and thus conquering time. The aging artist's survival, her victory over time, is an assertion of continuity, of growth throughout life, from randomness to meaningfulness, from pain to serenity, from loss to recovery. Harry Levin has suggested that the typical plot of realistic fiction is one of "systematic disillusionment,"[9] in which maturity and self-knowledge come about only through loss of innocence. Yet a Bildungsroman is by definition a story of progress: the post-Freudian Bildungsroman, accordingly, when written by novelists no longer young themselves, frequently shows the protagonist emerging from the unhappiness and the problems of youth to the freedom of adulthood and the ability to overcome victimization through experience (as in, for example, Anne Tyler's *The Accidental Tourist,* Margaret Drabble's *The Realms of Gold,* or John Updike's later *Rabbit* books). As Saul Bellow sums it up in *Herzog,* "But for this higher education survival is necessary. You must outlive the pain."[10]

Elaine is in fact so successful an artist that a Retrospective of her paintings is organized in Toronto, once her home. This Retrospective engages her in another one of even greater significance to her development, a retrospection of her own life: for, as Atwood remarks elsewhere, "All cultures are to some extent retrospective: we see where we are and where we're going partly by where we've been."[11] The return to Toronto is thus an important stage in Elaine's journey towards selfhood, as it was for Joan Foster; it enables her to evaluate herself as a person and an artist, and to lay the ghosts of the past that would otherwise have continued to haunt her. Now her first journey to Vancouver is no longer merely an escape, as it might have seemed to her earlier; set in the right perspective, it appears as her route to serenity and equanimity.

The Retrospective arouses memories that help Elaine to "exist in two places" at the same time, for "You don't look back along time but down through it, like water. Sometimes this comes to the surface, sometimes that, sometimes nothing. Nothing goes away." (3) This is why she tells her story in, in Alice Walker's picturesque phrase, a "crazy quilt" fashion,[12] an archetypally feminine form of narration.[13] Her use of the present tense throughout the novel suggests the interpenetration of the past and the present indicated by this water-image. Water is, moreover, traditionally associated with femininity, birth and rebirth, and the image reinforces the idea of the immersion in life and the death-by-drowning motif which are such significant markers of survival in Victorian literature.[14]

Echoing as it does Leopold Bloom's metaphor of "the stream of life we trace. Because life is a stream,"[15] the water-image also helps to establish the link between Elaine's story and the twentieth-century *locus classicus* of the Künstlerroman, James Joyce's *A Portrait of the Artist*. As in the earlier novel, for one thing, the protagonist of *Cat's Eye* is the only character: everyone else is filtered through Elaine's consciousness and is important only because he or she arouses certain emotions within her and pushes her forward along her path of growth. Elaine's story is thus seen by the reader, too, as though through water, transparent but fluid, changing its implications and focus.

Water and its associations—whether religious, sensual or scatological—are significant in both Künstlerromans. Thus, for instance, in both *A Portrait* and *Cat's Eye* the youthful protagonist is forced into the water by bullying schoolmates; both emerge from the water with much difficulty, and fall ill thereafter; and the bullies apologize to them in much the same way and for the same reasons. This incident is a turning-point in both their lives. Stephen realizes the reality of his isolation and the fear and hypocrisy of a society that does not understand artistic genius, while Elaine learns to outgrow the pain and hurt, rejects for the first time her victimization, and opens out to an intensely emotional and religious experience that contrasts so strongly with the pettiness of the conventional piety of the Smeaths. Throughout her life thereafter Elaine turns Our Lady of Perpetual Help for succour; the God of Christian iconography is always male and cannot provide the emotional support she needs.

At each stage in her life, then Elaine finds emotional strength in water, while for Stephen water provides for both his dissatisfaction with conventional ideas about Virgin Mary and his epiphanic vision of a wading girl, seen as a sea-bird and a dove, but something that transcends her appearance and passes into his soul; and he realizes that he is destined to become a poet. Both reject conventional religion, but where Stephen learns to dissociate femininity from Virgin Mary, Elaine dissociates her from patriarchal notions of the godhead, and links her, instead, with the Earth Mother and the Mother Goddess, reasserting thereby the close interrelationship between femininity and creativity. The difference between Elaine's paintings and Jon's art represents more than the difference between masculine and feminine art; as Elaine points out in an interview, art is androgynous, universal and timeless. (94-95)

Indeed, by making Elaine a painter rather than the usual writer- protagonist of most Künstlerromans, Atwood takes an even harder look than in *Lady Oracle* at the position of women in a so-called post-feminist society, for women take to writing rather than to the other arts primarily because, as Virginia Woolf suggests in *The Death of the Moth*, writing materials are cheap, and writing itself less disruptive of conventional social requirements for women.[16] Elaine's otherwise unconventional parents see no future in art as a profession and would prefer her to be a biologist, a more conventionally 'serious' occupation. They agree to her studying art only because it leads to a university degree and a "safe" job. Her struggle towards achievement of identity as woman and as artist is obviously harder, more painful, because she is a painter. When she tries to conform to the accepted artistic attire of her fellow students, for example, it worries her mother and her mother's friends that she is "letting herself go": "*Letting yourself go* is an alarming notion; it is said of older women who become frowzy and fat, and of things that are sold cheap." (291) But letting go is the first step towards selfhood, as she realizes.

Atwood's shift in focus from writing to painting is in a sense also a reflection of the way in which the Künstlerroman genre itself has concentrated on writers and has only from the late nineteenth century onwards begun to use other kinds of artists. Perhaps the early preference for writers was because, as Beebe believes,[17] they had achieved social respectability at a time when the other arts were considered merely crafts, Elaine is, however, very particular about being called "painter" rather than "artist," (93) a pretentious term that overlooks the labour and the pain of creativity—an important statement about the nature of art that the novel as a Künstlerroman makes. Another interesting statement is her belief that words are imprecise, ambiguous, especially when compared to the immediacy and exactitude of the graphic arts even in their surrealistic manifestations. After having trained as a biologist, with a scientist father who demands accuracy, Elaine is a careful and accomplished draughtsperson, and is very particular about her effects. That she communicates her meaning at once is evident from the response her art receives from the general public. The surrealistic quality of Elaine's imagination, incidentally, makes her the archetypal female protagonist and her creator a typical woman novelist.[18]

Bearing in mind the autobiographical background behind most Künstlerromans, moreover, it may be recalled that Atwood herself draws and paints, and that many of the paintings described in the novel resemble the artistic responses her own literary work has evoked.[19] Elaine's experience of male reactions to her paintings often echo Atwood's own. In "Paradoxes and Dilemmas, the Woman as Writer," Atwood points out what Elaine too discovers for herself, how only too often women's artistic accomplishments are reviewed only by women and only as women's work rather than for its own intrinsic merit, and is often dismissed as being "feminine" in style and sensibility. In "The Lady Painter Syndrome" that society suffers from, "good equals male, bad equals female," and "there is no critical vocabulary for expressing the concept 'good/female.'" A conversation between Elaine and a few male art-students (293) is a transcript of one the novelist herself had with a male painter: "'When she's good,' he said, 'we call her a painter: when she's bad, we call her a lady painter.'"[20] And Elaine's discomfort with labels echoes Atwood's own; commitment to selfhood inevitably implies the rejection of any kind of stereotyping. Nevertheless, Elaine Risley is not Margaret Atwood but a fully realized fictional character, presented with empathy and detachment, embodying through the confessional mode of first-person narration the paradoxical duality of the artist and her participation in common humanity, thereby fulfilling the novelist's belief that her female characters should be able to have "emotions all human beings have . . . without having [them] pronounced as a monster, a slur or a bad example."[21]

There is, accordingly, considerable irony in the way Atwood uses the Bildungsroman/Künstlerroman conventions. The traditional Bildungsroman/Künstlerroman, for instance, posits the stability and security of a childhood in a small provincial town against the dangers and challenges of a precarious adolescence and the periis and uncertainties of a journey to the sophistication and loss of innocence of the destination of identity. Following this model, Elaine's childhood is a happy one until they come to Toronto; the conventional assurance of a physically stable childhood is here replaced, however, by emotional and moral stability in a gipsy existence, as the Risleys move from forest to forest, from tent and motel to camp and cabin, wintering in remote northern towns, never putting down roots anywhere, in their search for the truths of nature. Her unusual childhood and her unconventional family, to whom, unlike the typical Künstlerroman protagonist, she always remains deeply attached, help to develop her imagination and to make her aware of the wonder and the vitality of natural things and bodily functions that her new bourgeois environment with its copy facade of moral superiority regards as dirty or disgusting even while it slyly instils an unhealthy prurience in its members. Elaine's realization of the harsh reality of this world, its cruelty and destructiveness, its politics of power, leads to a loss of innocence and to her dreams of isolation, death and destruction. Consequently, illness is a relief and a source of comfort here. (146) It gives her the time to ponder over how women's lives, even as adults, are straitjacketed into formulas from which there is no escape: "no matter how hard you scrub, whatever you do, there will always be some other stain or spot on your face or stupid act, somebody frowning." (148) Blind obedience to patriarchal demands makes people move "like bright animated dolls, their mouths opening and closing but no real words coming out": even the young are turned into "puppets," with faces "like moldy eggs." (165) With her realization that even her parents cannot help her, that she has to assert herself, also comes the belief, as she cuts up pictures from popular women's magazines and rearranges the parts in new designs, that the artist has the power and the ability to arrange her own life. Then occurs the incident at the creek and the vision of Virgin Mary, and her discovery of her ability to reject the victim's role as well as the victimizer's. She can resist them because "I can see right into them." (206) She has taken her first step towards identity and survival.

At first Elaine achieves an equanimity by shutting out feeling: "I am happy as a clam: hard-shelled, firmly closed." (213) She begins to use her "mean mouth," (247) the traditional feminine response to attack. But as she participates in the conventional sexual games of adolescence, she finds—unlike Stephen Dedalus, who must learn to transcend his sexual appetite before he finds his artistic vocation—that her interest in boys is not sexual but physical, the interest of the artist for whom "The body is pure energy, solidified light," (254) and animal bodies "breath- taking" (262) in their wonders. In another ironic contrast to Stephen's visionary epiphany, her epiphanic moment is "like a sudden epileptic fit" (270) and occurs in the middle of a school Botany examination, as she decides that she is not going to be a biologist but a painter. Again, though Elaine does leave home in order to fulfil her destiny, she does not do so because her bourgeois family does not understand her but because she wishes to be easily available to Josef Hbrbik, her seducer and art-teacher; in fact, she does not even leave town at all at this stage.

Josef is a refugee from the War, and therefore a victim; but as a man he is very much a part of the patriarchal power structure and uses her as much as he uses Susie, as Elaine soon realizes. Together with her new knowledge about the ambiguity of such terms as "iron lung," "empire bloomers" and "pressure cooker"—titles she gives her paintings and later to the different sections of her narrative—comes her awareness of the meaning of "fallen women":

> Fallen women were women who had fallen onto men and hurt themselves. There was some suggestion of downward motion, against one's will and not with the will of anyone else. Fallen women were not pulled-down women or pushed women, merely fallen. Of course there was Eve and the Fall; but there was nothing about falling in that story, which was only about eating, like most children's stories. (282)

Art thus expands Elaine's heart and understanding and shows her how to sublimate her suffering. She is soon able to reject Josef and her own complicity in her (and Susie's) suffering, and take another step towards self-recognition and autonomy by entering into what she imagines is an equal and loving relationship with a fellow-painter. With marriage and childbirth, however, her hopes turn sour. Participation in a feminist group does not give her the kind of support she needs either. Androgyny, she realizes, is what she is looking for. When Jon, her husband, dismisses her frustrations as being inevitable 'because she's a woman' she immediately refuses to accept gender stereotyping:

> Once it was a shaming thing to say, and crushing to have it said about you, by a man. It implied oddness, deformity, sexual malfunctions.
>
> I go to the living room doorway. "I'm not mad because I'm a woman," I say. "I'm mad because you're an asshole." (363)

The break with Jon is inevitable, and messy, but it takes her to her version of the Bildungsroman/Künstlerroman journey, away from home, certainly, but from a husband, not parents, and to another metropolis. In Vancouver her life stabilizes, she establishes herself, and, having "exhausted the notion that the answer to a man is another man," finds someone "uncomplicated and easily pleased," (210) and remarried: Atwood's translation of the archetypal "double-marriage" plot of the feminine Bildungsroman.[22] Elaine thus survives, as artist, as woman, as individual, though she may not have ended her quest completely. Indeed, this is the mark of her survival, that her quest continues, though she may have left her misery behind her: her quest and her zest for living life.

The title of the novel, so different from the traditional Bildungsroman/Künstlerroman use of the protagonist's name, is thus an extended metaphor for the survival that the genre celebrates. For cat's eyes glow in the dark, as Elaine's art does for her: cat's eye is also, moreover, the term for reflectors fixed on road surfaces that illuminate the way at night; and it is the name as well for the chatoyant mineral that is frequently used as a gemstone, and thus the image of art and of the precious identity that she has discovered. Elaine herself refers to a special kind of marble (used by boys, significantly, in play) when she talks of a cat's eye or paints it onto her canvases: from childhood this little ball—in a sense a symbol of her world—has been a source of security and selfhood for her, its beauty a sign of her artistic quest, its blue iridescence linking it with the traditional blue attire of the Madonna to whom she has always turned for succour. As Elaine flies back to Vancouver at the end of the Retrospective, therefore, victorious over the new Toronto and her memories of the past, sure of her survival in a world that will always be hostile, she looks out of the plane window and sees the stars in the night sky glowing like the cat's eye,

> Shining out of the midst of nothing.
>
> It's old light, and there's not much of it. But it's enough to see by. (446)

—a summing up of the meaning of Atwood's portrait of the artist as a woman and a survivor.

NOTES

1. Annis Pratt, *Archetypal Patterns in Women's Fiction* (Bloomington: Indiana Univ. Press, 1981), p. 14.
2. Rosalind Miles, *The Female Form: Women Writers and the Conquest of the Novel* (London: Routledge and Kegan Paul, 1990), pp. 102-3.
3. Joyce Carol Oates, comp., *First Person Singular: Writers on their Craft* (Princeton: Ontario Review Press, 1993), p. 85.
4. Sylvia Plath, *The Bell Jar* (NY: Harper and Row, 1971), p. 94.
5. Margaret Atwood, *Cat's Eye* (NY: Doubleday, 1988).
6. Pratt, p. 45.
7. *Ibid.*, p. 29.
8. Margaret Atwood, *Second Words: Selected Critical Prose* (Toronto: Anansi, 1982), p. 346.
9. Harry Levin, *Gates of Horn* (NY: Oxford Univ. Press, 1966), p. 48.
10. Saul Bellow, *Herzog* (NY: Viking, 1964), p. 319.
11. Introduction to *The New Oxford Book of Canadian Verse*, qtd. in M.F. Salat, *The Canadian Novel: A Search for Identity* (Delhi: B.R., 1993), p. 76.
12. Claudia Tate, ed., *Black Women Writers at Work* (NY: Continuum, 1983), p. 176.
13. Pratt, p. 11.
14. Jerome H. Buckley, *The Victorian Temper* (Cambridge: Harvard Univ. Press, 1951), pp. 97-108.

15. James Joyce, *Ulysses* (NY: Modern Library, 1934), p. 151.
16. Quoted in Miles, p. 1.
17. Maurice Beebe, *Ivory Towers and Sacred Founts: The Artist as Hero in Fiction from Goethe to Joyce* (NY: NY Univ. Press, 1964), p. 26.
18. Pratt, p. 11.
19. Oates, pp. 90-92.
20. Margaret Atwood, "Paradoxes and Dilemmas, the Woman as Writer," *Feminist Literary Theory: A Reader*, ed. Mary Eagleton (Oxford: Basil Blackwell, 1988), pp. 74-77.
21. *Second Words*, p. 227.
22. Pratt, p. 44.

Rudy Wiebe's *The Blue Mountains of China*: An Artistic Expression of a Bi/Multi-Cultured Experience

P.A. ABRAHAM

Born of Russian Mennonite parents on the Canadian prairie, Rudy Wiebe is the right spokesman to express the anguish, endurance, despair, faith and hope of a cultural minority in Canada. Though the experiences narrated in Wiebe's novel *The Blue Mountains of China* are of a particular group of people settled in an alien land, they transcend all barriers of nationality and culture. The book focuses on themes or experiences which are universal rather than regional or local.

Superficially the book looks like a collection of short stories. Each chapter projects an episode in the struggle of a number of Mennonite families to run away from the religious persecution and their yearning to find a new life. Each chapter is a self-contained unit. While the chapters can be read as a unit knit together, however loosely, they can also be separated from each other without loss of effect. In an interview with Robert Krotetche, Wiebe says:

> but the fact of the matter is that *Blue Mountains* . . . did not begin as a novel. It began as individual stories that I didn't at first think had any necessary connection . . . I simply got ideas for stories which . . . I had no sense were going to be of any particular pattern put together. I thought of a cycle, may be series of stories about the Mennonites wherever they might be . . . As a matter of fact many of the stories were published separately.[1]

One is reminded of the American writers of the twenties Sherwood Anderson, Hemingway and Faulkner who have adopted the same pattern in their books *Winesburg, Ohio, In Our Time* and *Go Down*

Moses respectively. These books are also a cycle of stories dealing with the themes of alienation, anguish, endurance and hope. However, Anderson, Hemingway and Faulkner have emphasized the need for hope, love and endurance indirectly through their absence.

To come back to Wiebe's *Blue Mountains*, his characters are exiled in the wilderness. They are in search of the 'promised Land of Moses' that will give them peace and religious tolerance. The quest extends over many decades and many places. Wiebe takes us from one generation to another, backwards and forwards in time between the old and the new worlds.

Wiebe's knowledge of the Mennonite community has enabled him not only to juxtapose events occurring at different times to different people in different parts of the world but also to develop the themes, to incorporate into them a large number of characters and finally to weave all these together into one unified whole. The changes in perspective are accompanied by dramatic shifts in narrative distance and style. The shifts between chapters make the reader increasingly aware of differences which lead to the question of identity in a multilingual situation and to understand the Mennonite ethnic culture in relation to the other cultures too.

The novel begins with the calm reminiscences of the aged Frieda Friesen narrating events from her childhood and adolescence on the prairie. It is Frieda who primarily acts as a yardstick for the rest of the Mennonite life depicted in the novel.

Wiebe places her story at strategic points, at irregular intervals, so that her presence is felt throughout. In fact, the multi-faceted narrative is unified in part by the recurrent reminiscences of Frieda. These memories act as a background material which helps the reader in juxtaposing the past of the Mennonites with that of the present.

Her agonizing journey to Paraguay has not shattered her equanimity. The undiminished faith of Frieda emerges immediately. She accepts her life in toto. She is convinced that "it all comes from God, strength, sickness, want and plenty."[2] This sentence occurs in all the chapters dealing with Frieda, as if to emphasize her faith. This belief has given her a detached outlook towards the events in her life, whether it be a sudden death of a worker at the beginning of the chapter or her betrothal in 1903. Facing a new culture has not changed her faith or conviction. She still adheres to the orthodox principles of her community.

While confronting a new culture, the Mennonites had to face

new tensions and conflicts—the tension between traditional faith and practice and the need for a change in the new world. There is also the tension between the need to preserve their identity and the need to assimilate with the culture of the new world. This is especially obvious in their use of language.

In the new world their own Low German language is almost on the verge of extinction. Yet there are echoes of Low German in their speech. For instance, Frieda Friesen talks about a visit to the "bone fixer" echoing the Low German "trach-moke" (one who makes right) rather than the English "Chiropractor." (43) Instead of referring to the threat of war she comments that it may "give war." (94) What is noteworthy here is that instead of using the Low German directly she translates it into English. Thus Frieda's narrative evokes the sound of two languages. Her world is divided. Magdalene Falk Redkop points out: "While this experience of being poised precariously on the frontier between two worlds is doubtless familiar to the many solitudes which constitute Canadian culture, it is particularly intense in Mennonite communities for theological and historical reasons."[3]

Frieda represents the anabaptist group of Mennonites who insist that the maintenance of a separate way of life requires a separate language. Some of these Mennonites left for Canada for Paraguay primarily in response to the threat of losing the language. Early Mennonite settlers in Canada were considered "Die stillen in Lande" (the silent ones in the land) not because they did not speak, but because they spoke a language which essentially isolated them from the larger culture by which they were surrounded. Rudy Wiebe himself speaks in this connection: "Russia had been vast, but Canada was not merely vast; it was impassively empty and lonely."[4]

In the second chapter of the novel, there is a sudden shift of focus from the simple and straight-forward narration of Frieda Friesen to the horrible and shattering world of Jakob Friesen. The location changes from Canada to Russia, from the expanse of prairie to the confinement of a dark cell. Violence replaces peace. The physical hardships of the Canadian Mennonites are juxtaposed with the terrible isolation and alienation of Jakob Frieda's first-person narrative to the complex third-person stream-of-consciousness of Jakob Friesen.

In the cell Jakob cannot see the brotherhood of Escha, the Russian servant. The two cultures of Escha and Jakob—Russian and

Low German—fail to recognize love and brotherhood which ultimately resulted in the killing of Escha and the self-destruction of Jakob. Similarly the chapter "Over the Red Line" also draws attention to arbitrary divisions. Like Jakob, Liesel Driedger is also tempted by a world of pleasure that lures her out of her own community. The ship is her other world or culture:

> She had never heard such happiness or imagined there could be so many people together laughing in the whole world. They did not even stop laughing. She could not understand what she thought perhaps Spanish or English or even French, but the German was as refined as somewhere she remembered her father and friends—just talked—Low German and German that would here sound like—like—she could think of nothing but the heavy felt boots some men still wore. (81)

Laughter and dancing dissolve the distinction between one culture and another one at least for the time being.

While Jakob's fall is the result of an assertion of identity, Liesel's is the result of a denial of identity. Both are proud characters, diminished by the shock of their immersion in a foreign culture, whether in a prison cell or in the ocean water.

The book also captures a crisis of identity for the Mennonites when the pattern of recurrent flight and separation comes into conflict with a modern technological society i.e. Canada. Their life pattern and style of living has been changed. They have become modern, attended schools and universities and learned English: "Our people came here with nothing and built up this land and worked through recognition, through two wars and we made it, we've got responsible men everywhere now, teachers, doctors, professors, engineers, civil servants, members of parliament, even provincial cabinet ministers." (148)

When Frieda reaches Winnipeg from Paraguay to see her daughter after many years, she found "Mary had a nice house, big and new with everything electric . . . and her Man worked eight hours a day." (148-49) The material progress has not affected their faith and prayer. They prayed and sang and read from the Bible. But as Frieda notices, "it was all English and not Mennonite, but the most people there came from US and to be it sometimes looked—they were stretching themselves around for what they weren't." (148-49)

It is very difficult to cut away entirely from the roots even if one is settled in a foreign land. The roots of the Mennonites are still in their native land. They have given Russian names to the villages where they have settled. In the new world also they longed for togetherness and fellowship. When she returns to Paraguay, Frieda Fricscn says: "And blessed be God, for our first Christmas in Schoenbach, our home in the Chaeo, we were all together." (92)

In fact among Mennonites, the discovery of family relationship is itself a kind of joke. It is said that whenever two Mennonites are gathered together they will inevitably discover that their mother's father's aunt is their uncle's cousin. This fascination with genealogy is due to their traditional emphasis on family relation and togetherness. Moreover the religious persecution in Russia which fragmented many families and estranged individual members like Friesen, has created an urge in them to come together.

While depicting the Mennonite qualities of togetherness, pacifism, endurance, hope and faith, Wiebe also juxtaposes them with the human degradation. At the end of the fourth chapter Jakob Friesen IV is arrested by the Russian soldiers. Several years later he emerges in Siberia. Here he becomes a witness to the degradation of human life. A nameless fugitive allows his equally nameless dying wife to be sexually assaulted by the Russian soldiers in an abandoned monastery. The helplessness of the man and his yearning for survival are pathetically depicted. He hopes that they will allow them to escape. The fugitive says: "There is the possibility as God is good. . . . There is only this: if you want anything survive. There is nothing else." (113) By not naming the fugitive, perhaps, Wiebe wants to generalize the human predicament—Man's yearning for survival at any cost: "You must survive. To him it is the most necessary possibility." (114)

Wiebe is of the view that the very idea of Mennonite is so ethnic and culture-oriented. According to him blood and culture and not belief make the Mennonite. He is of the view that the Mennonites have been held together by ethnic and cultural trappings. He wants his community to come out of the narrow domestic walls, and practice the principles of Christianity for the development of the society as a whole. While having tremendous faith in the Christian doctrines, he also wants his people to change their attitudes and work together for world peace. These views are expressed indirectly in the last two chapters of the novel.

Samuel Reimer, in the penultimate chapter of the book faces the same dilemma as faced by Thom Wien in Wiebe's previous novel *Peace shall Destroy Many*: the realization of the gulf between Christian theory and practice. It was during the time of the Vietnam war that the call came to Samuel in his sleep: "I am the God of your father, the Lord your God. Go and proclaim peace in Vietnam." (158) His Christian name Samuel draws parallel to the Biblical Samuel (I Sam. Ch.3). But the efforts of Samuel Reimer to obey the sublime order were not successful. He was issued a passport but valid "not in Vietnam": "though Canada was a free country and wanted its citizens to travel where they pleased, but it had to also think of their safety." (175) He used all his resources to fulfill the divine call but without hope. He drove to Winnipeg and a news$paper agreed to intervene, but finally the editors said 'no' to such a story about a minority religious group. A TV station did interview him thoroughly, but they cut it to one and a half minute news capsule when they got a sensational news about a sex scandal. Even his own Mennonite community discouraged him from his mission. Thus both his own community and the land of his choice were equally responsible for preventing him from becoming a God's witness in Vietnam.

The novel has universality in one sense that the problem is not entirely directed to a particular community. It is pertaining to people of any religious faith, for religions have divided man from man, brother from brother, inciting mankind to violence against each other. In the final analysis, Samuel almost loses his faith in an organized religion which exists just in name. In his will he writes: "I would like to leave part of my estate to the Inter Mennonite Church Service Society, Peace Section, but I cannot because that would be hypocrisy." (179-80)

In the last chapter Wiebe draws together various narrative threads involving faith and unfaith, peace and violence, conservatism and new ideas. The appearance of Jakob Friesen after generations becomes an important point and it seems to promise a discovery of the eventual kinship.

The airport setting shows us that English, more and more is becoming the common language of the world. The air plane, cars and motorcycles are signs of a technological world. At first Liesel plays the role of a friendly Canadian hostess to old Jakob Friesen by offering to translate from the Russian into English. But the need disappears when they discover that they speak a common language. Then the emphasis shifts to their mutual need to translate past into present. It is Liesel who draws attention to the newspaper article on John Reimer and points both Friesen and the reader to the figure of the man carrying the cross. Here Wiebe once again suddenly shifts the focus to John Reimer who becomes the focal point of the chapter. The setting is also shifted to the Alberta highway. The title "on the way" indicated that the ending is explicitly open. Here Wiebe catches a cross-section of his characters who have earlier appeared in various chapters. The absence of Frieda Friesen in the final reunion of Mennonites is conspicuous. Her absence represents the failure to discover the complete relation of estranged worlds. However, the other Mennonites provide a fleeting moment of unity in the novel.

Like many others in the novel, John Reimer is also an offspring of the captive exile community of Moscow. John walks along the Trans-Canada highway, carrying a plain wooden cross. He says: "I began it as a kind of walk of repentance. But walking along in the ditch, people looking, stopping, talking it's become more than that, I guess, what I don't know." (194)

Reimer's action of carrying the cross may be an act of a literal and moving imitation of Christ carrying the cross. The cross-carrying scene may also reestablish once again Kierkegaard's dictum that every man is a Christ and that we are all crucified. But his remarks about himself as a tired dying human being is an example to show his limitation as a human being. Of course, John has not been elevated to the status of a Christ figure. Yet as W.J. Keith points out: "his idea has the same combination of sublime simplicity and practical difficulty that we find in Christ's teachings."[5]

Though Reimer claims that "none of this is typical of Mennonites," (184) there is something characteristically Mennonite about his literal interpretation of Christ's order "to take up your cross and follow me." Reimer is a self-proclaimed prophet. His call to "repent and believe" (216) echoes the Biblical John the Baptist.

As Reimer talks about Frieda's prayer, Jakot Friesen keeps repeating: "It helped her exactly nothing." (225) Ironically "nothing" is the word which elicits the closing affirmation of faith. Wiebe seems to be suggesting that we still understand nothing. However, this very awareness is a step towards progress. In the words of Reimer:

> "Understand" is not the word; you are right. You can never really understand about some one, anyone, even yourself. It is best to believe in them as human, feel that they are alive like you and need warmth and concern . . . or let them know that you now believe you believe nothing. (225)

At any rate, the novel is not all pessimistic. The book is "a drama of flight into hope." In Mark Twain's *The Adventures of Huckleburry Finn*, Huck says that all he wants is to go somewhere, all he wants is a change. However, a change of place is no final solution to the human problems. The blue mountains symbolic of the Mennonite and human quest are visible on the horizon, but the real object of the quest, in the words of Reimer "isn't anywhere on earth." The title of the chapter "On the Way" poses yet another question: Where are we going? Wiebe has left the reader "in the middle of nowhere" i.e. on the way. We do not know where we are going. However, the quest is on, the journey is on and the hope is there. The words 'hope' and 'possibility' occur in many chapters of the book. After all it is the 'hope' and 'possibility' that sustains every human being in the midst of agonies and frustrations of life.

It is to the Bible that Wiebe is most indebted for its pilgrim model, motif and language. Biblical allusions proliferate throughout the novel. Friesen's meeting with Joseph Heibert at the well (ch. 7) reminds of a similar meeting between Rachel and Jakob in the 29th chapter of Genesis. Similarly, as mentioned earlier, Samuel Reimer's Vietnam call resembles the Biblical Samuel's divine call in 1 Sam, ch. 3 of the Bible and John Reimer's call 'to repent and believe' echoes the Biblical John the Baptist. Many such examples can be quoted from the novel.

In the last chapter the challenge of new ideas and responses is specially linked with the relation of the New Testament to the old. The conversation between Reimer and old Jakob is an eloquent example: "In the mountain Moses said—'Go over the river, there's the land God has given you for ever' but Jesus said, 'I am going to make a place ready for you and then I'll come and get you. You wait.' Moses gave his people Manna to eat. When they were hungry and Jesus did that a little but then changed. Then he just said 'I'm bread enough for you. Remember me.'" (227) To this old Jakob who has already lost faith in an institutional religion says: "That's the big trouble with Jesus. He never gives you a thing to hold in your hand." (227) Reimer's reply is pertinent: "There are things, many things that you can't hold in your hand." (227) The whole chapter reads like Christ's Sermon on the Mount. The language of *Blue Mountains* is at once Biblical and epigrammatic. To quote an example: "To have too much is to want more. The desire for knowledge leads to pride and self deception. To long for change is to forget one's destiny." (100)

Wiebe has also used effective imagery in order to evoke a variety of feelings. The central image is of course the journey. In fact the journey is the controlling pattern of the book. It stresses process and not completion, activity and not action. Images like Kremlin wall, dark building, shut windows are frequently used in the chapters dealing with the persecution of the Mennonites to suggest isolation and confinement and they give a claustrophobic atmosphere to these chapters. Above all the image of the Blue Mountains pervades all over the chapters. All these images act as a link between the chapters and the author makes an artistic use of them to give unity to the book.

Blue Mountains is not merely a story of an ethnic group in Canada. The book is Wiebe's affirmation of his belief in the durability of the human spirit and his assertion that hope, faith and endurance are necessary for meaningful human relationships. He indirectly points out that all men share the common bond of humanity and that they must recognize these values in order to survive in this harsh world. No doubt, the Mennonites are representatives of the aspirations and failures of all mankind.

NOTES

1. Shirley Newman, "Unearthing Language: An Interview with Rudy Wiebe" in W.J. Keith, ed., *A Voice in the Land* (Edmonton: New Westland, 1981), pp. 228-29.
2. Rudy Wiebe, *The Blue Mountains of China* (Toronto, 1970), p. 10.
3. Magdalene Falk Redekop, "Translated into the Past: Language in *The Blue Mountains of China*" in *A Voice in the Land*, p. 100.
4. Rudy Wiebe "Tombstone Community in *A Voice in the Land*," p. 18.
5. W.J. Keith, *Epic Fiction: The Art of Rudy Wiebe* (The University of Alberta Press, 1981), p. 60.

Value-Judgements in Literary Criticism: George Whalley

G.R. TANEJA

An attempt to provide an outline of the major critical concerns of George Whalley, to serve as an appropriate context for examining in greater perspective his attitudes to the question of the nature and basis of value-judgements in literary criticism, however brief and tentative, would amount to an assessment, involving extensive interpretation, of his entire oeuvres. Only some of the more readily noticeable directions in, and less controversial aspects of, his thinking are indicated here.

"A poem," Whalley wrote six years before *Poetic Process* was published, "is a fragment of human experience, in a universal rather than biographical or historical sense."[1] Here, an Aristotelian bias in Whalley's attitude is obvious and Whalley was to go on to absorb the *Poetics* into his "system" to a very great extent. Poetry, he later wrote, "realizes," — "bodies forth," — "incarnates" experience.[2] The experience embodies within itself its own Value (the upper case "V" is Whalley's) which becomes a measure of "reality" that poetry "expresses": "the art of painting, like the art of poetry, is a means of embodying states of feeling, vision of reality," (232) he maintained.

Despite these various attempts at definition, poetry, for Whalley, is not subject to formal definitions: "Whether or not it is important to be able to define poetry it is of paramount importance to be able to *recognize* poetry." He continues: "We recognize a poem when we encounter it in an appropriate attitude. An appropriate attitude is one that brings the poem to life for what it is; and only from the successive encounters with poems do we learn to adjust our attitude to any particular poem." (225)

Whalley, thus, recognizes the inevitable "dynamic triad poet-poem-reader." In a conversation he once expressed amazement at the paradox involved in the significance of a poem deriving itself from its impersonal character as well as its simultaneous dependence upon the crucible of the poet's mind for its creation. He observes in *Poetic Process:*

> When a poem is complete, it has been (as it were) secreted; it has been secreted; it has been extruded, is separate from the author and no longer belongs to him; but since the process both "remakes the poet and is a condition of survival, the author's name merely indicates a point at which time and poetic process intersect." (223)
>
> . . . the sign of a maturing cognitive process is the way the poem separates itself from the reader, becomes a "thing out there," unchanged by inquiry distinct and separate, with a life of its own—certainly not projection of ourselves. As the poem moves away from us we are aware that we are no longer merely "experiencing" the poem; we are getting to *know* it as it becomes less and less like ourselves. What seemed at first little more than an intriguing encounter with a dark stranger becomes a careful and faithful tracing out of the poem's existence, the universe it represents—or simply what it is and how it lives.[3]

Mind in the process of perceiving and creating offers immense fascination for Whalley. Writing on Aristotle, for instance, he writes about bringing to the reader "the revelation . . . of the driving energy of Aristotle's thought."[4] He sees in the *Poetics* "the drama of Aristotle's thinking . . . flow[ing] out."[5] In another article dealing with both Aristotle and Coleridge, he proposes to "consider the critical *thinking* of Aristotle and Coleridge."[6] When considering poetry, Whalley fixes his gaze upon the mind of the poet and, thus, poetic *process* becomes of supreme importance.

Of literary criticism, Whalley observes: "I like to think of criticism as a process of getting-to-discern." He explicitly points out that "The end of critical act . . . is an extension of awareness shaped by the work . . . under attention. . . . The end of critical theory is to prepare and stimulate one's means of sustaining critical reflection upon works of literature . . . good critical theory is strictly speaking *theoria*—vision, a way of seeing."[7]

Whalley does not ignore the moral end of poetry. "Literature," he observes, "is the opposite of an escape: imagination is a realizing process, making the world real, making us real; and as Collingwood has said, poetry is not enchantment, but a disenchantment." Whalley maintains that "it is through language as much as anything else that we discover integrity of purpose and integrity of action. . . . For we leave in our speech and writing as in our actions more than the gist of our meaning, but the physical and durable imprint of what we are, and what we care for, and disclose beyond what we have in mind,"[8] and, therefore, he believes, language realizes its greatest potential when "it is in a state of poetry."

At this point perhaps the very concept of value-judgement requires some consideration. Whether one subscribes to impressionistic criticism of Walter Pater, or genre criticism that dominated the two centuries from Vida to Dr. Johnson, textual criticism as developed and almost perfected by the Neo-Aristotelians, among others, or the historical criticism that made its greatest contribution to Shakespearean scholarship and was even more successful with minor poets, or the sociological, biographical, psychological or comparative criticism—there is bound to be, implicit or explicit, deliberately stated or unconsciously echoed, an element of value-judgement in any critical approach. As Brewster Rogerson puts it, "merely to recognize a literary phenomenon is to place it in some way, at least tentatively, and thus to have an attitude towards it."

What has always provoked immense opposition, whenever literary criticism has sought to become overtly judicial, is its supposed recourse, first, to non-literary, external standards of values; secondly, the suspicion that all evaluative criticism is personal, subjective and impressionistic. What has further complicated matters is the fact that a neat distinction, expressed, for example, by T.E. Hulme in this metaphor of the romantic well and the classical bucket, between so-called objective response to literature and an impressionistic, subjective and personal response to literature, has almost always been taken for granted and it has not always been clearly recognized that "to disagree with Tolstoy is by no means to agree with Oscar Wilde." The fact of the matter, I suggest, is that in practice, genuine critics in the past and present—whether a neoclassicist such as Dryden, a romantic critic such as Coleridge, or an avowed "classicist" such as T.S. Eliot, or writing in the tradition of

Coleridge, Arnold, and Eliot, a critic such as Leavis—have never recognized an insurmountable barrier between one's personal response and its objective, demonstrable validity. A single work of art provokes a wide variety of responses, but what is common to responses that critics like Dryden, Coleridge, Eliot or Leavis bring to bear upon a work of literature is the fact that while "dead laws" are never permitted to "judge" "living literature," as Eliot puts it, an instantaneous, impressionistic and subjective response has never been considered valid either. Dryden, for instance, maintains that, on the one hand, personal preferences or taste cannot be taken as the criterion of poetic value, and, on the other hand, suggests that it is possible to ground the rules on reasoned arguments. Also, he points out, such principles are not dogmatic since they are not claimed to be demonstrable. In short, for Dryden, there is a middle ground between individual taste or personal, subjective and impressionistic judgement, and the objective, impersonal laws or rules, and it is in this area—the one that combines the two—that sound criticism ought to operate. Since Dryden considers rules to be merely probable, his position cannot be called dogmatic; on the other hand, since they have sufficient plausibility to justify assent, he also avoids the opposite extreme of anarchic individualism.[9]

If we sometimes tend to look upon this merging of the opposites as a clever ruse by which "heterogeneous ideas are yoked as if by violence together," we have only to recall that this was the solution that T.S. Eliot, too, found acceptable to his genius, both as a poet and as a critic. If in his admiration for Donne and Dryden, and the eighteenth century in general, in his harsh treatment of the Romantic poets, and disparagement of D.H. Lawrence, and, of course, as an avowed "classicist in literature," Eliot gives the impression of neo-classical tendencies, his poetic practice, especially in the forms that he ultimately chose to embody his poetic vision in, yields some "romantic" flavour. And the resultant contradiction was consciously resolved by Eliot when he wrote in *The Dial* a year after *The Waste Land* was published that classicism is not an alternative to

> "romanticism," as of political parties, conservatives and liberal, Republican and Democratic on a "turn-the-rascals-out-platform." It is a goal towards which all good literature strives, so far as it is good according to possibilities of its

> sense, by turning away from the nine-tenths of the material which is at hand and selecting only mummified stuff from a museum. . . . Or one can be classical in tendency by doing the best one can with the material at hand. . . . And in this material I include the emotions and feelings of the writer himself.[10]

A few years later, writing in *The Criterion,* Eliot remarked that "modern tendency among contemporary literary journals is toward something which, for want of a better name, we may call classicism,"[11] and, for him, "it was a tendency—discernible even in art—toward a higher and clearer conception of Reason, and a more severe and serene control of the emotions by Reason."[12] Yet he warned the reader that "We must scrupulously guard ourselves against measuring living art and mind by dead laws of order. Art reflects the transitory as well as the permanent condition of the soul; we cannot wholly measure the present by what the past has been or what the future may be."[13]

While the detractors of value-judgement in literary criticism have taken its supposed illusory character for granted and have therefore sought a firmer ground from which to appreciate literature, and have presumed its total lack of any theoretical, objective or demonstrable basis, the fact is that sophisticated personal value-judgements have always been based, paradoxically, on certain objective principles. The resolution between these two apparent extremes is achieved through a critical sensibility which is essentially a literary sensibility, a sensibility which achieves its profoundly systematic character from the fine balance it achieves between "guiding principles and spontaneous response."[14] A critic's judgement may be personal yet it derives its strength and validity from carefully considered opinion and a sensibility that is nurtured on the works of literature hence, for instance, the essential objective criteria and concepts underlying the critical writings of Leavis. Writing about Leavis, Robert Boyers tells us how in Leavis's critique of Lawrence:

> The impersonality of text is answered by a disciplined impersonality in the collaborative commentary, so that values and standards beyond anything deliberately aimed at by the author or critic are brought into play. The judicial project fails when the over reaching value judgement obstructs the local dis-

> criminations upon which the critical thinking absolutely depends. . . . In both Lawrence and Leavis it is *disciplined* [sic] instinct that may be said to have been the determining factor. (122)

As Wellek and Warren point out, "reasoned judgement, in matters of literature cannot be formulated save on the basis some *sensibility*" and that sensibility "judge[s] in detail and judge[s] while analyzing instead of making the judgement a pronouncement in the final paragraph."[15]

The view of the nature and basis of the value-judgements in literature and the sensibility that is apt to exercise such a judgement (that I have sought to project by invoking the theories and practice of critics such as Dryden, Coleridge, and Leavis, and, of course, T.S. Eliot), is not far from the position that one detects in Whalley. Even though *Poetic Process* is replete with his views on the question of the nature and basis of value judgement in literary criticism, it is not surprising that Whalley's more trenchant observations were provoked by his response to Northrop Fyre's *Anatomy of Criticism* when it was first published with an immediate aim to demolish what Murry Krieger[16] refers to with a naive self-complacency as "traditional criticism" had stood so far. A whole body of scholars, critics and theoreticians felt threatened with obsolescence; Whalley appears to have been perhaps the only critic of some significance who closely examined Frye's proclamation of the need for a scientific framework and basis for literary criticism and his insistence, with which, in fact, *Anatomy* opens, that value-judgements in literary criticism are not only unscientific, but are, altogether, irrelevant.

To begin with, Whalley accepts value-judgements as integral to critical response because "without value-judgements there can be no sense of relevance," and he considers "one of the main educative virtues of criticism . . . in the refinement of value-judgements." In his comments on *Anatomy* itself, he pointed out that

> Without a sense of value, particularly in the field of archetype and myth, the critic is precisely in the position Frye assigns to the sociologist working on literary method: "Horatic Alger and writers of the Elsie books may well be more important than Hawthorne or Melville, and a single issue of the *Ladies Home Journal* worth all Henry James."[17]

Whalley, thus, freely indulges in value-judgements which are bold and drastic and are not merely polite disagreements or courteous agreements. He, for example "feel[s] personal regret at not finding *Anatomy of Criticism* . . . satisfactory" and maintains that "so much of it is perverse, ingenious, desolate, at crucial points gaining rhetorical speed and assuming a sharp edge to seek safety in irony."[18] Elsewhere speaking of Johnson he writes: "More than half-deaf, and more than half-blind, his response limited almost entirely to the conceptual aspects of poetry, Dr. Samuel Johnson does not surprise us with such a statement as "Nothing can please many, and please long, but just representation of general nature." (133)

In *Poetic Process* he writes: "There is an extensive shadowland in which are mingled poems scarcely realized and highly wrought but vain struggles towards poetry. . . . Society may require for nourishment second- and third-rate art and qualities of what looks like art but isn't; but the critic's main activity belongs . . . outside the shadowland." (230)

Whalley repeatedly points out that value-judgements in literature, when exercised under right condition, are not merely subjective and impressionistic but have an objective validity about them. Consider his view of "Poetic (on the analogy of Logic—and there is good Aristotelian authority for it)" to indicate "the method of making relations in art":

> Poetic differs from Logic most markedly in this: it has no rules of procedure and never can. Rules belong to the technical and not to the contemplative way of mind; rules can be applied only "from outside," but Poetic must grow from within.
>
> Where then do we find the consistency and solidity in poetry that can make reliable judgement possible? Language is—in one sense at least—an abstraction; but a poem is not an abstraction, it is not a structure of concepts. . . .
>
> The poem as the physical incarnation of an experience is the only means of recovering that individual experience; and that experience can only be recreated when the reader can regard the poem, not as a "piece of stuff," but as containing within itself the power to regenerate a particular experience. . . .
>
> What the reader experiences is not a repetition of the process of construction, but the state in which that process

> terminates. . . . A poem is inexhaustible to analysis because it terminates in a "vision of reality." Whatever judgements of reality we may make rest upon judgements of value. There are strictly speaking degrees of reality to correspond with the degrees of value; for reality and value are inseparable.

Whalley concludes:

> Critical judgements, then, are internal; referable only to the internal nature of the poem when it is wholly and directly grasped, and to the internal nature of the reader when he is grasping the poem integrally. There is no qualitative test for the value of a poem; there is no way of being certain except through "the holiness of heart's affection," through one's own integrity and a conviction of the poem's integrity. (131; 235)

And yet George Whalley enjoins upon the critic a "sense of fact" (236); "something beyond extraordinary sensibility and intelligence"; "an impulsive contemplative attitude . . . more comprehensive than refined connoisseurship; a restless centre of emphasis guided by a flair for relevance; a subtle tact in discovering and gently unfolding, self-revealing process." He interprets Aristotle's description of poetry as "serious and philosophical" to mean "morally profound and passionately concerned with wisdom (or truth)." (237) A critic, for Whalley, must respond to poetry with "a serious attitude, a posture of responsible delight, devoid equally of dilettante levity and morose earnestness." (327-28) "Fact, sensitive apprehension, and the sense of relevance," Whalley maintains, "are . . . inseparable. And truth no longer appears as a set of acquisitions, bits of information to be picked up and carried about, but as value." (238)

It is, then, the controlled sensibility of a wary critic which is capable of responsible value-judgement. As Eliot warns the critic against judging "living literature" by "dead laws," Whalley, too, sees the danger of the extremes of both internal critical judgements and external intellectual (rational/scientific/rule-bound?) controls and points out that "The critic must indeed be wary . . . against his own prejudices, his own cliches of thought and perception, his use of language. He must constantly refresh his images and analogies; words, phrases, and theories must be abandoned as soon as they begin to clot the blood-stream of reflection." (239)

Whalley, in fact, denies "the pseudo-antithesis between objective and subjective—sometimes falsely identified with the pseudo-antithesis between classical and romantic"[19]—"the object of the theoretical critic is not to supplant Logic with Poetic; we need both." (231)

Whalley believes that the only valid value-judgements in literary criticism are literary judgements and do not derive their validity from external, non-literary standards or frameworks. His very attitude to "poetic process" testifies to this idea. He observes:

> Mallarme once remarked to Degas that poetry is not made with *ideas* but with *words*. Every word carries some charge of feeling, even though in some cases the charge be subliminal; and every word can . . . be made to carry a precise and complicated charge of feeling provided the time is ripe and the writer can invent and control an appropriate context. . . . The meaning of the poem is not what the *words* mean, but what the poet means. (230)

Elsewhere he writes:

> Poetry is a human business, not divine; and I hold with St. Augustine and others that "creation" and "creativity" are not properly within human compass. What poets do is to select and arrange and by various means intensify and find significance in what they find or what is given to them, and what at a certain level of energy haunts the dark places of the mind.[20]

Complex, tentacular and multifaceted as Whalley's views on poetry, poetic process, reality and Value are, one can barely suggest the varied directions that an examination of his views reveals. It is, though, apparent that his view of the nature and basis of value-judgement is quite compatible with similar pronouncements made by major critics since Dryden. Whalley's total vision is his own, yet one can discern parallels in Eliot, whom Whalley constantly quotes, and Leavis, whose influence was at its highest during the period when *Poetic Process* was being written.

NOTES

1. George Whalley, "The Poet and His Reader," *Queen's Quarterly*, LIV (Summer, 1947), p. 213.
2. George Whalley, *Poetic Process* (1953; rpt. Conn.: Greenwood, 1973), p. 222.
3. George Whalley, "Teaching Poetry," Unpublished, Undated, p. 5.
4. George Whalley, "On Translating Aristotle's *Poetics*," *University of Toronto Quarterly*, 39 (1969-70), p. 77.
5. *Ibid.*, p. 83.
6. George Whalley, "The Aristotle-Coleridge Axis," *University of Toronto Quarterly,* XLII (1973), p. 94, emphasis added.
7. *Ibid.*, p. 95.
8. George Whalley, "Literature: An Instrument of Inquiry," The James A. Cappon Inaugural Lecture delivered before Queen's University on 28 November 1977, Unpublished, pp. 2 and 3.
9. Cf. Dryden:
   The liking and disliking of the people gives the play the demonstration of good or bad, but does not really make or constitute as such. To please ought to be the poet's aim because the plays are made for their delight; but it does not follow they are always pleased with good plays, or that the plays that please them are always good.
   . . . if nature be to be imitated, then there is a rule for imitating Nature rightly otherwise there may be an end and no means of conducing to it.
   . . . So having laid down that nature is to be imitated, and that proposition proving the next, that then there are means which conduce to the imitation of nature, I dare proceed no further positively; but having laid down some opinions of the ancients and the moderns, and of my own, as means which they used, and which I thought probable for attaining that end. "A Defence of An Essay of Dramatic Poesy" [1688] in W.P. Ker, ed., *Essays of John Dryden* (1900; rpt, Oxford: OUP, 1926), vol. i.
10. T.S. Eliot, "Ulysses, Order and Myth," *The Dial*, 75 (Nov. 1923), p. 482.

11. T.S. Eliot, "The Idea of a Literary Review," *The Criterion,* 4, i (January 1926). p. 5.
12. "Ulysses, Order and Myth," p. 482.
13. "The Idea of a Literary Review," p. 5.
14. The expression is M.M. Badwai's. See *Coleridge: Critic of Shakespeare* (Cambridge: Cambridge University Press, 1973), p. 29.
15. Quoted in [S.J. Kahn], "Evaluation," *Princeton Encylopaedia of Poets and Poetry* (1965; Princeton: Princeton University Press, 1974), Cf. T.S. Eliot: "The true generalisation is not something superimposed upon an accumulation of perceptions; the perceptions do not, in a really appreciative mind, accumulate as a mass, but form themselves as a structure; and criticism is the statement in language of this structure; it is development of sensibility."
16. "Northrop Frye and Contemporary Criticism" in Murray Krieger, ed., *Northrop Frye in Modern Criticism: Selected Papers from the English Institute* (New York and London: Columbia University Press, 1966), p. 7, for example, and throughout.
17. George Whalley, "Frye's *Anatomy of Criticism*," *Tamarack Review,* No. 8 (1958), p. 100.
18. *Loc. cit.*
19. Cf. Coleridge: "I should call that investigation fair and philosophical, in which the critic announces and endeavours to establish the principles, which he holds for the foundation of poetry in general, with the specification of these in their application to the different classes of poetry. Having thus prepared his canons of criticism for praise and condemnation, he would proceed to particularize the most striking passages to which he deems them applicable, faithfully noticing the frequent or infrequent recurrence of similar merits or defects, and as faithfully distinguishing what is characteristic from what is accidental, or a mere flagging of the wing. Then if his premises be rational, his deductions legitimate, and his conclusions justly applied, the reader . . . may adopt his judgement, and in the independency of free-agency. If he has erred, he presents his error in a definite place and tangible form, and holds the torch and guides the way to their detection." (*Biographia Literaria*, ed. J. Shawcross [Oxford: OUP, 1907], p. 85.)
20. "Literature: An Instrument of Inquiry," p. 7.

Index